Ecological Poetics;
or, Wallace Stevens's Birds

Ecological Poetics;
or, Wallace Stevens's Birds

CARY WOLFE

The University of Chicago Press | Chicago & London

The University of Chicago Press, Chicago 60637
The University of Chicago Press, Ltd., London
© 2020 by The University of Chicago
Published 2020
Printed in the United States of America

29 28 27 26 25 24 23 22 21 20   1 2 3 4 5

ISBN-13: 978-0-226-68783-4 (cloth)
ISBN-13: 978-0-226-68797-1 (paper)
ISBN-13: 978-0-226-68802-2 (e-book)
DOI: https://doi.org/10.7208/chicago/9780226688022.001.0001

The University of Chicago Press gratefully acknowledges the generous
support of Rice University toward the publication of this book.

Portions of chapter 2 first appeared in "The Idea of Observation at Key
West: Systems Theory, Poetry, and Form beyond Formalism" in *What Is
Posthumanism?* (Minneapolis: University of Minnesota Press, 2010) and
are reprinted here by permission of the publisher. A version of chapter 4
appeared in *Angelaki: Journal of the Theoretical Humanities* 23, no. 6 (2018)
and another version of chapter 4 appeared in *Eco-Deconstruction: Derrida
and Environmental Philosophy* (New York: Fordham University Press, 2018).
Robert Frost's poem "Never Again Would Birds' Song Be the Same" from
The Poetry of Robert Frost, edited by Edward Connery Lathem, copyright
© 1969 by Henry Holt and Company, copyright © 1942 by Robert Frost,
copyright © 1970 by Lesley Frost Ballantine, reprinted by permission of
Henry Holt and Company, all rights reserved; and from *The Collected Poems*,
published by Vintage Classics, reprinted by permission of The Random
House Group Limited, © 2013. Robert Morgan's poem "Mockingbird"
from *Trunk and Thicket* (L'Epervier Press, 1978) is reprinted here courtesy
of Sagehill Press.

Library of Congress Cataloging-in-Publication Data

Names: Wolfe, Cary, author.
Title: Ecological poetics; or, Wallace Stevens's birds / Cary Wolfe.
Other titles: Ecological poetics
Description: Chicago : University of Chicago Press, 2020. | Includes
    bibliographical references and index.
Identifiers: LCCN 2019035377 | ISBN 9780226687834 (cloth) |
    ISBN 9780226687971 (paperback) | ISBN 9780226688022 (ebook)
Subjects: LCSH: Stevens, Wallace, 1879–1955—Criticism and interpretation. |
    Ecocriticism. | Ecology in literature. | Nature in literature. |
    Birds in literature.
Classification: LCC PS3537.T4753 Z955 2020 | DDC 811/.52—dc23
LC record available at https://lccn.loc.gov/2019035377

♾ This paper meets the requirements of ANSI/NISO Z39.48-1992
(Permanence of Paper).

Contents

Preface: "An Affair of Places" vii

PART I : READING STEVENS, ONCE MORE

1. Poems (and Critics) of Our Climate 3

2. "Like Seeing Fallen Brightly Away": A New Theory for the Emerson/Stevens Genealogy 26

PART II : FROM EPISTEMOLOGICAL TO ECOLOGICAL POETICS

3. "There Is No World": Deconstruction, Theoretical Biology, and the Creative Universe 61

4. "Never Again Would Birds' Song Be the Same" 84

PART III : "FAREWELL TO AN IDEA": SOME LATER LONG POEMS

5. Scapes and Spheres 119

6. "Premetaphysical Pluralism": Dwelling in the Ordinary 138

Coda: Indirections, on the Way 166

Notes *171*   *Index* *211*

"An Affair of Places"

ROUGHLY HALF OF THIS BOOK IS about the work of Wallace Stevens (poetry and prose, but by no means all of it), and half consists of a theoretical recasting of the problem of ecocriticism in relation to poetics. Suitable working subtitles for this book thus might be something like, "Can Wallace Stevens Be Read as an Ecological Poet?" or "How Does Reading Stevens as an Ecological Poet Change Our Idea of Ecopoetics?" I make no attempt in this book to cover the entire body of Stevens's corpus in poetry. Many important poems by Stevens that I love are discussed very little or not at all ("The Rock" is a good example, but there are many others), and I am not interested in marshaling evidence for my argument from every poem Stevens ever wrote. What I *am* interested in is tracing a coherent, unfolding trajectory in Stevens's poetry that moves toward ever more sophisticated conjugations of the relationship between poetics and ecology, and in a way that is quite different from how we usually think of it—nearly unique in my experience, in fact.

In the service of describing that trajectory, I have found the work of an older generation of critics to be invaluable—a generation that helped elevate Stevens's status in the years following his death in 1955 to the canonical, "philosophically serious" poet that he is today. Helen Vendler and Harold Bloom lead the list, but there are several others who appear in these pages. I have found their criticism more valuable and more useful to me than most because they are above all exquisite *readers* who unfailingly locate the most important moments in the poetry, even if they do not always agree about the significance of those moments or unpack their philosophical implications in a way that we are positioned to do today. In a contemporary context of academic knowledge production that often seems predicated upon the tacit assumption that the job of one generation of critics is to expose the blindness of the previous one (deconstructive readings of Romantic poetry give way to New Historicism, which in turn gives way to the New Formalism, and so on), I think it is important to honor the work of these most readerly of readers, representatives of an art of reading poetry that has suffered greatly over the past thirty years. I won't go into my opinions about why this has been the case (that would be a book on its own, and a very different one). Instead, I want to emphasize that the work I am doing in this book would have been impossible without the foundational readings of Stevens laid down by that generation of critics from the late 1950s into the mid-1970s—roughly up until the rise in the US academy of "theory" of the sort that I am using here to frame not just my reading of Stevens, but also my reinterpretation of the readings of Stevens by that earlier generation of critics. In one sense, what I see myself doing in this book is extending and refining their work, seizing upon many of the same moments in Stevens's poetry and their insights about those moments, but pursuing the ramifications and implications of those moments for understanding Stevens by putting to use theoretical tools they scarcely had, or had not at all, at their disposal.

Above all else, I am arguing here for a reconceptualization of ecopoetics by seeking it out in a poet not often associated with the terms "ecology" and "environment." More specifically, I am arguing that only a *nonrepresentational* understanding of ecopoetics can enable us to grasp the most profound sense in which Wallace Stevens is an ecological poet—a sense that does not exclude but reaches well beyond the thematics and imagery of seasons and climate, palm trees and snowy scenes, and what he called his poetic "mundo." Upon reflection, this nonrepresentational emphasis should not surprise anyone—and indeed might be seen as long overdue—because, as we know from contemporary theoretical biology, no organism has a representational relationship to its environment, in the sense of a neutral, transparent access whose veracity and usefulness is calibrated to the degree of this neutrality and transparency. To get on in the world, organisms must exclude (largely unconsciously) most of what is "out there" to make a structured and functional world possible.

This fact about any living being's "world" (a term that will carry for us both philosophical and biological resonance) is foregrounded, relentlessly and paradoxically, in Stevens's poetry, framed as it is by an extreme tension between, on the one hand, a desire for "things as they are," things without human mediation, and, on the other, constant reminders of the supreme value of the imagination and how the mind of the poet makes its world. In my view, any serious engagement with Stevens's poetry has to begin with this tension (though "tension" is far too weak a word for how this paradox galvanizes Stevens's poetics), and more specifically with how Stevens refuses to resolve it, dialectically or otherwise. He takes that lack of resolution and makes a poetics out of it, and he refines it as his career stretches on.

For me, the most lucid and rigorous way to systematically describe how Stevens handles this problem, and how he handles it in an increasingly sophisticated way as his body of work develops, is through second-order systems theory, specifically its description of the paradoxes that arise (unavoidably) through the self-referential structure of observation. To put this in the language of social systems theorist Niklas Luhmann, the distinction between system (or organism) and environment is, paradoxically, a product of one side of the distinction (namely, the system); "self-reference" and "hetero-reference" are themselves a product of the system's (or organism's) self-referential schema, and so what look like opposites on the surface of things—subject vs. object, let's say, or mind vs. nature—turn out, upon closer inspection, to share a deeper, paradoxical unity. They are two sides of a distinction that gives *form* to the world, but here "form" is indissociable from function, enaction, and performativity. The issue isn't about getting an accurate picture of the world, it's about *getting on* in the world, and the shift in emphasis is from "being" to "doing" (to borrow from Humberto Maturana).[1] This is a dynamic that Stevens relentlessly foregrounds and exfoliates as few poets ever have.

Now one might well object that if this foregrounding of the paradoxical nature of the organism/environment relationship is what makes Stevens "environmental" or "ecological," then *all* poets may be called ecopoets in a sense, whether they are interested in the "green" world or not. There is a touch of truth to that assertion, but perhaps the simplest retort to this objection would be to cite Stevens's own assertion (or admission) that "[l]ife is an affair of people not of places. But for me life is an affair of places and that is the trouble."[2] Stevens is indeed a poet of places and not people, but it is the peculiar nature and texture of this "affair of places" that makes his ecopoetics what it is (and not the fact, say, that he writes a group of poems about Florida). Stevens's characteristic ecopoetic mode is to focus intensely on a particular place, or feature of a place, and then ask, "what is its relationship to this thing we call 'reality'"? That question usually prompts a reflexive questioning of the possibilities and limitations of the one asking the question—it leads to an intense engagement of the problem of *observation* (in the most capacious sense I can invite you to imagine), an engagement for which the most iconic Stevens poem is perhaps "Thirteen Ways of Looking at a Blackbird."

What makes this process an especially instructive ecopoetics in Stevens is the extraordinary power of *virtualization* that he exerts in such moments. Why is this important? Because, as we know from the contemporary life sciences (as we'll see in chapter 3), ecological space is above all *virtual* space. Why? Because any such space is populated by myriad wildly heterogeneous life forms that create their worlds, their environments, through the embodied enaction, unfolding dynamically and in real time, of their own self-referential modes of knowing and being, their own autopoiesis (a process for which birds and birdsong will be privileged tropes in Stevens). It's a wild, crisscrossing dance of an almost unimaginable heterogeneity of living beings, at different scales and at different temporalities, doing their own thing, and a hallmark of Stevens's mode of attention is to look, listen, and follow where this dance leads him. Paying attention to this multidimensionality and overdetermination of ecological space means understanding that here "virtual" doesn't mean "not real" or "less real"; it means "*more* real." Indeed, Maturana calls such a perspective "super-realist," in the sense of one "who believes in the existence of innumerable equally valid realities," which cannot, however, be called "relativist" because "asserting their relativity would entail the assumption of an absolute reality as the reference point against which their relativity would be measured."[3] Such an assertion would entail the all-too-familiar humanist desire to escape our own ecological embeddedness and finitude (to use Jacques Derrida's term)— what Donna Haraway, in a famous essay, characterizes as the "situatedness" of our knowledge and experience of the world.[4]

My own particular intervention in this book is thus not just resolutely theoretical and philosophical; it also takes place at a level both "below" and "above" the main line of ecocritical discourse ("below" in the sense of not allowing questions of diversity and difference in relation to the environment to *ever* separate themselves from the question of the diversity of nonhuman forms of life; "above" in the sense of not taking for granted the thing called "world" in which such forms of life interact in what may not best be characterized as a common plight). Were one to amplify this point about virtuality and individuation in a more cultural-studies direction, one might say that what Stevens refuses— what he *radically* refuses—is what Stacy Alaimo has characterized as the "externalization" of "world" and "environment" in relation to the ongoing embodied enaction of living beings, rather than the mutual entanglement and embeddedness of organism and environment whose main name here (taken from theoretical biology) will be "autopoiesis." As Alaimo notes, this partition is a dominant (if unintentional) feature of much contemporary environmental discourse about the Anthropocene and climate change: "the world" that we care about and want to save, *over there*, and those of us doing the caring, *over here*. As she puts it, the most characteristic discourses of the Anthropocene imagine the species as having a more-than-human-scale impact on the earth, "colossal" and "unthinkably vast in duration, on something that we externalize as 'the planet,'" which in turn "removes us from the scene and ignores the extent to which human agencies are entangled with those of nonhuman creatures."[5] As she argues, this removal and externalization is, ironically enough, extended in the standard formulations of "sustainability," where what is sustained above all is "our" ability to remain insulated from— the better to manage and steer—this entanglement. This presumption, as we'll see in a moment, is the target of both Heidegger's and Sloterdijk's critiques of "man" as the "rational animal," who easily morphs into Man the Manager.[6] It pushes ecological critics such as Elizabeth DeLoughery toward other ways of thinking about the question of "world"— in Maori culture, for example, in which, as she puts it, "knowing and being are constitutive and interrelated."[7]

Stevens pursues precisely this realization in his poetry, but my point is not, of course, that Stevens's mode of enacting this is "like" the Maori. On the contrary, I am interested in his *particular* way of taking up this ecopoetic challenge—from the belly of the beast, you might say, of a canon that has rarely been associated with the concerns voiced by Alaimo and DeLoughery. (And here I'll mention that Stevens's situatedness in what Sloterdijk calls the "immunological" regimes of modern developed societies, of which insurance is a prime example, is very much to the point.) One of the captivating things about Stevens's late mode, in particular, is his removal of all the furniture and all the toys that the reader might rely upon for distraction, all those "stabilizing apparatuses," as Derrida puts it, that are calculated to never let the question of "world" arise in the first place.[8] In the increasingly spartan later work, it's as if Stevens sucks all of the excess air out of the room and says to the reader, "*You*. I'm talking to *you*. It's up to *you* to listen, watch, observe, learn, and be—not your cellphone, not your iPad—*you*." And thus, to me, the resonance and force—the challenge, really—of Stevens's ecopoetics, in the context of our multitasking, ultra-distracted mediascape, is all the more timely. One of the meanings of "ecological" in Stevens is "pay attention to the details; focus on your way of being where you are, what you see and don't see."

And here is where I insist that the concept of "world" continues to be useful, because it draws our attention to precisely those details, those particulars, upon which poetry depends. We all may be "entangled" in the world on the level of physics, for example, but that has nothing to tell us about the *particular* embodied ways of being in the world that Alaimo and DeLoughrey foreground. It's a simple distinction of "necessary" versus "sufficient," and it directs us, again, to the nongeneric details of what it means to be *here, now,* as *this* form of life and not some other. Derrida draws out this radically nongeneric challenge embedded in the concept of "world" late in the second set of seminars on *The Beast and the Sovereign,* in pedagogical engagements that are by turns poignant, luminous, and humorous. As he writes there, "the vague comforting feeling of understanding each other . . . for example in the use of the words 'world' (*Welt, world, mundo*), 'our common world,'" does not "suffice for it to be true and for anything other to be happening than an agreement inherited over millennia between living beings who are more or less anguished by illness, death and war and eating-each-other-alive"—"an agreement to ensure for oneself the best, and therefore the longest *survival* by a system of life insurances. . . . For example, the word 'world' as totality of what is, etc. That no one has ever come across, right? Have you ever come across the world as such?"[9]

A virtual world, then, not unreal but *super*-real. This power of virtualization, at least in part, gives Stevens's poetry a quality that often borders on "clairvoyance" (to borrow Harold Bloom's wonderful characterization)[10]—his ability to disclose how that virtual space is paradoxically more "real" than "reality," precisely because the "out there" and the "in here" become so dynamically, intimately, conjoined in real time. The ecological point here is not simply epistemological, not simply about Stevens's insistence that the paradoxical relationship of organism and environment emphasizes the inescapable co-implication and mutual enfolding of self and world. Rather, it actually aligns with the understanding of system (or organism) and environment that we find in contemporary life science—a point I take up in some detail in chapter 3.

In Stevens's poetics, the "operating program," so to speak, *reproduces* rather than *represents* the complex logic of physical (and, specifically, biological) systems in ongoing acts of meaning-making that are, at the same time, processes of individuation.[11] But because that reproduction takes place in the domain of language and culture (in shorthand), it can hardly be called "natural" or "ecological" in the traditional sense of those terms (a point made with great force, of course, by Derrida)—hence the necessity of a posthumanist understanding of what "ecological" and "ecopoetics" mean.

What I have in mind, then, when I say "nonrepresentational" reaches well beyond the considerable literature that attempts to complicate our understanding of representation as *mimesis* stretching from Plato and Aristotle to Erich Auerbach, Walter Benjamin, and René Girard (and beyond)—with its emphasis on the performative and framing elements, rather than the imitative aspects, of *mimesis*. And it even reaches beyond Derrida's considerable engagements of the question in texts such as *Glas, Dissemination*, and "Economimesis," because I am interested in articulating the problem in relation to recent work in theoretical biology (and, in chapter 4, ornithological literature about bird song), in a way that Derrida sometimes gestured toward but never really pursued, given all his other engagements. I suggest that, in rethinking the "ecological" and "environmental" aspects of poetics, what's crucial is not just the performative iterability of difference (*différance*) at the heart of Derrida's deconstruction of mimesis-as-representation, but an infrastructural *poetics*, in the deep historical and etymological sense of *poiesis*, a "making," by which both Stevens's poetry and current theoretical work in biology on "life" may be understood as creative, enactive, and performative.

I hasten to add that, in deploying this scientific literature, I am not claiming to give the reader a snapshot of "the way things really are" in the biological domain, or to suggest that literature and criticism are "grounded" (and thereby, so the story goes, legitimized) by the empiricism of science, simply because my theoretical approach to these questions is not a philosophically "realist" one. Another way to put this, as I do later in these pages, is that there can be no neat division between the "ontological" and the "epistemological" domains, or the "empirical" and the "interpretive." For the realist or idealist thinker, this would be a scandal, of course, but for the pragmatist orientation I began developing in my second book, *Critical Environments* (1998), it is no scandal at all. To put the matter somewhat differently, as Richard Rorty does when distinguishing pragmatism from realism and idealism, "holism takes the curse off naturalism," and I add here that attention to the autopoiesis and embodied enaction out of which "worlds" emerge takes the curse off holism, in the sense that the "naturalism" of a living being's "world" is a product of the "holism" of its particular way of structuring (and thereby being affected by) its environment.[12] On offer here, then, instead of a realist or idealist account, is a robust and coherent framework within which to rethink the question of "ecological poetics" in ways that stretch beyond literary criticism, and finally beyond philosophy, by drawing upon the theoretical life sciences. To put this in the most brazen way possible, in the poetry and in the biology, *there is nothing to represent* because there is no "there" there, no antecedently given "subject" or "object," "mind" or "nature." And because there is nothing to represent, there is *plenty* to do—an endless amount, as Stevens shows us again and again in his poetry. This approach separates my project decisively from many reductionist contemporary attempts to "ground" literary interpretation in science (and, in particular, in more recent evolutionary arguments, often quite reductive neo-Darwinian ones that attempt, for example, to trace the cultural pervasiveness of certain literary conventions or patterns to an evolutionary or adaptive driver). How does this change how we read poems, and how we locate the "ecological poetics" of poetry, when we do? We'll see.

This connection on the terrain of "poetics" between the philosophical and theoretical, on the one hand, and the biological and ecological, on the other, is crucial for reasons noted a few years ago in an essay called "Ecocriticism: Some Emerging Trends," by Lawrence Buell, the dean of American ecocriticism. As he notes, the development of ecocriticism in the United States since around 1990 has been a two-stage affair. After an initial focus on either "nature writing" (of the American variety, featuring authors such as Thoreau, or the British, focusing on Romanticism and especially Romantic poetry) or, conversely, on seeing representations of nature as a "discursive and/or ideological screen," ecocriticism moved in its first phase toward "reorienting literary-critical thinking toward more serious engagement with nonhuman nature in two different although related ways":[13] post-Heideggerian "deep ecology" (associated with philosopher Arne Naess, and others in the United States, such as Bill Devall and George Sessions), which suffered in no small part because of suspicion about privileging "subjective perception/experience as against social context/human collectivities"; and what he calls "the second most distinctive path," which was to make it "more scientifically informed," seeking to "bridge the gap between the humanities and the sciences by means of a literary theory obedient to conceptual models derived from the life sciences."[14] As he notes, however, the latter "has not won many adherents," and the tendency has thus been to give way to models derived less from science *per se* than from "science studies," which steered away from the possible pitfalls of "scientific reductionism," but often at the expense of resorting to the far less intellectually ambitious project of analyzing the cultural narratives and genres of discourse that condition science's representation of nature and the ecological.[15] And while, in Buell's view, ecocriticism has continued to receive upgrades in theoretical sophistication by scholars such as Dana Phillips and Timothy Morton, "the aspiration continues to run strong to enlist scientific method and theory in the service of humanistic-literary analysis while avoiding the opposite pitfalls of scientistic reductionism (e.g., genetic-determinist explanations of consciousness) and the 'humanistic reduction' of science as cultural construct."[16]

This is precisely where this work intervenes, in bringing together the approaches set in opposition to each other by Buell. My use of the Heideggerian idea of "world" is not "phenomenological" (it derives, in fact, from a thoroughgoing critique of the phenomenological project by Derrida), and it is a concept that is operative at a level beneath and beyond "the human" (and not in a manner that lines up in any neat way, as Derrida argues, with terms such as "human" and "animal"). And my use of scientific material (in this case, theoretical biology) is not "constructivist" in the sense invoked by Buell with reference to "science studies," even though it well understands that scientific knowledge is generated by a specifically modern form of social complexity, with its institutions, disciplines, discourses, and protocols for what counts as knowledge. To foreground this fact about scientific knowledge does not in the least delegitimize it because—again—the issue here is not the veracity of science from a realist point of view, but rather (from a pragmatist vantage) its ability to help us understand the ontogenetic and adaptive processes of organisms, the operations of the biosphere, the complex dynamics of perception and consciousness, and so on. Is this relationship between social complexity, the scientific and philosophical discourses produced by it, and the biology and ecology studied by both, circular? Of course it is. As Gregory Bateson points out, nowhere do we see that circularity more in evidence, and unavoidably so, than in biological phenomena— a problem that poetry can handle more effectively, he suggests, than philosophical logic. That is exactly why we need second-order systems theory (both social and biological) and deconstruction to address the matters at hand. But that is also, most of all, why we need poetry, because what I hope to show—with sociologist Niklas Luhmann playing the role of *amicus curiae* alongside the literary critics—is that poetry is a privileged site for thinking the ecological precisely because it can convey the complexity of ecological meaning in ways that scientific and philosophical discourse cannot directly and denotatively elucidate.

This is, in part, Amitav Ghosh's point in *The Great Derangement*. As he notes about climate change, our cultural mores do not allow us to think the uncanny otherness of the radical "outside" of the environment (brought home for him in natural catastrophes).[17] In that light, one might object (from *either* a realist or idealist point of view) that the formulation of the "outside" in my work—and in systems theory and deconstruction generally—is contentless and empty in a way that Ghosh's is not. I will leave aside for the moment the technical rejoinder to this assertion, which I take up later (in brief: that it is unwarranted to assume that something that can't be described or perceived by a particular set of coordinates or in terms of a particular schema does not exist). For now, I will simply assert, with Ghosh, that this resistance to representation by the "outside" is a good thing, because all attempts to found in it a positive content or a concrete image are domestications of something that is unthinkable and yet at the same time must be thought. The task is rather to preserve for that "outside" the space and force of the unthought, the unformulated, the unimaged. And this is, I think, where we can locate Stevens's "outside" and his intense desire for it: an "outside," as he puts it in the opening salvo of "Notes toward a Supreme Fiction," that "has expelled us and our images."[18]

There is no doubt, as Ghosh notes, that those cultural mores and literary conventions (figuratively inventoried by Stevens in poems such as "The Man on the Dump") lead us to burrow ever more deeply into that myopia that wants to reduce the unthinkable, the unrepresentable, to the representable and knowable.[19] And while Ghosh is focused on the novel, he suggests that poets have always been at the forefront of resisting what Bruno Latour has called the "partitioning" of nature and culture that characterizes modernity (and he cites a genealogy that runs from Hölderlin and Rilke to W. S. Merwin and Gary Snyder in the contemporary moment).[20] Stevens is certainly exemplary in this regard, but I locate Stevens a bit differently—or a bit *additionally*, you might say—in this larger drama of the regime of "calculations of risk" and "statistics and probability" whose domesticating effects on the novel Ghosh plumbs so well.[21] Why? Because not only was Stevens writing at the historical peak of what Peter Sloterdijk calls "insurance societies" (the peak, because those have obviously been eroded in the period between the New Deal and the Reagan revolution and its aftermath), he was also eventually vice president of Hartford Accident & Indemnity Company, after working in the insurance business for many years.[22] How to understand the relationship of this fact to his poetry?[23]

As Ghosh writes about experiencing a tornado in India, the sense of its radical otherness, the sheer ahuman nature of the "outside," was "something that was not a property of the thing itself but of the manner in which it had intersected with my life."[24] I think this is the case as well with Stevens's experience of the "outside"—which might be something as dramatic as the aurora borealis in "The Auroras of Autumn," or as minimal as "a shade that traverses / A dust" at the end of his great late poem, "An Ordinary Evening in New Haven."[25] What I think we find in Stevens—and it would require another, very different kind of book to make this case—is the registration of the greater and greater "inward" pressure of the mechanisms of "calculation" and "risk" touched on by Ghosh, the immunitary regimes analyzed on a grand scale by Peter Sloterdijk in his *Spheres* project, that generates what you might call an "autoimmune" response in Stevens's enactment of a poetics in which "Snow sparkles like eyesight falling to earth, / Like seeing fallen brightly away," where "we reach / The last purity of the knowledge of good."[26] One of the main sources of Stevens's lyricism, perhaps, is an intense *resistance* to that immunitary pressure and its deadening effects on the life of the everyday, a life that gives way to "the celestial ennui of apartments"[27]—hence the brilliance and urgency of Stevens's recovery mission of the "ordinary" in "An Ordinary Evening in New Haven," so different from his recourse to the exotic and the florabundant in his earlier poetry. To put it telegraphically, Stevens pits his aurora borealis of the opening section of that great long poem against "the wax flowers on the mantelpiece" in the essay "Insurance and Social Change," a "world in which nothing unpleasant can happen,"[28] and we know exactly where his heart lies, what quickens his pulse.

Here is where Sloterdijk's perhaps unexpected presence in the later pages of this book is important. In his revision of Heidegger in his massive *Spheres* project, he argues that "being-there" (a rough translation of Heidegger's *Dasein*) is above all, for human beings, an environing, a "being-in" and "being-with," that starts (literally) in the dyadic relationship of the womb, from which we are jettisoned at birth into an "outside" in which we forever try to reconstruct a sphere of immunitary security and protection by making space manageable, knowable, livable, navigable. (For Stevens, such immunitary spaces are often troped in terms of the house, the home, and dwelling—as in some of the most famous passages in "The Auroras of Autumn"—but they are also operative more generally for Stevens in the form of literary tradition, social conventions, religious cosmologies, and all the habits that go with them.) We need not buy into the rather fanciful ontological foundations of Sloterdijk's project to see that it enables us to link the inner and the outer worlds of Stevens—the Stevens of the ceaseless conjugation of "mind" or "imagination" and "reality," and the Stevens of insurance and obsolesced religious tradition. We might be reminded here of the role that "privacy" plays in Frank Lentricchia's reading of Stevens, but what is important here is less (as in Lentricchia's argument) the grounding of the idea of privacy in private property, or the feminization of the private sphere over and against the masculinized rough-and-tumble of so-called public life (the life of corporations and law firms, for example), than the paradoxical immunitary core that makes these two sides of Stevens not so much "schizophrenic" (to use Lentricchia's phrase) as *systematically* linked.[29]

We can see *how* they are linked—to move now from the "inner" to the "outer" world of Stevens—when we remember that, for Sloterdijk (as Timothy Campbell puts it), "the contemporary moment is characterized principally by the construction and protection of increasingly fortified internal spaces, indeed, of a multiplicity of interiors that are premised on the centrality of individual life as the contemporary agent of protection."[30] What we find in these "individually designed immunity regimes"—to move now to the outermost domains of Stevens's situation—is the "securing of man's essence based on a form of technology now understood as schemes of private insurance that substitute for one's own national community" (something with which Stevens was, of course, intimately acquainted).[31] Though it will not be my quarry in this book to make such an argument, I think that what we find in the course of Stevens's career—sometimes as a backdrop and sometimes in the foreground—is a poet reacting to, and very often rebelling against, immunitary regimes, both cultural and social, as those develop from the fabled "death of the gods" and the passing of religion to the gradual development of what Stevens called "an insurance era," perhaps characterized by nationalization, perhaps not.[32] Stevens wanted immunitary protection—as we all do—and he also bridled against its deadening effects. Poetry was his way of having both.

At a deeper level, Sloterdijk's centrality to the later parts of the book has to do with the challenge to humanism that he poses—an *environmental* challenge of a particular kind—in his effort to think the questions of "world," "environment," "life," and so on in a rigorously posthumanist fashion. Here—to broaden the context for a moment in terms of my own work—we should remember the discussion of "humanist posthumanism" in chapter 4 of *What Is Posthumanism?* My point there was that the fundamental issue is not just the decentering of the human in relation to nonhuman life, but also *how* one thinks that decentering. "Humanist posthumanism" is an apt characterization for much of what passes for ecocritical discourse in the estimation we glossed earlier from Alaimo, in which the central questions seem to be, as Heidegger and Sloterdijk remind us, questions of *use*, management, distribution of goods, and extension of rights, with the discourse of "sustainability" as perhaps the most familiar example. Thus, what looks like a decentering of the human, what looks like a posthumanism (taking the question of environment seriously), ends up anchoring itself in a fundamental and familiar form of humanism, in which the ecological question, as it is framed in this book, is never actually fundamentally raised.

The underlying problem here, as Heidegger insists in the "Letter on Humanism," is that the question of the human in relation to its world is never philosophically interrogated. Over and against what Sloterdijk calls "the edifying character of humanism conveyed at school and Sunday politics," Heidegger's point in the "Letter" is that the humanist picture of the "rational animal" "makes do with relating two apparently familiar dimensions: he believes he knows what animals are, and he thinks he understands what reason is; in adding these two trivialities together, he comes to believe that he has acquired a view of the whole and that he finds himself home at his place."[33] This is "the fundamentalism of our culture," the "political religion of globalized western man," which manifests itself in "a planetary projection of the question of power and the total utilization of the Earth and of the living for production, circulation, and consumption," which is merely fine-tuned, not fundamentally challenged, in most versions of the dominant ecocritrical discourses of sustainability, environmental justice, and the Anthropocene.[34] (This is not to declare wholesale that such discourses are worthless, of course; it is simply to specify the horizon that they take for granted and in which they are operative.)

It's this arrogance and this blindness—about the human, but also about the so-called "animal"—that Heidegger, in Sloterdijk's view, fundamentally challenges. For Sloterdijk, the radicality of this challenge is that it forces us to fundamentally revise our understanding of terms like "environment" and "world" in a way that is opposed at its core to all the familiar variations of modernity "as a project of taking power and of progress won through technology and political reason."[35] For Heidegger, "man is no longer the important thing in the modern world, but instead something that exceeds human being and of which the latter can only be the medium or the resonance-ground."[36] What makes this move both posthumanist and environmental (or rather, it will be made posthumanist after Derrida's fundamental deconstruction of Heidegger) is that, as Sloterdijk puts it, "it is radically oriented against every sort of human vanity," with "man" now situated on the "periphery" of the fundamental question of Being: "being in the center and being-there relegated to the margins."[37] The injunction here is that "men must be even more restrained and more gathered than they have ever been"; they must learn "to fear themselves as the *Unheimliche*, the uncanny strangers."[38]

The next step, then, in this "ecologization" is Derrida's radicalization of this exposure of the human to its outside and its decenteredness by taking away Heidegger's ontologically partitioning assertion, at the opening of the "Letter on Humanism," that "[l]anguage is the house of Being. In its home man dwells." I will explore this in more detail in my discussion of Derrida's writings on the *oikos* as a frame for reading Stevens's later long poems, but for now, I note that what makes Derrida more "environmental" than Heidegger is that he casts us outside without the reassurance of the primordial protection of the house of Being that is language.[39] To put this succinctly: Heidegger dedomesticates the humanism of the "rational animal" and the management relationship to environment that it underwrites, exposing the human to the challenge of the Clearing, the Open. But Derrida dedomesticates Heidegger by getting rid of the support and enclosure of language as the house of Being.

And here I locate the—or at least *a*—deep theoretical background to this study: the assertion, common to Derrida and Sloterdijk, and traceable back to Heidegger—that "world" is a philosophical, not empirical, question, and that a posthumanist understanding of the question of "world" in relation to "life" has to proceed from the ground up. In one sense, all Derrida adds to this Heideggerian assertion is an interrogation of Heidegger's partitioning of the human versus other forms of existence in relation to this question—a partitioning that actually goes *against* the radicality of Heidegger's posing of the question of world and Dasein as *not* reducible to an empirical derivation. Derrida then radicalizes this decentering by taking seriously the Heideggerian challenge that "the Being of beings is not a being" but then interrogates Heidegger's "dogmatic" assertion that this could only be a problem—more strictly speaking, a "question" (to evoke Derrida's reading in *Of Spirit: Heidegger and the Question*)—for human beings alone.[40] For Derrida, we can never be sure, "dogmatically" (because of an unwarranted assertion of language's securing of access to the "as such" of Being, as Heidegger thinks), that the question of the Open or the Clearing is always and only a question for human beings—a point that is staged, I think, in many of Stevens's bird poems, where the issue of human versus nonhuman access to this space is posed as a question and an enticement.

So the importance of Derrida's deconstruction of Heidegger can be stated quite precisely, and it consists in a double move. First, Derrida respects what Sloterdijk identifies as Heidegger's radical "decentering" of the human—a decentering that entails a fundamental ethical shift (of restraint, of respect) on the part of the human being toward its world. And he respects Heidegger's insistence that this decentering is not simply empirical but also fundamentally philosophical. But, second, Derrida rescues this intervention of Heidegger's from its ontotheological hangover by getting rid of Heidegger's insistence that language, as the "house of Being," is what enables an ontologically singular relationship, over and against all other forms of life, of the human to this role as "guardian" or "neighbor" of Being. This is the second "dedomestication" I spoke of earlier, and it allows us to reopen the question of Being, *as* a question, nondogmatically, while at the same time radicalizing Heidegger's intervention by making it *more* "environing."

If Sloterdijk's analysis of immunitary drift is right—that we are driven more and more inside our own competing bubbles, our microspheres of immunitary protection—then we might see Stevens's relationship to this phenomenon as on a par with Emerson's in "Self-Reliance": an ongoing movement of "aversion" to "conformity" (to borrow the terms Stanley Cavell highlights in his many writings on Emerson) that turns us away from "the sepulchers of the fathers" and toward what we used to call "Nature," as Emerson did at the opening of that famous essay in 1836.[41] Given the biographical details of Stevens's own life (which seem rather conformist, indeed), perhaps it was a process, as the poet James Dickey once put it of his work in an advertising agency in New York, of "selling my soul to the devil all day . . . and trying to buy it back at night."[42] But it provides a context in which to take seriously Stevens's otherwise odd claim—but it is a pragmatist claim, after all—about the function of the poet, that "certainly it is not to lead people out of the confusion in which they find themselves. . . . His role, in short, is to help people to live their lives."[43]

PART I

Reading Stevens,
Once More

CHAPTER 1

Poems (and Critics) of Our Climate

WALLACE STEVENS IS NOT TYPICALLY TAKEN to be an ecological poet, but were you to make that ascription, you would probably begin by drawing attention to what Stevens called his poetic "mundo," which is structured by the seasons and their changes, motifs that, in turn, body forth the more abstract poetic commitments (often called "philosophical") for which Stevens is famous. As Sebastian Gardner has noted, the world of winter in Stevens's poetry is "not the everyday world, but the world stripped of all human, anthropocentric features," and we typically arrive at it through "an operation of subtraction" of the everyday, creating a kind of "contraction" of the ordinary world, one that "involves exchanging the *world*, in the sense of something that a human subject can properly 'be in,' for mere *reality*" (to use one of Stevens's favorite terms, whose problematic nature we will pinpoint later).[1] Stevens's world of winter answers to his ceaseless desire—announced throughout his poetry, beginning to end—to know the world as it is, in itself, without human mediation or transfiguration, but (or perhaps we should say "and") it sets going a dialectical movement (though that is not the word we will want, eventually) that makes us long for a habitable world, a world full of life and light. Hence, we have Stevens's world of summer, the world associated with his other great theme, the imagination, but, as Gardner points out, the world of summer also does not correspond "to the ordinary world, of which it is rather a *transfiguration*" and a kind of intensification. Rather, the world of summer "restores the character of worldhood to reality and intensifies its habitability."[2] In between these two seasons, these two worlds, Gardner writes, "hovers the *ordinary* world," which Stevens associates with "a sense of reality that is provisional and uncertain," a "place of transition between the great antitheses of winter and summer." Stevens's expression "the plain sense of things" captures "the uncertainty about reality that Stevens locates in the ordinary world," sometimes denoting the everyday and the mundane, and sometimes tending toward the "*hard* sense of reality which characterizes the contracted world of winter."[3]

Among Stevens's critics, no one has written more about the seasonal motif than George Lensing, who observes that the seasons in Stevens are "more than pastoral backdrop or lyrical evocation"; they form "a larger mythos that lends a unity to what Stevens eventually came to call his cumulative 'grand poem.'" But they also embody "a highly personal psychodrama, even a mode of survival, for a poet who found himself for the most part estranged from the supporting ties of family (parents, wife, siblings, daughter), friendships, and religious faith."[4] While Lensing, at least in part, indexes Stevens's seasonal cycles to biographical facts, J. Hillis Miller has seen them as part of the larger cycle of "decreation" and "recreation" in Stevens's "endlessly elaborating poem," from the poetry of autumn, where the leaves fall and eventually, in winter, "man is left face to face with the bare rock of reality," to the "reconstruction of a new imagination of the world" in spring.[5] But this new world of spring obsolesces in its turn, and "in this rhythmic alternation lies our only hope to possess reality."[6] It's as if Stevens realizes in his later poetry that the poem of winter, once written, rapidly ossifies and becomes "part of the dead past long before he has finished it," and so, for Miller, the poet is forced to "make sterile vibrations back and forth between one spiritual season and the other, always a little behind the perpetual flowing of reality."[7] Stevens's solution to this impasse, Miller writes, is to achieve in the late poetry an increasingly rapid "oscillation" between the two poles of decreation (autumn/winter) and re-creation (spring/summer) that "becomes a blur in which opposites are touched simultaneously, as alternating current produces a steady beam of light."[8]

Richard Macksey, for his part, combines elements of both Lensing's and Miller's interpretation in his own version of Stevens and the seasons, when he writes that "for Stevens, man lives in the weather as he lives in the changing light of his moods and new redactions of reality."[9] As he notes, this dynamic unity "is open to change from both quarters, the turning seasons and the spinning mind," and one end of that spectrum, "rare in the tropics of *Harmonium* and dominant in the northern world of *The Rock*—is represented by the nothingness of winter, the 'basic slate.'" Here we find the world increasingly privileged in Stevens's later poetry, one of "immense clarity and intense poverty, an abandonment to pure content of consciousness unrefracted by convention or individuality," a "moment of contraction" from which the poet returns "without baggage or clothing to the bare fact of the world, a winter world of unmediated perception."[10] Precisely here, however (though many such moments could be cited in many writings on Stevens), we run aground, as I have noted elsewhere,[11] on a conundrum that has dogged Stevens criticism from the beginning to the present day, a conundrum one might associate with the terms "epistemology" and "phenomenology."[12] For here—to put it bluntly—one is forced to ask, "Well, which is it?" The "bare fact of the world" or rather "unmediated perception"? Here, it seems to me, we need another theoretical vocabulary to describe what Stevens is up to, and that vocabulary is *not*, I think, the vocabulary of phenomenology on which so many fine and nuanced engagements of Stevens's work have foundered.

That vocabulary is mobilized by Macksey as the solution, you might say, to the various philosophical conundrums that animate Stevens's poetry: "Enmeshed in the world, open to the future and the concreteness of experience, the phenomenologist chooses Husserl's 'third way' between the dangers of absolute realism or idealism. His cry of 'to the things themselves' and his insistence that all consciousness is intentional, that every *cogito* is an act, reveal fundamental aspects of Stevens's approach to writing poetry."[13] There is much to preserve here in Macksey's observation—not least of all, his emphasis on the "act" of the *cogito*, which I will amplify a bit later—but *not* his emphasis on intentionality, convincingly dismantled just a few years later by Jacques Derrida's patient unraveling of the chimera of intentionality in his engagements of Husserl, Saussure, and J. L. Austin (among others). Indeed, as we will see, Derrida's critique of intentionality and consciousness finds poetic dramatization in Stevens's handling of syntax, grammar, and vocabulary as analyzed by critics such as Helen Vendler, Roger Gilbert, Robert Lehmann, and others; and we can trace a direct line, I think, from Stanley Cavell's penetrating engagement with Emerson's thought (taken by

Harold Bloom to be the central precursor to Stevens's poetic orienta-
tion), in which intentionality is one of the very first casualties, to Ste-
vens's fundamental posture toward the relationship between mind and
world.

The title of one of the most famous books on Stevens, Bloom's *Wallace
Stevens: The Poems of Our Climate*, directs us toward a clue about how we
might articulate the ecopoetics of Stevens's work in light of the above
reservations and considerations. For the title of Stevens's "The Poems of
Our Climate" seems to have little to do with the fact of "climate" in any
literal sense, much less in the pitched sense of the word that animates
our current obsession with the Anthropocene and global warming. Here,
it's useful to read the poem in light of Stevens's well-known passage in
"The Figure of the Youth as Virile Poet":

> It is easy to suppose that few people realize on that occasion, which
> comes to all of us, when we look at the blue sky for the first time, that
> is to say: not merely see it, but look at it and experience it and for the
> first time have a sense that we live in the center of a physical poetry, a
> geography that would be intolerable except for the non-geography that
> exists there—few people realize that they are looking at the world of
> their own thoughts and the world of their own feelings.[14]

Stevens's poem seems to suggest, as this passage suggests, that the "cli-
mate" in question is finally our own internal climate of what the poem
calls "the never-resting mind."[15] And yet both poem and prose pas-
sage subtly but insistently determine that we complicate this seemingly
straightforward declaration: not just by remembering the etymology of
"geography" in the prose passage above ("earth" + "writing" in the Greek),
and not just by noting Stevens's insistence that a "non-geography" ex-
ists "there."

Let's pause for a moment and ask, where is this "there"? Inside the
organ called the "brain"? In that thing called "mind" that is coupled to
(through language, through culture, through much else),[16] but irreduc-
ible to, the physical organ itself? If so, then that means that the "world
of their own thoughts and feelings" is both inside and outside the per-
ceiving subject, at the same time, directing our attention to the dynamic
coupling of organism and environment. And, more important, Stevens
seems to suggest—in his evocation of a "physical poetry" of which "ge-
ography" and "non-geography" are, as it were, two sides—that an un-
derlying formal dynamics, an underlying poetics, joins these domains:

an "earth writing" in which form (the "non-geography" which is not a thing, not a substance) allows us to "tolerate" that geography that *is* a thing, a substance, a medium. Or consider, in the poem itself, the curious etymology of "climate," from the Greek *klima*, meaning not just "region" or "zone" but more specifically "inclination" or "slope," from the root *klinein*, meaning "to slope" or "to lean": again, an invocation of *form*, not substance. And consider as well the curious persistence of this inhuman, even ahuman, formal principle—a leaning, a disposition—that dwells within the restless mind on which the poem focuses, and how that persistence is underscored by the utterly canonical contrast (utterly canonical if we believe perhaps the greatest essay ever written on English rhyme, W. K. Wimsatt's "One Relation of Rhyme to Reason") between "simplicity" and "I," itself set against (and set up by) the dissolving similarity of the only other rhyme in the poem, "light" and "white." The issue here, in this climate, is apparently not so much how the restless human mind, in its freedom from nature and the naturally given, is anything but simple (hence the canonical function of semantic contrast, if we believe Wimsatt's thesis, in the rhyming of "simplicity" and "I"), but rather that it is "evilly compounded" and "vital," with all its "torments." But "vital" turns out to be as weird as "geography" and "climate," because what makes the "I" what it is—and where its "torments" come from—is the *opposite* of the domain of vitality and vitalism: that is, the opposite of the domain of nature, of life. But where does this restlessness come from—the desire, "torments," the "imperfect," the "bitterness" "flawed" and "stubborn"? From a bad attitude? From a psychological complex of some kind? I don't think so. It's more infrastructural (indeed, more inhuman) than that, and we find a hint in the fact that we can't help but hear—if we've read Bloom on Stevens—in this "compounded" "I" the echo of the compound *eye* that we find in flying insects, the *omateum* (to use the Latin scientific term) that A. R. Ammons—the central inheritor of the Emerson/Stevens line in contemporary American poetry, according to Bloom—chose as the title for his first book (trafficking, as all Emersonians do, in the fecundity of the "I"/"eye" topos). That "eye" takes the "I" in Stevens's poem back to nature, perhaps (by means of the insect world), but it is a denaturalized naturalism at work here, because the eye that *sees*, and the I that *says* (as we know from Emerson) are riven by paradoxical self-reference (as in Emerson's famous "transparent eyeball" of *Nature*: "I am nothing. I see all").[17] The motor of specification, of differentiation, of individuation—what Derrida calls the "*machinalité*" of any semiotic code that is underneath any enunciation, any utterance—is what makes the "never-resting mind" inescapably, and infrastructurally, restless.[18] Seeing is not seeing; the "eye" decomposes the "I" even as it composes it.

We find a similar co-implication of what we thought were opposites (the domain of nature over *here*, the domain of the mind and the emotions over *there*) in the echoes of both "carnal" (body) and "incarnation" (process) in the "pink and white carnations" themselves; in the folding of the "light" (natural givenness) of the second line into the "delight" (unpredictable emotion) of the last stanza; the punning echo of "sense" and "scents"; and the persistence of "-scape" (as in "landscape," but also—and more on this later—"*inscape*" in Gerard Manley Hopkins's strange terminology) in the "escape" one would want in the face of "what had been so long composed." So maybe the "brilliant bowl," which is also and at the same time "a cold porcelain, low and round"—the formal container, too simple—is really just the bottom half, as it were (a kind of spectral half, implying its other half) of the "orb" of Stevens's late poem "A Primitive Like an Orb," "the essential poem at the centre of things," which focuses our attention not on the simple givenness of form (all too pretty), but rather on *form as process*: "the poem of the composition of the whole": "composition" versus, in the earlier poem, "what had been so long composed."[19] And perhaps the bowl is a spectral half, too, of "The Planet on the Table" (one of Stevens's very last poems), which begins, as "The Poems of Our Climate" seems to begin and end, with the speaker's inclination—"Ariel was glad he had written his poems. / They were of a remembered time / Or of something seen that he liked"—but only to end with the very different kind of inclination (thinking back now to the etymology of "climate" as a slope or a leaning). For what matters about the poems written by the speaker of "The Planet on the Table" is that "they should bear / Some lineament or character" of "the planet of which they were a part."[20]

And so, to sum up, when Stevens writes, "we live in the center of a physical poetry, a geography that would be intolerable except for the non-geography that exists there—few people realize that they are looking at the world of their own thoughts and the world of their own feelings," we have to unpack what Stevens is up to here in two stages. Stage one is that the most obvious candidate for the "non-geography" is the self-reference of the mind and imagination—"the world of their own thoughts and their own feelings"—which itself *already* deconstructs the holism of Stevens's "mundo." But stage two directs us, upon closer scrutiny, toward Stevens's "non-geography that exists *there*," which for my purposes reaches back to Emerson's interest (in *Nature* and elsewhere) in the question of *form*, but form as process, as performative (whether that form be the vehicle of either scientific or spiritual forces, as Joan Richardson has noted),[21] and forward to the relationship between form and "world" that we'll explore in chapter 3 by cross-conjugating contemporary continental philosophy and theoretical biology. To put this telegraphically for the moment, the dynamic, formal, and material principles at work in "their own thoughts and feelings" are not *only* at work in the domain of the subject (leave aside "intentionality"), but are in fact pervasive in a way that joins the human and nonhuman domains.

For Stevens, then, to insist on the "non-geography" of the mind, the imagination, and so on is to insist that the deeper that commitment, the more we can tease out its fundamentally inhuman and ahuman formal dynamics (as we'll see in some detail in our discussion of "The Irrational Element in Poetry"). And this gives us a way to take seriously Stevens's insistence, in "The Planet on the Table," that the poems should body forth "some lineament or character" of "the planet of which they were a part": not by embracing holism, with the poet as its designated mouthpiece, but by foregrounding what we will later call a "topological" (or "mereological") rather than "topographical" sense of ecological relations.[22] And we can thus surmise—to return to the question of "climate" raised above—that if Stevens could address the era of the Anthropocene, he would say that there is a precipitous "earth-writing" here, to be sure (literally, of course, as a stratigraphic registration of anthropogenic activity), but that "earth-writing" is never a generic or given antecedent (a thing, a substance) that is separable from the "non-geography" that animates particular forms of life, including ours (and not just ours, as we'll see in our discussion of birds, bird song, and bird poems in chapter 4).[23] In short, we are talking not about "nature" but about "environment," or, perhaps even better, "environ*ing*." "Earth-writing" is "earth-*writing*."

Richard Poirier, in his influential *Poetry and Pragmatism*, comes at the "flawed words and stubborn sounds" of "The Poems of Our Climate" from the standpoint of a fundamental "linguistic skepticism" that orients the Emerson/Stevens/pragmatism genealogy, with William James as the key intermediary. Poirier's reading is framed by what he sees as the commitment of the Emerson/Stevens line to writing as an "act of self-erasure, of disowning the words by which just a few seconds ago you may have identified yourself"—a process that "becomes in fact, and paradoxically, an indication of selfhood."[24] To help make his point about skepticism, Poirier quotes a remarkable passage by the distinguished textual scholar G. Thomas Tanselle (which must seem even more remarkable in the current context of literary study, given its obsession with archives). Tanselle emphasizes the enormous gulf between any text "embodied on paper or film or in memory—of a literary, musical, choreographic, or cinematic work" and "the 'work' or performative activity or thought," as Poirier puts it, "that produced it." And so, Tanselle continues, "those most emphatic in holding that the meaning of literature emerges from a knowledge of its historical context—those most likely, that is, to believe themselves scrupulous in the use of historical evidence—are in fact hindering their progress toward their goal if they do not recognize that artifacts may be less reliable witnesses to the past than their own imaginative reconstructions"—hence the "linguistic skepticism" foregrounded by Poirier.[25] (And hence, too, as we shall see in the next chapter, the need to articulate much more carefully the relations, and disrelations, between what Niklas Luhmann characterizes as "psychic" vs. "social" systems, "consciousness" vs. "communication.")

The issue here is not just the mundane one described by Poirier—that "the same work gets repeated throughout history in different texts, each being a revision of past texts to meet present needs"[26]—but the more complex question of how to articulate the relationship between this "beyond" toward which the performativity of the writer moves, to which both language and its historical, textual monuments are inadequate (hence the skepticism), and the contingency of the particular enunciation in the here and now that declares it to *be* inadequate—a problem in which Stevens is conspicuously invested in important poems such as "Sunday Morning" and "The Auroras of Autumn." How do we describe this enunciation—which Stevens formalized with the prescriptions for "The Supreme Fiction" that "It Must Change," "It Must Give Pleasure," and "It Must Be Abstract"—in a way that can draw out the rigor of its poetics? And how might this "beyond"—of the enunciation, of the writing and speaking subject—be described as intensely and ecologically real even though not yet (and not ever) completely known or knowable to the speaking and writing subject of the enunciation?

The relationship of this process to the question of language—*and* to the question of the difference between language and the broader domain of meaning-making, *and* to how *those* questions are related to the differences between human and nonhuman forms of life—presents a challenge that Poirier's work is able to direct us toward but not really resolve. He makes a first attempt by quoting William James on how any new reality created in the present world must "build out" on "previous truths." James writes that "man *engenders* truths" upon the world. Thus, in Poirier's words, a text "is like a newborn baby: authored by its parents, its origins are lost, as are theirs, within untraceably ancient genetic codings." And thus, "because it is a copy it can be recognized and understood, and yet as to its ultimate source it carries within itself a mystery that neither we nor it can ever fully know or articulate."[27] There is much to admire here, and as we shall see in chapter 3, current work in theoretical biology is more germane to the simile than Poirier might imagine. But for that very reason, the claim must be handled quite carefully. For we have to remember that, whatever "texts" are, they are in an important sense the *opposite* of organic, biological processes, even if these latter are subtended in part by semiotic codes (genetics, for example), the formal *"machinalité"* that we touched on earlier. And this is why any suggestion that the literary language of Emerson or Stevens somehow represents biological or organic process (such as Joan Richardson's suggestion that "the signal, if implicit, move of Pragmatism is the realization of thinking as a life form, subject to the same processes of growth and change as all other life forms") must be handled very carefully, to say the least.[28] The key distinction here, again, is production—*poiesis*—versus *representation*.

This is the problem with Richardson's claim that for writers in the Emerson/James/Stevens line, the fundamental task was "taking into full account and translating into their stylistic practices as accurate a representation as possible, within a linguistic system, of the structure of the natural world as it was known in their moments."[29] The issue here is not—indeed, as we shall see in chapter 3, *cannot* be for biological systems— "representation" or "accuracy." Rather, it is the more complicated question of how poetry may be understood as both "natural" (as a biological and psychic phenomenon of consciousness) and radically unnatural (as a process made possible only through the prosthetic machinery of the "dead letter" of social forms and conventions such as language, replete with all their own self-reference, historicity, and intertextuality). Beyond that, what remains to be done is to articulate with greater precision not only the biological and nonbiological components of those ways of meaning, but also their relation to other, broader modes of meaning-making beyond the human domain—a relationship that Stevens is keenly interested in, and nowhere more obviously, perhaps (as we'll see in chapter 4), than in his bird poems.

This set of problems percolates underneath Poirier's engagement with James—and underneath James himself: for example, in James's "Pragmatism and Humanism," which is interested in the relationship between linguistic and textual phenomena, psychic states and "experience," and that other entity called "reality." Poirier has just argued that "the repeated anagnorisis or recognition in the story of soul is that its progress is forever threatened by textuality, by contraction of work into a text"—"the dump is full of images," as Stevens put it[30]—and then he quotes James, who suggests that

> when we talk of reality "independent" of human thinking, then, it seems a thing very hard to find. It reduces to the notion of what is just entering into experience and yet to be named . . . It is what is absolutely dumb and evanescent, the merely ideal limit of our minds. We may glimpse it, but we never grasp it; what we grasp is always some substitute for it which previous human thinking has peptonized and cooked for our consumption. If so vulgar an expression were allowed us, we might say that wherever we find it, it has been already *faked*.[31]

There's a deep, deep Emersonian background to the animating spirit here, of course. As Stanley Cavell reminds us in his spectacular reading of Emerson's essay "Experience" with regard to the question of skepticism, Emerson's characterization as "unhandsome" of the state of affairs described by James prepares us not just for how we should hear "grasp" in the passage quoted above, but also for the pragmatist recalibration of what philosophy is taken to be in such a situation: philosophy not as a "grasping" or capture of the world by propositions and concepts (which could be precisely calibrated, as it were, by epistemology), but as a rather more "literary" matter of letting the world reveal itself in a process of what Emerson calls "reception."[32] Stevens himself is in the thick of this conversation, of course, and nowhere more so than in the late poems, including the posthumous "The Region November," where "the way things say," "that which is not yet knowledge," is "like a critic of God, the world // And human nature, pensively seated // On the waste throne of his own wilderness."[33]

The problem here can be stated quite precisely, and it consists of three components: first, James's invocation of the difference between psychic experience and social communication; second, how historical inheritance and cultural legacy bear upon that difference (something that Emerson and Stevens are keenly interested in, of course, as are perhaps all "Romantic" poets); and third (and most important for my immediate purposes), the assumption that psychic experience *can* be "faked" by what is "named"—an assumption that will wither, as we'll see in the next chapter, under Niklas Luhmann's more precise description of the difference between psychic and social systems and how they are structurally coupled through media such as language. In the light of which, there can be no talk of psychic experience being "faked" by the "named," since it is, on principle, impossible for psychic experience to be *represented*—fakely *or* accurately—by language.

James's swerve toward "independent," on the one hand, and "faked," on the other, leads us away from a much more promising formulation in Poirier's engagement of the Emersonian line—more promising because it emphasizes not the representational but the performative aspect of language and textuality. He reads Emerson as "not *describing* a situation in which 'previous human thinking has peptonized and cooked' reality, including such reality as is just flickering across the mind. Rather, his writing *enacts* the struggles by which he tries to keep his own language from becoming 'faked.'"[34] And here again we need to ask what the relationship is between this "enacting" and the world "outside" or "beyond" toward which it is directed. How are these two domains connected or disconnected? Poirier reads Emerson as engaging in a kind of "sacrificial" practice in which he offers himself over to the struggle of bridging the two; he imagines Emerson saying this "is how I have learned, before your very eyes, to cope with the one medium essential to the conduct of human life in culture, the medium whose invention and reinvention distinguishes us, as Kenneth Burke suggests, from other animals," about which Poirier editorializes: "Of course other animals have languages of their own, but they have not, so far as anyone can tell, evolved cultures of their own, and for the reason that their languages are biologically transmitted, and therefore do not change; the languages are not recreated by activities of the soul. They have no literary or artistic inheritance to transmit."[35]

My aim for the moment is not to take up the efficacy of this claim, or the more egregious contention that "the invention of consciousness is simultaneous with the invention of language, which, in turn, measures both the restraint upon and the expression of human freedom"[36]—something I have done in some detail elsewhere.[37] It is rather to suggest that this is not where the emphasis really falls in Stevens's engagement of nonhuman and "animal" reality—a point made sometimes obliquely (as in "Autumn Refrain") and sometimes quite explicitly (as in section IX of "Credences of Summer," or in the "scrawny cry" and "new knowledge of reality" of "Not Ideas about the Thing but the Thing Itself," both of which I will discuss in some detail in the chapters to come). I think that Stevens's concern at such moments is not so much with the human struggle with human language (to paraphrase Poirier), the struggle of the human with itself and its legacies, as with the question of how the inhuman or ahuman domain can be brought into poetry, or how poetry (to put it another way) can be responsive—maybe even uniquely responsive—to the nonhuman world. The complicated problem here is that such a response to the nonhuman world is taking place, necessarily, in a poem, in language, even as the issue for Stevens is not, as Poirier puts it, "the actual *inadequacy* of language to the task of representing reality," simply because the issue here is not—and could never be—"representing reality."[38]

I will address this problem in copious detail in the next chapter, in my discussion of Stevens's essay "The Irrational Element in Poetry," but let's stay with Poirier a moment more as he explores one more strategy for thinking about how we can locate the nonhuman or ahuman in a poetry that cannot, by definition, *represent* it. What writers in the Emersonian line realize, he suggests, is that "the customary structures of sentences give precedence to substantives, while transitives, including prepositions, conjunctions, and adverbs, merely speed the way toward nouns, more or less expending themselves in the process." But for writers like Emerson and Stevens, he argues, "superfluity, itself an abstract noun, points to a human desire to go beyond these usual stopping places in sentences, these nouns, abstractions, concepts that serve the function of homes or still points, making us their dependents."[39] Poirier here captures something of what Stanley Cavell will call the "onwardness" and "abandonment" of the Emersonian posture or "climate" (which will help us, in turn, to rethink the question of dwelling in an ecological sense—a point I will explore in the final chapter).[40] And his point of emphasis takes us in a rather different direction—one I am tempted to call more "machinic" or "prosthetic"—from James, whom he quotes in this context. James writes:

> We ought to say a feeling of *and*, a feeling of *if*, a feeling of *but*, and a feeling of *by*, quite as readily as we say a feeling of *blue* or a feeling of *cold* ...
> There is not a conjunction or a preposition, and hardly an adverbial phrase, syntactic form, or inflection of voice, in human speech, that does not express some shading or other of relation which we at some moment actually feel to exist between the larger objects of our thought.[41]

Poirier's angle of questioning here actually pushes us *away* from James's interest in a correlation of language with experience, and toward a focus on the heightened rhetoricity and artificiality of those prepositions, adverbs, conjunctions, and transitives that operate in the services of "superfluity"—an "onwardness" that will, in Stevens, turn out to be a crucial part of an ecological poetics, though not in the usual sense. These are not representations, pictures of a world; they are *doings*, ways of being *in* the world, connected with it—and in quite particular ways.

Several critics have explored this aspect of Stevens's style, reaching back to Helen Vendler's early essay on Stevens's "qualified assertions" and her emphasis on "the frequency with which he closes his poems on a tentative note," resorting "repeatedly to some of the modal auxiliaries—may, might, and must, could, should, and would—to conclude his 'statement.'"[42] One effect of this, she notes, is that "the texture of Stevens' language is such that it shifts from 'reality' to the realm of the 'as if' very easily, making the two almost interchangeable at times," so that he is able to use logic "not as a logician but as a sleight-of-hand man . . . delighting in paradoxical logic"[43]—a point we'll unpack in greater detail in the next chapter. Beverly Maeder, who has written the most extensive book on Stevens's grammar and syntax, similarly draws our attention to Stevens's salient use of "'function words,' such as prepositions, modal verbs, and certain uses of the verb *to be*"—words that are "weak in semantic content but that bind other words and parts of sentences together in special ways," and so are "central to the poems' tentative, speculative edge."[44] Roger Gilbert has calculated that roughly one in every twenty-seven words in Stevens's *Collected Poems* is some form of the verb "to be" and, significantly, roughly one-third of those occurrences are preceded by what linguists call "dummy subjects," words such as "there," "this," and "here": significant because the designation of the ontological claim "to be" gets referred to the provisional and contingent performativity (the "location," if you will) of "there," "this," and "here."[45] And even though most studies of Stevens's diction, he notes, have focused on its "florabundant" aspects, much of Stevens's diction is centered on what Maeder calls the "functional core" of English, words that are performative and grammatically *enactive* rather than denotative and representational.[46]

The result, Maeder writes, is that in Stevens, word choice "means less the search for the right word or *le mot juste* than the experimental combination . . . to draw attention to, and to stimulate pleasure in, the poem's constructedness or artifice."[47] Indeed, as she notes, Stevens's later poetry takes "some distance from the exotic flourishes he included in his early poems."[48] Mac Hammond puts it even more forcefully: "after the gorgeous vocabulary of the 1923 *Harmonium* volume, the bareness of vocabulary in poems beginning with 'The Man with the Blue Guitar' (1937) seems something of a desert." And when we ask, "Of what does this desert music consist?" his answer, like Maeder's and Vendler's, is astute: "to lay bare the grammatical structure of the speech and to place a heavy burden on the grammar in respect to the communication of meaning. The late poetry of Stevens is, in short, a poetry of grammar."⁴⁹ All of the foregoing helps to underscore the difference between how I locate the ecopoetics of Stevens's work and how that project has been understood by recent critics such as Joan Richardson; and it is one of the reasons, but an important one, why I will spend much more time in this study on Stevens's late rather than early poetry.

My emphasis on this "functional" or "weak" or "rhetorical" quality of Stevens's poetics is meant to emphasize that the point here is not "accuracy" or "representation" in relation to the natural world, but rather a *performativity* that highlights at every moment the contingency of the observing subject and its construal of the world, which then gets handled within the specific (and nonnatural) technology of the poem, foregrounding the relationship between the world of "fact" (Stevens's "reality") and the *factum* of the poem itself—literally an act, a making, as Simon Critchley has pointed out (about which more in the next chapter).⁵⁰ And *this* fact directs our attention to a very different understanding of the "ecological" dimension of the poetry, because it foregrounds, as does Stevens's "functional" and rhetorical core, the "machinic" and "iterative" nature of meaning that inheres not just in poems, and not just in human language, but across ontological domains (as we'll see in the discussion of bird song and bird poems in chapter 4). Performativity and iterability, in other words, are far larger domains of meaning-making than "language" proper. And in this light we can see that the problem with Poirier is not his emphasis on performativity—which opens onto the Emersonian poetic project of "onwardness"—but rather his suggestion that all of this is, in the end, simply a *linguistic* phenomenon, in which we are enjoined "to participate as readers in a recurrent discovery about the language we inherit: that by a conscious effort of linguistic skepticism it is possible to reveal, in the words and phrases we use, linguistic resources that point to something beyond skepticism, to possibilities of personal and cultural renewal."⁵¹ To put it more precisely, Poirier does not sufficiently *disarticulate* questions of language, strictly speaking, and questions of meaning (which is not, of course, a strictly linguistic phenomenon)—a task that has to be undertaken *before* we can describe how the two are conjoined in the domain of "consciousness," "experience," and the like by means of the medium called "language" and the workings of the poem.

We find a slightly different problem in one of Stevens's most important recent critics, Joan Richardson, whose body of work on Stevens (it should go without saying, but I'll say it anyway) is invaluable to my (our) generation of critics. She argues in *Pragmatism and American Experience* that Stevens's relationship to the knot of problems I have been discussing reaches back to his *father*'s reading of a series of articles published by Charles Sanders Peirce in *Popular Science Monthly* under the title "Illustrations in the Logic of Science," which became, she writes, "the core of what would come to be called 'pragmatism.'"[52] She invokes Poirier's *Poetry and Pragmatism*—and *his* invocation of James, too—but then ends up, I think, in precisely the wrong spot when she anchors Stevens's poetics in what Peirce calls "the 'I' as zero, 'origin of all coordinates.'"[53] The problem here is not the focus on the "I" (as the brief discussion above of the Emersonian eye/I attests); the problem is that the status of that "I" is equated with intentionality, rather than with the division of intentionality that resides at its core because of the "*machinalité*" of its enunciation by means of something—call it language, call it code—that is radically *not* the "I," and indeed that is radically ahuman, nonliving. Richardson is right to note that the task of "the pragmatic method" of James, Peirce, and Stevens "is to navigate from where we are to where we want to go, plotting a course into the cosmic weather," but wrong, I think, to follow Peirce's suggestion that in this process, "*intention* is central = 'I' = the 'storm center.'"[54] The problem can be put quite succinctly: while it is true that performativity in the general sense invoked by Richardson and Poirier requires intentionality, it is also true that intentionality is never "master in its own house," for well-known (even canonical) reasons reaching back to Marx, Freud, and Nietzsche and forward to Derrida and Luhmann (who will be my main coordinates here).

There is, I think, a fundamental, and irreconcilable, tension between the indexing of pragmatist performativity to intentionality (or for that matter, and by extension, to Jamesian "experience") and the more promising direction suggested by Richardson when she reminds us of the *other* side of pragmatism (and of James) in quoting his address "The Experience of Activity" from 1904. There, James plumbs the Darwinian background of pragmatism in the following way: "No philosophic knowledge of the general nature and constitution of tendencies, or of the relation of large to smaller ones, can help us to predict which of all the various competing tendencies that interest us in this universe are likely to prevail."[55] The point here is not just the theoretical one made by recent thinkers such as Elizabeth Grosz, who points out that for Darwin, the question of origin for life and species is thus "the point where Darwin's own account uncannily anticipates Derridean *différance*."[56] It is also the case for quite good scientific reasons, which we will unpack in some detail in chapter 3 when we explore theoretical biology's recent reconceptualization of the evolution of the biosphere as a "nonergodic" process without "entailing laws."

To put it this way is not just to sharpen our sense of the irreconcilability of "intentionality" and "belief," on the one hand, and a more complex understanding of performativity, on the other—and in doing so, to sharpen our sense of what (and how) pragmatism means; it is also to open up a space in which we can pursue by other means Richardson's astute observation that in Stevens's poetry she "found and continues to find answers to 'Where do we find ourselves?' in this extended moment," a continuation of the Emersonian question posed at the opening of his essay "Experience" that leads to one of the most intelligent things I have ever read about Stevens's poetic pursuit: that "reading or hearing Stevens's lines in memory always puts me in mind simultaneously of the limitation and the wonder of knowing anything at all."[57] Though Richardson might not think of it in these terms, that is a very deconstructive point to make. And in Stevens's poetry, it opens onto questions not of representation but of *strategy*: hence Stevens relentlessly calling our attention, as we saw above, to his "weak" or "functional" poetics and the excessive rhetoricity thereof.

Angus Fletcher's portly book *A New Theory for American Poetry: Democracy, the Environment, and the Future of Imagination* shares Richardson's interest in poetic forms of knowledge and their underlying ecological conditions of possibility and emergence. Even though Stevens does not figure prominently in Fletcher's account, he does appear in the opening pages, where Fletcher suggests that we need to drive a wedge between the Romanticism of which Stevens (and Hart Crane) are thought to be the inheritors, and "a deeper, a more truly underlying strain of English poetry that both precedes and grounds English Romanticism and later subtends for us what Emerson called the transcendental and the extraordinary in our American poetic vision."[58] Now, what is odd about Fletcher's book is that its central thesis—which he associates with Emersonian pragmatism and its apotheosis in the poetry of Whitman—centers on what he calls "the *environment-poem*," in which "the poet neither writes *about* the surrounding world, thematizing it, nor analytically represents that world, but actually shapes the poem to *be* an Emersonian or esemplastic circle."[59] And yet that thesis is seen to be *opposed* to the poetics associated with Stevens. This is even stranger because, for Fletcher, the "environment-poem" ends up having essentially the same formal characteristics as recursive self-organizing systems in complexity theory and chaos theory. The effect they create is "to surround the reader, such that to read them is to have an experience much like suddenly recognizing that one actually has an environment, instead of not perceiving the surround at all."[60] Crucially, he argues, coherence in the context of the environment-poem is like the so-called coherence theory of truth in philosophy, "as distinct from the opposed, exceedingly powerful theory which defines truth as accuracy and adequacy of representation."[61]

This is certainly a step in the right (that is to say, antirepresentationalist) direction, but one that makes it all the more curious why—*especially* given the details of Fletcher's framework, ballasted as it is by the paradigm of self-organizing, emergent complexity—Stevens is not Exhibit A in this "environment-poem" tradition, with its "inward dialectical questioning of opposites."[62] A fundamental problem with Fletcher's analysis[63]—and it is perhaps the source of the disconnection from Stevens in his theory—is its insufficient attention to the difference (and the stakes of the difference) between first- and second-order systems theory, and a tendency to lapse into first-order modes of analysis when only a second-order approach can advance us deeper into an understanding of the poetics. For example, Fletcher writes that "sometimes, when we perceive things, we notice we are crossing back and forth between an inner self and a world out there . . . Such mental activity is both inside and outside at the same moment, while we the perceivers stand between." Or—to take another example—"the scientist looks at the ways in which such co-ordination requires hidden skills that give the system (birds, fish, ants, buyers) new information needed for modeling new and ever changing conditions."[64] But second-order systems theory rejects the semantics of both information and modeling and "inside" versus "outside." As theoretical biologists Humberto Maturana and Francisco Varela note, "The most popular and current view of the nervous system considers it as an instrument whereby the organism gets information from the environment which it then uses to build a *representation* of the world," but in fact, "representation" is not what it at issue.[65]

More important, second-order theory foregrounds the inescapable—and dynamically productive—role of paradoxical self-reference in bringing forth a world in a process of what Maturana and Varela call embodied enaction: paradoxical because (as we'll see in detail in the next two chapters) the "inside"/"outside" distinction is itself what we will call a "topographical" misconstrual of a "topological" relationship between "inside" and "outside," "mind" and "world." (And this paradoxical and topological relationship is never far to seek, of course, in Stevens's poetry.) I say "topological" here because what seem opposites (inside/outside, mind/world) are, paradoxically, the two sides of a deeper unity, the same form. The inside/outside distinction is itself, paradoxically, a product of one side of the distinction: the inside. Or, to put it in biological terms: organisms don't "represent" the "outside" world, they bring it forth in their dynamic and recursive autopoiesis. I belabor the point because, while Fletcher is certainly right about the importance of Emersonian pragmatism in the "environment-poem" tradition, what decisively *binds* rather than separates Emerson and Stevens is their shared emphasis on the paradoxical self-reference of the imagination (often troped as vision, as underscored in Joseph Riddell's masterful study of Stevens from the 1960s titled *The Clairvoyant Eye*[66]—the famous eye/I of Emersonianism, of course, already touched upon above). This is the radical—and radically "ecological," I would argue—conclusion that Fletcher's essentially *first-order* deployment of complexity theory is unprepared and unable to address: the second-order understanding that paradoxical self-reference, precisely because of its contingency, is a reservoir of environmental complexity.[67]

Fletcher's recourse to theories of complexity, emergence, self-organization, and so on constitutes an admirable attempt to get at what Roy Harvey Pearce finds intensified in Stevens's "late," even "final" mode, from *Transport to Summer* through poems such as "The Rock" and "Not Ideas about the Thing but the Thing Itself": a kind of swerving away or subversion of "the dialectical compromise" between "mind" or "imagination" and "reality" that, "although it is still wished for, is no longer conceivable. The poet will do one thing or the other. He will celebrate mind or celebrate things themselves."[68] Pearce observes that, as philosophy, this may seem a naïve way of dealing with the subject-object problem at the core of Stevens's Romantic inheritance, but, as he cannily notes, "it seems naïve only on first glance—as it seems to be philosophizing only on first glance."[69] Indeed, as Pearce points out, in a late essay, "A Collect of Philosophy," Stevens argues that although both the philosopher and the poet seek to "form concepts" in the service of the "integration of thought" (itself in the service of "a general will to order"), the philosopher "intends his integration to be fateful" (in the sense of "sufficient in itself"), while "the poet intends his to be effective."[70]

Two issues are posed here: the underlying problem—let us call it, in shorthand, the subject-object/mind-world problem—and the different *solutions* to the problem that are possible for poetry vs. philosophy. Regarding the latter issue, Pearce focuses our attention on one of the last poems Stevens ever wrote, "The Region November," touched on earlier, which was published the year after the poet's death. There, the speaker observes the "north wind" and the swaying of the treetops, and finds the trees "Saying and saying, the way things say / On the level of that which is not yet knowledge," and concludes, in that beguiling Stevens manner, "Deeplier, deeplier, loudlier, loudlier, / The trees are swaying, swaying, swaying."[71]

Now let's keep in mind here, once again, that the fundamental question taken up by the poem is the one broached in "The Planet on the Table," *also* one of the last poems Stevens wrote: that "what mattered" was that the poems should bear "Some lineament or character" of "the planet of which they were a part."[72] In a wonderfully suggestive engagement with this posthumously published poem, Pearce writes, in a passage worth quoting at length:

> The poem see-saws between "sway" and "say"—the movement of meter and sensibility being enforced by the outrageous adverbs, "deeplier" and "loudlier" . . . The effort of the treetops is "So much less than feeling, so much less than speech." Yet it proves a feeling and speech of some sort; and the poet can suppose that they "say / On the level of that which is not yet knowledge." "On the level of . . ." is "philosophic" diction, and so bids us think with this lyric, not sing mournfully with it. The "not yet intended" of the seventh line is in fact a bit of technical language out of Stevens' dabbling in phenomenology, in whose logic all revelations are nothing if not "intended." Now he decides that, spontaneously, without intention, to be is to say: to say what "It is hard to hear." In short, Stevens is claiming that if the treetops do "say," it is not in the language of any "speech" . . . He will not let himself be trapped in the anthropocentrism, as often as not masked as theocentrism, of his "romantic" forebears and contemporaries. He will be a radical humanist to the end. But his humanism now forces him to acknowledge both the virtual life of the non-human and its virtual capacity to "say."[73]

I've already dwelt upon the resonance of the term "virtual" above, so here, let me pick up on two quite precise locutions by Stevens in both of these late poems—"not yet intended" from "The Region of November" and "only half-perceived" from "The Planet on the Table"—and add them to what Pearce draws our attention to in this passage: a kind of "saying" or meaning-making by the "non-human" world, one not reducible to speech and thus "hard to hear." I do so as an invitation to pursue a theoretical framework quite different from phenomenology, one that had been taking shape during the same period in which Pearce's essay on Stevens appears: namely, Gregory Bateson's work in systems theory on what he called "ecology of mind." Bateson's interest is in forms of meaning— what he calls "ideas"—for which human "speech" is not a constitutive element, and in which various nonhuman living systems participate quite robustly, all the time. Bateson's work will allow us to begin to understand why we will need a posthumanist rather than humanist framework to understand, as Pearce puts it at the end of this wonderful passage, "the virtual life of the non-human and its virtual capacity to 'say.'"

Pearce's gambit sets the stage for Bateson's much more rigorous reframing of the differences between the logical, the epistemological, and the ecological in the broader context of poetry vs. philosophy. Bateson reminds us, in "Epistemology and Ecology," of the Liar's Paradox familiar to us from the philosophical tradition's confrontation with the problem of paradoxical self-reference. "If Epimenides was right in saying that Cretans always lie," Bateson writes, "and he was a Cretan, was he a liar or not a liar? If he was a liar, then he was not a liar. If he was not a liar, then it was untrue that Cretans are always liars, and so on. Now," he continues, in a crucial advance on Pearce's quarry,

> look at the "then" in that paradox. If yes, then no. If no, then yes. If the "then" is logical, there is a paradox, but if the "then" is causal and temporal, the contradiction disappears. The sequence is like that of the electric bell on the front door. If the circuit is complete, then a magnet is activated which will break the circuit. If the circuit is broken, then the magnet will not be activated, and the circuit will be restored. If the circuit is restored, then the magnet will be activated, and the circuit will be broken, and so on. We get an oscillation, and the paradox "if yes then no; if no then yes" contains a real *temporal* "then."[74]

This, it seems to me, is *already* a major step. Bateson is describing here the "recursiveness" that is constitutive of "oscillating" systems that use their own outputs as inputs, and such systems include, but are not limited to, biological, computational, and mental systems. And the temporalization of the "then" means that the same element in such a system can have a different, even opposed, meaning at a different point in time, depending on the dynamic state of the system as a whole. Such systems do not operate with, and are not constituted by, *substances* that have fixed and permanent meanings. And this is one of the reasons, Bateson writes, that "*logic is a very poor model of the world of mental processes*. We used to ask whether computers could simulate all conceivable steps of logic, but it turns out that this was precisely a wrong question. The truth of the matter is that logic cannot simulate all the steps of causal systems operating in time."[75]

We will examine this crucial fact of the temporalization of the "then" in biological and evolutionary systems in much more detail in chapter 3, but for the moment I only want to amplify two points: first, Bateson's account gives us a robustly naturalistic way to understand the problem that captivates so many of Stevens's critics (and captivated Stevens): how poetry can take on and explore philosophical problems that philosophy *qua* logic can't handle because it isn't complex enough; and it isn't complex enough because, for logic, *time* is not a constitutive element. To put it bluntly, therefore, poetic strategies for handling the philosophical problems Stevens is so interested in may be less "logical" but, for that very reason, more "effective" (and here Fletcher's hunch about "pragmatism" is spot on) insofar as they are more *ecological*: that is to say, they partake of the same nonlogical "integration" (to use his term) that characterizes biological, ecological, and evolutionary systems. Or, as Luhmann puts it in a formulation we'll explore in the next chapter, they don't make sense, they make meaning.

It is worth emphasizing one last time that such systems *are not representational* because they operate not with fixed substances but rather with elements whose function and significance in the system will always vary in the context of the temporalized complexity emphasized by Bateson. But they are also not representational in an even more important sense elucidated by Bateson—important, given the habitual recourse to phenomenology and intentionality in the critical literature on Stevens. If it is true that meaning-making systems and biological systems are nonrepresentational in the first sense just discussed, then it is also true, as Bateson puts it, that "mind always operates at one remove away from matter," at "one *derivative*" from the so-called "'external' world." "The primary data of experience are *differences*," he continues. "From these data we construct our hypothetical (always hypothetical) ideas and pictures of that 'external' world."[76] This is not primarily a philosophical or epistemological assertion—and it is certainly not about "correlationism" (a point I'll return to later on); rather, it is an evolutionary and adaptive necessity. As Bateson notes, "you have sense organs specially designed to keep the world out," but "very few people seem to realize the enormous theoretical 'power' of this distinction between what I 'see' and what is out there."[77] Most people, Bateson continues, assume that "they see what they look at and they assume this *because* there is total unconsciousness of the processes of perception . . . My mental machinery provides me not with the news of its processes, but with news of its products. Indeed, there is a certain common sense in a world so constructed that organisms shall not be bothered with news of processes and they shall be given the product only. But, in fact, the processes of *making* images are of a very great complexity, and can be experimentally investigated," as in, for example, the famous false parallax experiments of Adelbert Ames that Bateson describes.[78]

Interestingly enough, Bateson, in the essay "The Creature and Its Creations," points to Stevens's "The Man with the Blue Guitar" as a meditation upon this process: "The poet sees himself as divided from 'Things as they are,'" Bateson observes. "*But this, after all,*" he continues, "*is the circumstance for all organisms* . . . The 'Blue Guitar,' the creative filter between us and the world, is always and inevitably there. This it is to be both creature and creator. This the poet knows much better than the biologist."[79] And at this juncture, I want to emphasize two further points made by Bateson, points that I think have considerable bearing on understanding Stevens's poetic sensibility and procedure. First, if "the primary data of experience are *differences*," then the process of experiencing "things as they are" takes on a quite different character.[80] "Consider a difference between two objects," Bateson writes, "say, a sheet of paper and a desk top. One is white and the other is brown; one is thin and the other is thick; one is flexible and the other is rigid; and so on. But these 'characteristics' are not really *in* the paper and the desk top." He continues:

They are *embodied* in the interactions between paper and desk top *and* in interactions between desk or paper and your sense organs. Consider now these embodiments of differences. Rub the paper on the desk top; try to cut the wood with the edge of the paper, and so on. Get a "feel" of the aggregate of differences between the paper and the wood. Call this feeling "news" of the difference A/B (where A was paper and B was wood). Now take two quite different objects, say plate and butter, and go through the same drill to get a feeling of the difference C/D (where

C was plate and D was butter). Now meditate to get a feeling of the difference between A/B and C/D.[81]

I think this captures something of Stevens's poetic procedure, especially in his later poetry (sometimes this procedure is nearly literalized, as in "Study of Two Pears," or "So-And-So Reclining on Her Couch," and sometimes it is more oblique, as in the many moments we will discuss in "An Ordinary Evening in New Haven"). And I think it also goes a long way toward explaining what Stevens means when he says of his "Supreme Fiction" that "[i]t must be abstract."

My second point has to do with how all of the above is related to what I have elsewhere called the "second-order turn" of "openness from closure."[82] In Stevensian terms, this might be rephrased as follows: our intense concentration on what Stevens called the "august" activity of the mind's formation of its perceived reality actually makes us more attuned to the world, and to our ongoing immersion in it, precisely because of the contingency of our self-reference. Or, as Bateson puts it, "most people are not aware that they do this, and as you become aware that you are doing it, you become in a curious way much closer to the world around you . . . The world is no longer 'out there' in quite the same way that it used to seem to be." What we find instead, he writes, is "neither pure solipsism nor its opposite" (which is, of course, the impasse in which we land in an epistemological framing of the problem). As Bateson sketches it, in solipsism, you are "ultimately isolated and alone, isolated by the premise 'I make it all up,'" but at the other extremity (what is often called "realism"), "you would cease to exist, becoming nothing but a metaphoric feather blown by the winds of external 'reality.'" And "between these two," he continues, "is a region where you are partly blown by the winds of reality and partly an artist creating a composite out of the inner and outer events"[83] Or, as Stevens will write about driving home in the lights of the highway, late on a Friday night, in "Reality Is An Activity of the Most August Imagination"—one of the many poems that wonderfully exemplifies this "composite" process—"It was not a night blown at a glassworks in Vienna," something "gathering time and dust." On the contrary, we found that "things emerged and moved and were dissolved," "An argentine abstraction approaching form / And suddenly denying itself away."[84]

CHAPTER 2

"Like Seeing Fallen Brightly Away":

A New Theory for the Emerson/Stevens Genealogy

STEVENS HAS TYPICALLY BEEN TAKEN, AMONG the major modernists, as an inheritor of the Romantic tradition. As Robert Lehmann has summarized it, "what matters, to Harold Bloom and Hillis Miller as to Frank Kermode and Helen Vendler, is Stevens's restatement, in chastened, qualified, and ironic form, of the Romantic position, his Emersonian (for Bloom), or Coleridgean (for Kermode), or Keatsian (for Vendler) ethos."[1] I shall focus here on the Emersonian strand of this legacy, because I hope to provide us with a theoretical vocabulary that can not only more usefully describe what it means to call Stevens an "Emersonian" poet, but also explain the systematic quality of some of that genealogy's more puzzling and vexing characteristics.[2] This task is all the more pressing because Emerson's writing (as Stanley Cavell has noted) has often been described by critics as a kind of "mist" or "fog" lacking denotative precision and overall coherence;[3] and Stevens's poetry (especially his late poetry) has often been viewed, even by admiring critics such as Joseph Riddell, as "a questionable poetry even by generous estimate," where "almost anything said against it can be supported."[4] What binds the Romanticism of Stevens to Emerson is not just what has been described (variously) as a denaturalized naturalism, or a detotalizing holism, but more specifically, as I suggested in the last chapter, an intense focus in both writers on the paradoxical forms of observation and self-reference that systems theory (but also, of course, in its way, deconstruction) enables us to theorize with some depth and precision. Both Emerson and Stevens go out of their way not just to declare that fact, but also to unfold its consequences rigorously as they work through the relationship between imagination and reality, mind and world.

For Stanley Cavell—whose reading of Emerson has been especially influential for my own—this central dynamic originates in Emerson's confrontation with the problem of philosophical skepticism: the fact, as Cavell puts it, "that the world exists as it were for its own reasons."[5] As Cavell characterizes what he calls Kant's "settlement" with skepticism, "to settle with skepticism . . . to assure us that we do know the existence of the world, or rather, that what we understand as knowledge is *of* the world, the price Kant asks us to pay is to cede any claim to know the thing in itself, to grant that human knowledge is not of things as they are in themselves."[6] The irony of the Kantian settlement with skepticism—an irony that will in no small part, in Cavell's view, structure Emerson's reinvention of philosophy—is that if "reason proves its power to itself, over itself," by discovering the difference between the mere appearances of which it can have knowledge and the *Ding an sich* of which it cannot, then the triumph of philosophy is also, at the same time, its failure (a final failure, as it turns out), because knowledge secures itself only by losing the world.[7] Or, as Emerson puts it in a famous passage from "Experience" that Cavell returns to time and again, "I take this evanescence and lubricity of all objects, which lets them slip through our fingers then when we clutch hardest, to be the most unhandsome part of our condition."[8]

As we will see, this is an especially apt starting point from which to explore the Emerson/Stevens connection, not least because of Stevens's well-known obsession with "reality"—"a word I wish Stevens had renounced," writes Harold Bloom, "since it takes away more meaning that it tends to give."[9] As Bloom points out, Stevens "was addicted to it in prose; he used some form of it well over a hundred times in his poetry."[10] But what does it mean? He cites Frank Kermode's gloss as perhaps the best:

> *Reality*, in Stevens' use of the word, may be the world supposed to be antecedent in itself or the world created in the specific occurrence of thought,

including the thinker himself and his mind forming the thought. Often the term offers the assumption that if the self is the central point of a circle of an infinite radius, then reality is the not-self, including all except the abstract subjective center . . . Stevens usually means by *reality* an undetermined base on which mind constructs its personal sense of the world. Occasionally he will use the word *real* as a term of approval, as a substitute for the word *true*, and, therefore, no more than an expression of confidence.[11]

The complex described by Kermode and its "abstract subjective center" is most insistently troped in Emerson and Stevens as the eye/I of vision (as in the very first line of Stevens's greatest long poem, "The eye's plain version is a thing apart"—and we note the paradox imported by the homophone "a part"), and our starting point will therefore be to lay bare the theoretical infrastructure of that trope and its generative force for Stevens's poetics, systematically generating, as it does, a quite consistent network of paradoxes in Stevens's poetry that are anything but fanciful.[12] And this infrastructure and the network it generates will open, in turn—in Stevens and in the philosophical literature—onto the crucial differences between poetry and philosophy, how poetry can achieve a kind of knowledge and engagement of the world not available to philosophy.

Or at least, if we believe Cavell, philosophy before Emerson. This is because Emerson, in his confrontation with the "unhandsomeness" of the settlement with skepticism, inaugurates a rethinking of thinking that will eventually lead, as Cavell points out, to Heidegger's assertion that "thinking is a handicraft," but a handicraft carried out in light of "the derivation of the word thinking from a root for thanking . . . as giving thanks for the gift of thinking."[13] (And eventually—as Cavell does not point out—it will lead not only to Jacques Derrida's analysis of the gift, but also to his critique of Heidegger's humanism in relation to the question of species difference in the essay "*Geschlecht* II: Heidegger's Hand.")[14] Thinking with Emerson, then, becomes not active apprehension (prehensile grasping and fixing of the world by our philosophical concepts, as it were), but rather an act of *reception*, a reception in which passivity—because it consists of a capacity to be affected by the world in manifold ways that exponentially outnumber the choked bottleneck of thought as philosophy has traditionally conceived it—becomes, paradoxically, a maximally *active* passivity. That process is everywhere testified to in Emerson's work from beginning to end, from the "transparent eye-ball" passage in *Nature*, to the seemingly paradoxical assertion in "Self-Reliance" that "self-reliance is God-reliance," to his assertion in "Experience" that "All I know is reception. I am and I have: but I do not get."[15]

But as crucial as Cavell's work has been for enabling an entirely new and deeply compelling understanding of Emerson and his relationship to continental philosophy, I suggest that a more rigorous analysis of Emerson's work is available to us if we reframe Cavell's account itself within a more comprehensive view of Emerson's Romanticism as a response to the condition of *modernity* and its epistemological and ethical fallout—a phenomenon marked in Cavell's reading by the broad brush-stroke of "skepticism." A hallmark of modernity and a keystone of modernization theory, of course, is the process of secularization, and Emerson is caught squarely in the middle of it, as his famous resignation from the Unitarian ministry in Boston makes clear.[16] For Habermas, for example, in *The Philosophical Discourse of Modernity*, secularization means that thought "can and will no longer borrow the criteria by which it takes its orientation from models supplied by another epoch; it has to create its normativity out of itself"; for Foucault—and here we return to Kant once more—it means that thought must put its "own reason to use, without subjecting itself to any authority."[17] If the upside of the philosophical situation of modernity is, as Paul Jay puts it, that "the present represents an exit or a way out of subordination to traditional sources and modes authority," then the downside, already traced in Kantian transcendentalism, is that the ungrounding of reason invites the various forms of idealism that have been attributed to Romanticism in the all-too-familiar narratives of secularization, where Mind, Spirit, Imagination, or the equivalent comes to take the place of self-generated knowledge and its authority previously reserved for God.[18]

The relevance of this last point for Stevens's preoccupation with "the death of the gods" and his conception of poetry as "the Supreme Fiction" as an answer to it is probably clear enough. They are taken up meditatively in many prose pieces, such as "Two or Three Ideas" from 1951, where he writes of "poetry and the gods" that "I do not mean to refer to them in their religious aspect but as creations of the imagination," which in turn means that "in an age of disbelief . . . it is for the poet to supply the satisfactions of belief, in his measure and in his style."[19] But here I'm interested less in the fallout of this process in the form of a cultural thematics than in the seismic shift in strategies of philosophical and poetic practice that rise to meet it—strategies that, in Stevens's case, are far more interesting as a poetics than the thematics of "the Supreme Fiction."

We find a similar process at work in Emerson's career, as he moves from his work in the ministry, to the essay *Nature* of 1836, to the mature work of the first and second series of essays, which begin to develop as well new strategies for what had seemed, at an earlier moment, culturally and philosophically manageable. As Cavell puts it, "I would characterize the difference by saying that in *Nature* Emerson is taking the issue of skepticism as solvable or controllable where thereafter he takes its unsolvability to the heart of his thinking."[20] It is precisely this "unsolvability" that generates what we can call, following Richard Rorty, an increasingly—and increasingly demanding—*antirepresentationalist* mode of philosophical practice in Emerson, one that anchors the pragmatist enterprise more generally as it develops into the twentieth century. As Rorty explains it, the problem with philosophical representationalism is the assumption that "'making true' and 'representing' are reciprocal relations," as if "the nonlinguistic item which makes S true is the one represented by S."[21] For philosophical idealism, that "item" will be something in the changeless character of the subject; for realism, it will be something in the nature of the object that "has a context of its own, a context which is privileged by virtue of being the object's rather than the inquirer's."[22] In either case, what representationalism fails to see is that "'determinacy' is not what is in question—that neither does thought determine reality nor, in the sense intended by the realist, does reality determine thought."[23] Both positions, as Cavell might say, find themselves unduly, even preeningly, "handsome"—hence the strange, insistent movement of Emerson's prose, which takes for granted, as it were, Rorty's contention that "words take their meaning from other words rather than by virtue of their representative character" and their "transparency to the real,"[24] that "'grasping the thing itself' is not something that precedes contextualization."[25]

Precisely this kind of embeddedness is everywhere under intense scrutiny in essays of Emerson's such as "Fate." And so—to return now to Cavell—to take the unsolvability of skepticism to heart is not *just*, at the same stroke, to abandon the representationalist philosophical project; it is also to change our view of the relationship of thinking and language, already discussed in some detail in chapter 1. What Kant confronted as "merely" a problem of thought, Emerson will grapple with under the additional rigors of writing and language—of philosophy as a writing practice—so that the "stipulations or terms under which we can say anything at all to one another" will themselves be subjected to endless—and endlessly unfinalized—scrutiny.[26]

One striking example of this new philosophical practice that Cavell finds in Emerson—this time in relation not to Kant but to Descartes—occurs in "Self-Reliance," when Emerson writes, "Man is timid and apologetic; he is no longer upright; he dares not say 'I think,' 'I am,' but quotes some saint or sage." If the central feature of the Cartesian subject is, as Cavell writes, the "discovery that my existence requires, hence permits, proof (you might say authentication) . . . requires that if I am to exist I must name my existence, acknowledge it," then the real rigor of Emerson's confrontation with these "terms" is that it "goes the whole way with Descartes' insight" by insisting on the proof of selfhood—including its proof in and through the "terms" of thinking—without providing a fixed, *a priori* subject on which such a proof could rely and of which it could be, as it were, the representation, "as if there were nothing to rely on," Cavell writes, "but reliance itself."[27] The "beauty" of Emerson's answer to Descartes," Cavell continues,

> lies in its weakness (you may say in its emptiness)—indeed, in two weaknesses. First, it does not prejudge what the I or self or mind or soul may turn out to be, but only specifies a condition that whatever it is must meet. Second, the proof only works in the moment of its giving, for what I prove is the existence only of a creature who *can* enact its existence, as exemplified in actually giving the proof, not one who at all time does in fact enact it.[28]

The "self" of Emersonian "self-reliance," then, is "not a state of being but a moment of change, say of becoming—a transience of being, a being of transience."[29]

In Cavell (and this marks quite precisely one of his differences with Rorty) the paradoxical self-reference of the "proof" of the Emersonian self is crucial to what we might think of as its generative incompleteness. This movement of the Emersonian self—in which the self might be said to be alive only to the extent that it *is* moving—is crucial to what Cavell sees as the political import of Emerson's work. But I want to mark how it is also crucial to the vein of Emersonianism that Stevens will develop in his late long poems, and crucial to the ecopoetics of rethinking the question of *dwelling* in relation to cultural legacy, as we'll see in chapter 6. As Cavell describes it, "I do not read Emerson as saying . . . that there is one unattained/attainable self we repetitively never arrive at, but rather that 'having' 'a' self is a process of moving to, and from, nexts . . . That the self is always attained, as well as *to be* attained, creates the problem in Emerson's concept of self-reliance . . . that un-less you manage the reliance of the attained on the unattained/attainable (that is, unless you side that way), you are left in precisely the negation of the position he calls for, left in conformity."[30] In its "onwardness," the Emersonian self must constantly surpass the selves it has already be-come, but not to attain an ideal, fixed selfhood. And yet, "since the task for each is his or her own self-transformation," Cavell sensibly observes, "the representativeness implied in that life may seem not to establish a recognition of others in different positions, so as to be disqualified as a moral position altogether." Emerson's remarkable twist on this problem, however, is that his writing "works out the conditions for my recognizing my difference from others as a function of my recognizing my difference from myself."[31]

As Cavell's reading of Emerson makes clear, an unavoidable cor-ollary of this "aversive" movement of the Emersonian self is that the world—as we know from the Kantian anatomy of skepticism—always already "vanishes from me," as Cavell puts it. But what Cavell empha-sizes is that that vanishing horizon is in an important sense dependent upon the terms we use, not to apprehend it, but rather to allow itself to disclose itself (as Heidegger might say), or to *receive* it (as Cavell puts it, to "acknowledge" it).

Here, I think, we can begin to get a sense of the usefulness of Niklas Luhmann's work for helping us to read the full letter of Emerson's think-ing, which is all the more important because Cavell's reading of Em-erson under the master rubric of "skepticism" remains tied, one might argue, to the representationalism he would otherwise seem to disown. Why? Because "skepticism" holds onto the desire for a representational adequation between concepts and objects even as it knows that desire to be unappeasable (how else are we to understand Cavell's insistence on taking seriously the "mourning" of the loss of the world, as a result of skepticism, in Emerson's "Experience"?).[32] Luhmann puts acute pres-sure on the relentlessly paradoxical and confounding dynamics of "ob-servation" that are so central, and so increasingly vexing, in Emerson's work—dynamics that usually get thematized in Romanticism under the rubric of "Imagination," and, in Emerson, in his well-known theatrics with the trope of vision (as in the famous "transparent eye-ball" passage in the opening pages of *Nature*: "I am nothing; I see all.").[33]

Luhmann's work on modernity and observation helps us to see that we need to honor, rather than paper over, Emerson's insistence on the contingency, not transcendence, of observation—what Maurice Gonnaud calls his effort to "fling out a new bridge—less ethereal, less har-monious perhaps, but tougher—between the One and the Many," with a "toughness" purchased by taking it upon himself "to be the champion of the acknowledged facts, honored in their richness and diversity," all of which led to Emerson being even less understood than he had been be-fore 1840.[34] Remarking on "The Method of Nature," Gonnaud writes that "his listeners confessed to understanding very little of it; the word 'ecstasy' recurs like a leitmotif, applied now to Nature and now to human beings and thus compounding the confusion," not just for his contemporaries but even for later critics such as Stephen Whicher, who finds that such work "incorporates two irreconcilable perspectives and suffers from a profound incoherence."[35] I suggest, however—and we will need Luhmann's work to fully explain why—that it is precisely at these moments that we find Emerson at his most systematic, rigorously extrapolating in his later work the paradoxical dynamics and consequences of observation that were—as both Gonnaud and Cavell rightly observe in their different ways—certainly central to the Emersonian corpus from the beginning, but were finessed by the more conventional idealism that we find in essays such as *Nature*. And while Gonnaud regrets in the post-1840 Emerson "the au-thor's centrifugal disposition of mind, which keeps him from transforming the profoundly contradictory impulses within him into dialectical move-ment," Luhmann's work on observation will help to make it clear why Emerson's relentless exploration of these problems cannot and should not resolve themselves into a dialectic. Here again, we find not so much an in-coherence or vagueness of thought, but rather the rigor of what we might call Emerson's undoing of Romanticism—calling its hand, as it were.

A reader of Emerson who comes close to realizing this fact about Emerson's work is Lee Rust Brown in his book *The Emerson Museum: Practical Romanticism and the Pursuit of the Whole*. As he observes about Emerson's contention in "Compensation" that "[t]he value of the uni-verse contrives to throw itself into every point," such moments "have been cited by readers who attack or applaud Emerson as a cheerful mys-tic who vaguely sees everything in everything."[36] What we have here in-stead, he suggests, is a more complicated process in which Coleridgean "multeity in unity" is subordinated to the workings of observers, where "the sense found in natural objects is precisely the viewer's own original *means* for seeing them . . . By virtue of these means, vision rises to a place of authority over objects, to a kind of perspectival remove sufficient to reveal relations within the whole scope of things."[37] And this, of course, is a matter of *form*. Yet, such an observer is not transcendent in the usual idealist sense—indeed, in any sense. Instead, we find here the more complicated dynamic of Emersonian "transparency"—that ability to perceive the "unity" of the "multeity"—which "is the one fatal condition of moving on intellectually; it is the way we pay for all worthwhile adjustments of attention," and the only way we achieve what Emerson calls "new prospects" (in Brown's words, "at once the new object and the prospect of its future conversion into transparency").[38] Far from being transcendent, then, "we see one object only at the cost of another," and "transparency, far from signifying a passive state or continuity or unity, testifies to the way the eye manufactures its own discontinuous intervals."[39]

We are now in a position to move to Niklas Luhmann's more highly technical description of this process, which is valuable for two reasons. First, observation in Luhmann (despite its connotations) is *disarticulated* from the familiar trope of vision *per se*; and, second, the problem of observation is assimilated here to the larger problem of complexity, which is described in Romanticism under the familiar (and finally somewhat mystical) rubric of multeity in unity. It is this convergence—the paradoxical dynamics of observation and the related problem of complexity, how observation both reduces *and* produces complexity—that Emerson's writing insists on more and more strenuously as his career unfolds, rendering it, in his mature work, literally *unavoidable*. Luhmann can help us to see how, in the apparently outlandish and fanciful paradoxes for which he is famous, Emerson quite clear-headedly registers the epistemological fallout of the very modernity to which his "Romanticism" is responding—not as a mystification or "imaginative" solution, but as a kind of relentless anatomy.

Emerson insists, in other words, on the radical contingency *and, at the same time*, the radical authority of self-referential observation, whose positive existential valence gets figured in the "whim" of "Self-Reliance," while its more vexing effects are registered in the isolation and vertigo of the opening of "Experience" and, finally, in the paradoxical fatedness to freedom of the late essay "Fate."[40] Such paradoxes are, from Luhmann's point of view, masked in the theological tradition Emerson inherits and famously rejects early in his career as a minister. Were we to follow Luhmann's suggestion, the closest thing we could find to Emerson's work in the theological tradition would be the line of medieval theology that works its way from Saint Augustine through John Scotus Eriugena to the fifteenth-century theologian Nicholas of Cusa. "No traditional epistemology," Luhmann writes, "could dare to go this far—obviously because the position from which it would have had to deal

with distinctness was occupied by theology."[41] But with the seculariza-
tion of these questions in Romanticism's philosophy of the subject—
itself, Luhmann argues, a product of the unavoidable movement from
hierarchical to functionally differentiated society under modernity, in
which the Church no longer has a centering role—they begin to become
unavoidable. "With the retreat of the religious world order," Luhmann
writes, the "question of how the world can observe itself" becomes more
pressing and vexing, and it typically gets answered in Romanticism and
its forerunner, German Idealist philosophy, by such makeshift terms as
"Spirit," "Idea" and so on.[42]

The problem with these "solutions," of course, as Harro Muller, among
others, has pointed out, is that in an increasingly "acentrically" organized
society (the society of modernity), "it is difficult to preserve the notion
of an Archimedean point from which and towards which both world
and society might be understood," such as "God, Spirit, History, Man,
Nature, the subject, the individual or intersubjectivity at the center of a
foundational discourse." But these foundational discourses—whether of
an ontological, natural, or anthropological nature—"are predominantly
a matter of self-attributions or self-simplifications that are functionally
in need of explanation."[43] And this is where we need systems theory.

We need, in other words (to use Luhmann's shorthand), to replace
"what" questions with "how" questions.[44] And this enables us, in turn, to
deepen and renovate our understanding of the pragmatist tradition of
which Emerson is, by nearly all accounts, a central if not founding fig-
ure. For both pragmatism and systems theory, the world is not given but
made, and this helps us take a different, less traditionally phenomenolog-
ical angle on the question of what Derrida in his reading of Heidegger
will call "world" and the paradoxes attendant upon "worlding"—and the
kinds of strategies in philosophy and poetry that must be developed to
meet it. In Stevens, meeting these challenges will lead first to his doc-
trine of the "Supreme Fiction," and later, and more important, to his
pragmatist claim that the function of the poet is "to help people to live
their lives."[45]

The process of secularization within which Stevens's doctrine arises
(as he himself emphasizes in the first two essays in *The Necessary An-
gel*) is, for social systems theory, but one manifestation of modernity
as a process of what Luhmann calls "functional differentiation" (what
other critical lexicons will call the increasing "specialization" or, more
moralistically, "fragmentation" associated with the process of moderni-
zation), which itself arises as an adaptive strategy to meet increasing

social complexity. And here it is worth lingering for a moment over a few fundamental postulates. The first is that systems theory replaces the familiar *ontological* dichotomies of humanism (mind/body, spirit/matter, and so on) with the *functional* distinction of system/environment—a distinction that is, crucially, *asymmetrical*. All systems find themselves, commonsensically enough—second postulate—in an environment that is always already more complex than they are, and all systems attempt to adapt to this complexity by filtering it in terms of their own self-referential codes. The point of the system is to reproduce itself, but no system can deal with everything, or even many things, all at once. And certainly, no system—either a psychic one or a social one—can establish and maintain point-for-point representational correspondences between its own internal elements and every single element in its environment. Or, as Luhmann will put it in *Social Systems*, "systems lack the 'requisite variety' (Ashby's term) that would enable them to react to every state of the environment . . . The system's inferiority in complexity [compared to that of the environment] must be counter-balanced by strategies of selection."[46]

Two subsidiary points need to be accented here. First, in responding to environmental complexity in terms of their own self-referential codes, systems build up their own internal complexity (one might think here of the various subspecialties of the legal system, say, or the specialization of disciplines in the education system); in doing so, they become ever more finely grained in their selectivity as they attempt to achieve resonance with their environments. And thus—in increasing the fineness of their filters, as it were—they buy *time* in relation to overwhelming environmental complexity. But, second, if the self-reference of the system's code reduces the flow of environmental complexity into the system, it also increases the system's "irritability" and thus, in a very real sense, its *dependence* on the environment and environmental change.

Here—and this is crucial to understanding the "engine," if you like, of what Cavell calls Emersonian "transience," "onwardness," and "abandonment"—the term "complexity" should be understood neither as an aggregation of particular substances (a big pile of lots of things), nor only (though this is better) as an abstract set of *relations*, but rather, and more importantly, as a set of dynamically changing *temporalized* relations. Systems use self-reference not just to build up their own internal complexity, but also to stabilize themselves in the temporal flow of events and render events meaningful for the system—and this is an adaptive necessity. As Luhmann explains, "We need a concept of meaning . . . as the simultaneous presentation . . . of actuality and possibility";[47] "the totality of the references presented by any meaningfully intended object offers more to hand than can in fact be actualized at any moment. Thus the form of meaning"—the copresentation of the difference between the actual and possible—"through its referential structure, *forces* the next step, to *selection*."[48] As Luhmann writes in a key passage, "the genesis and reproduction of meaning presupposes an infrastructure in reality that constantly changes its states. Meaning then extracts differences (which only as differences have meaning) from this substructure to enable a difference-oriented processing of information. On all meaning, therefore, are imposed a temporalized complexity and the compulsion to a constant shifting of actuality, without meaning itself vibrating in tune with that substructure."[49] Read against this background, the rigor of moments such as this one in Emerson's "The Method of Nature" becomes, I believe, all the more apparent:

> The method of nature: who could ever analyze it? That rushing stream will not stop to be observed. We can never surprise nature in a corner; never find the end of a thread . . . The wholeness we admire in the order of the world, is the result of infinite distribution . . . Its permanence is a perpetual inchoation. Every natural fact is an emanation, and that from which it emanates is an emanation also, and from every emanation is a new emanation. If anything could stand still, it would be crushed and dissipated by the torrent it resisted, and if it were a mind, would be crazed, as insane persons are those who hold fast to one thought, and do not flow with the course of nature.[50]

Subordinating the problem of self-referential observation to the larger problem of complexity is not only useful for moving us away from the phenomenological register, the philosophy of the subject, consciousness, intentionality, and so on (although nothing prevents the questions that animate phenomenology and the philosophy of consciousness from arising in this framework). It also helps clarify why it is misguided at best to charge systems theory in general and the theory of autopoiesis in particular with asserting a kind of solipsistic relationship between the system and its environment. As we saw with Gregory Bateson's admonition at the end of the previous chapter, what such a characterization misses is the seemingly paradoxical fact that the autopoietic closure of a system—whether social or psychic—is precisely what *connects* it to its environment. As Luhmann explains it in *Art as a Social System*,

> autopoiesis and complexity are conceptual coordinates . . . Dependency and independence, in a simple causal sense, are therefore not invariant magnitudes in that more of one would imply less of the other. Rather, they vary according to a system's given level of complexity. In systems that are successful in evolutionary terms, more independence typically amounts to a greater dependency on the environment . . . But all of this can happen only on the basis of the system's operative closure.[51]

Or, as Luhmann will put it in one of his more Zen-like moments, "only complexity can reduce complexity."[52]

All of this leads to a paradoxical situation that is central to Luhmann's work, and central to understanding the line that runs from Emerson to Stevens: what links the system to the world, what literally makes the world available to the system, is also what hides the world from the system, what makes it unavailable. Why? Because if all systems interface with their environments in terms of, and only in terms of, their own constitutive distinctions, self-referential codes, operational closure, embodied enaction, and so on, then the "environment" is not an ontologically *given* category but a functionally *produced* one. That is to say, it is not an "outside" to the system that is antecedently given *as such*—it is not, in other words, "nature" in the traditional sense—but is rather always the "outside" *of* a specific inside. Or, as Luhmann deftly explains it, the environment is different for every system, because each system excludes only itself from its environment.[53] And "with this turn," he writes, "the distinction between self-reference and hetero-reference is relocated within the observed observing system"; or, to put it another way, "the distinction between self- and hetero-reference is nothing other than the re-entry of the distinction system/environment into the system itself."[54] As we shall see, this is precisely the structure of the "globe" in Peter Sloterdijk's massive *Spheres* project—a sort of architectonic rendering of the logic at work here (with Emerson's essay "Circles" as a sort of halfway house, as we'll see in a moment) that will enable us to make significant headway in redescribing Stevens's "mundo" and its associated tropes of "sky," the "heavens," and so on.

The constant, dynamic precipitation of an outside by ongoing acts of distinction and selection enables us to understand more clearly what Emerson is reaching for in "Nominalist and Realist," when he writes that "excluded attributes burst in on us with the more brightness, that they have been excluded. 'Your turn now, my turn next,' is the rule of the game. The universality being hindered in its primary form, comes in the secondary form of *all sides*."[55] This might sound, at first blush, Hegelian, but the key difference is Emerson's strident insistence on the primacy and paradoxical contingency of the observer, an insistence that reaches its peak in *Essays: Second Series*. As Luhmann explains the relationship between observation and what Emerson, in "Circles," calls the "horizon":

> The source of a distinction's guaranteeing reality lies in its own opera-
> tive unity. It is, however, precisely as this unity that the distinction can-
> not be observed—except by means of another distinction which then
> assumes the function of a guarantor of reality. Another way of express-
> ing this is to say the operation emerges simultaneously with the world
> which as a result remains cognitively unapproachable to the operation.
>
> The conclusion to be drawn from this is that the connection with
> the reality of the external world is established by the blind spot of the
> cognitive operation. Reality is what one does not perceive when one
> perceives it.[56]

Or, as he puts it in somewhat different terms, the world is now conceived, "along the lines of a Husserlian metaphor, as an unreachable horizon that retreats further with each operation, without ever holding out the prospect of an outside."[57] This is the way Emerson's essay "Circles" begins: "The eye is the first circle; the horizon which it forms is the second; and throughout nature this primary figure is repeated *without end . . .* Our life is an apprenticeship to the truth that around every circle another can be drawn; that there is no end in nature, but every end is a beginning."[58] "In this twofold sense," Luhmann writes, as if in an analytic gloss on Emerson's essay, "the notion of a final unity—of an 'ultimate reality' that cannot assume a form because it has no other side—is displaced into the unobservable . . . If the concept of the world is retained to indicate reality in its entirety, then it is that which—to a second-order observer—remains invisible in the movements of observation (his own and those of others)."[59]

We are now in a position to mount a rather different understanding of the significance of the Kantian "settlement" with skepticism from what we find in Cavell, reframed now in terms of the signal importance of the formal, temporalized dynamics of observation. As Luhmann puts it succinctly, if we ask "what new insights the concept of observation (first- and second-order observation) has to offer," the answer is "it traces the problem of unity back to the ultimate form of paradox."[60] In a way, he notes,

> All this can be handled with the de-reification of the concept of the world introduced already by Kant. World is no longer a totality of things, a *universitas rerum*, but rather the final, and therewith unobservable, condition of possibility of observations, that is, of every sort of use of distinctions. To formulate this another way, the world must be invisibilized so that observations become possible. For every observation requires a "blind spot," or more precisely: it can only indicate one side of the distinction being used, employing it as a starting point for subsequent observations, but not the distinction itself as a unity and above all not the "unmarked space," precisely the world from which every distinction, as soon as it is marked as a distinction, must be delimited.[61]

Here, Luhmann gives us an especially technical version of the same "world" that will occupy Jacques Derrida throughout much of the second set of seminars on *The Beast and the Sovereign*—a set of meditations on "world" that reaches back to Kant, then to Jakob von Uexküll, and thence forward to Heidegger. And Luhmann's mention of Kant is fortuitous for my purposes as well, because, as Derrida notes in the very last of those seminars, Kant, in the context of the concept of "world," "said some terribly seismic things about the 'als ob'[the "as if"]," not the least of which is that "the world is a regulative idea of reason and it hangs by a mere *als ob*."[62] For Kant, he continues, "the point is to consider the way phenomena are linked '*as if* they were the arrangements made by a supreme reason of which our reason is a faint copy.'"[63] From here, it is but a small step to the juncture at which both Derrida and Luhmann deliver us: namely, that the contingency and constructedness of "world" is precisely what ensures that the "unmarked space" (in Luhmann's terms) against which "world" asserts itself is not exhausted by, but *replenished* by, that contingency and constructedness. And in this unfolding process, art and poetry, in Derrida's discussion of Kant, have a special role to play. As he puts it in the last *Beast and Sovereign* seminar: "where there is no world, where the world is not here or there, but *fort* [gone]," what "I must do . . . is make it that there be precisely a world . . . as though there ought to be a world where precisely there is none, to make the gift or present of this *as if* come up poetically."[64] Or in Stevens's words, again, the function of the poet is "to help people to live their lives."

Luhmann's work can help us extend and refine Derrida's observations on the differences between art (including poetry) and philosophy in relation to these questions. When Luhmann died, he left behind scattered notes for a project on "Poetry and Social Theory," which were published in 2001 in the special issue of *Theory, Culture and Society* devoted to his work.[65] Central to his understanding of the specificity of poetry is his well-known articulation of the autopoietic closure and difference of psychic systems and social systems, consciousness and communication. It is within the context of this difference that Luhmann understands the significance in poetry of characteristic themes such as incommunicability, ineffability, silence, and so on. But he understands them specifically within a posthumanist context—not as expressions of a psychological or emotional interiority or intentionality that reveals itself in language (even if only to gesture toward language's inadequacy in the face of the "ineffable"), but rather as expressions of a set of differences—most important, the difference between communication and perception, which in poetry are "miraculously" made to coincide (as he puts it) when the material form of the signifier seems to duplicate the semantics of communication (in familiar devices such as rhyme, rhythm, and so on). Or we might say even more precisely (in light of W. K. Wimsatt's famous thesis about the differential relations of semantics and acoustics in rhymed English poetry in his classic essay "One Relation of Rhyme to Reason"): in which the material form of the signifier has a *systematic* relation to the semantic content of words, even if that relationship is (systematically, as Wimsatt suggested, in English rhyme) one of difference or contrast.[66]

But this is only part of the story, and I emphasize here that in Luhmann's scattered writings on poetry, we need to separate and disarticulate two main strands that tend to become confused: on the one hand, what we might call the perceptual or the phenomenological (which has to do with the familiar prosodic aspects of poetry that I just mentioned), and, on the other hand, what we might call poetry's abstract, formal aspect. What I want to bring out here, in other words, is how in Luhmann's analysis, the perceptual and the material are radically subordinated to the problem of *form*, and to the relationship of form to the paradoxical dynamics of observation. I argue, more forcefully, that the former is even, in a fundamental sense, superfluous to what makes poetry art at all in Luhmann's sense—and is superfluous in a way that helps us understand how, paradoxically, poetry that is *least* replete with prosodic features, such as stanzaic regularity, rhyme, alliteration, and so on (and here one could choose among any number of modernists—Marianne

Moore would be representative, but so would much of Stevens), can in a sense be regarded, *for that very reason*, as *most* poetic in the specific sense developed by Luhmann. This is particularly useful for helping us to tease out and formalize the poetics of the mature Stevens, which for many readers takes on an increasingly paradoxical and spartan cast as his career unfolds.

To understand why poetry that is least poetic in prosodic terms may be seen as *most* poetic in Luhmann's terms, we have to remember that, for Luhmann's theory of art (including poetry), the difference between perception and communication is paramount. The meaning of a work of art cannot be reduced to its perceptual, material, or phenomenal aspect (this is, after all, the lesson for Luhmann of a Duchamp, a Cage, or, one might add, of conceptual art in general). Instead, the work of art copresents the difference between perception and communication, and "re-enters" that difference on the side of its *own* communication, its *own* meaning. To understand how this happens, we need to recall that perception (and, beyond that, consciousness) and communication operate in mutually exclusive, operationally closed, autopoietic systems (though they are structurally coupled through media such as language), and that the relationship between them is "asymmetrical."[67] The mind (and here I mean the brain, strictly speaking, despite the foibles of translation) is its own, operationally closed (biological) system, but because it is also a necessary medium for communication, "we can say that the mind has the privileged position of being able to disturb, stimulate, and irritate communication."[68] The mind (the psychic system), in other words, constantly produces "noise" (in systems theory parlance) for the communication system (the social system), and the challenge for communication is thus how to secure the (necessary) participation of psychic systems while at the same time ensuring its own continuation through the autopoiesis of its own structures (and not those of the psychic system).[69]

This irreducibility and asymmetry of perception to communication is crucial for several reasons. First, perception and communication operate at different speeds—and art puts this to use. The faster speed of perception and neuronal processing makes it appear that perception confirms, stabilizes, and makes immediate, while communication, which operates with a sequential selective process, differs and defers.[70] Luhmann observes that "perception (in contrast to thought and communication) can decide *quickly*, whereas art aims to *retard* perception and render it *reflexive*—lingering upon the object in visual art (in striking contrast to everyday perception) and slowing down reading in literature, particularly lyric poetry."[71] In the work of art, this difference between perception and communication is then "re-entered" on the side of the artwork's communication[72]—a communication that "accomplishes this goal or fails to do so by facing the usual, and perhaps even increased, risks involved in all communication. Art communicates by *using perceptions contrary to their primary purpose*."[73] As a "re-entered" element in art's communication, then, perception serves the following role: "what strikes us in an art form—as, in a different way, does the conspicuous character of acoustic and optic signals—engenders a fascination that turns into information by changing the state of the [observer's] system—as a 'difference that makes a difference.'"[74]

As I have already noted, this difference is what allows art to have a special relationship to what is commonly invoked as the "ineffable" or the "incommunicable." As Luhmann puts it, "the function of art would then consist in integrating what is in principle incommunicable—namely, perception—into the communication network of society . . . The art system concedes to the perceiving consciousness its own unique adventure in observing artworks—and yet makes available as communication the formal selection that triggered the adventure."[75] With regard to poetry specifically, Luhmann writes, "the reader might assume that all of this holds exclusively for the so-called visual arts. On the contrary, it holds—much more dramatically because less evidently—for the verbal arts as well, including lyric poetry."[76] Paradoxically, it is all the more true (and all the more counterintuitive) that for art made of words, "we must focus on types of nonverbal communication that realize the same autopoietic structure as verbal communication . . . but are not bound by the specific features of language and thus extend the realm of communication beyond what can be put into words."[77] Or, as he puts it succinctly, "art functions as communication although—or precisely because—it cannot be adequately rendered through words (let alone through concepts)"; it "permits a circumvention of language."[78]

Thus, "text-art," Luhmann writes, "organizes itself by means of self-referential references that combine elements of sound, rhythm, and meaning."[79] But poetry "is not just rhymed prose," he continues:

> If one reads poetry as a sequence of propositions about the world and considers the poetic only as beautification, adornment, or decoration, one does not observe it as a work of art . . . Only at the level where symbols, sounds, meanings, and rhythms conspire—a level that is difficult to "read"—do poems *refer to themselves* in the process of creating forms.

They generate contextual dependencies, ironic references, and paradoxes, all of which refer back to the text that produces these effects.[80]

In other words, the poem begins with a radically contingent distinction, and then gradually builds up, through recursive self-reference, its own unique, nonparaphrasable character—its internal necessity, if you like. As Luhmann characterizes it,

> the artwork closes itself off by reusing what is already determined in the work as the other side of further distinctions. The result is a unique, circular accumulation of meaning, which often escapes one's first view (or is grasped only "intuitively") . . . This creates an overwhelming impression of necessity—the work is what it is, even though it is made, individual, and contingent, rather than necessary in an ontological sense. The work of art, one might say, manages to overcome its own contingency.[81]

But here (and this is my main point), the recursive self-reference of *form*—and not the materiality of language as medium, the perceptual material *per se*—is key.

Here, we need to remind ourselves once again that for Luhmann *any* observation "renders the world invisible" in relation to its constitutive, self-referential distinction in the sense that the thing that makes the world cognitively or communicationally available is also the thing that occludes it and renders it invisible by its selectivity; and that invisibility must itself remain invisible to the observation that employs that distinction—which in turn can only be disclosed by *another* observation that will also necessarily be doubly blind in the same way.[82] "In this twofold sense," Luhmann writes, "the notion of a final unity—of an 'ultimate reality' that cannot assume a form because it has no other side—is displaced into the unobservable . . . If the concept of the world is retained to indicate reality in its entirety, then it is that which—to a second-order observer—remains invisible in the movements of observation (his own and those of others)."[83] So on the one hand, he explains, "a work of art must distinguish itself externally from other objects and events, or it will lose itself in the world"; it "closes itself off by limiting further possibilities with each of its formal decisions." On the other hand, "whatever distinction is used at any given time cannot be indicated as a unity—this condition reproduces itself with every distinction. It merely displaces the blind spot" of observation.[84]

As Luhmann summarizes it in a key formulation, "*with this media-tion we arrive at a world extant in the difference* between the sameness and otherness of observations (of the first and second order). As so often elsewhere, it is also true here: reducing complexity [by deploying obser-vations] is the means to generate complexity."[85] Art can thus "no longer be understood as an imitation of something that presumably exists along with and outside of art," but, more important for our purposes, "to the extent that imitation is still possible, it now imitates the world's invis-ibility, a nature that can no longer be apprehended as a whole."[86] "The paradox unique to art, which art creates and resolves," Luhmann writes, "resides in the observability of the unobservable."[87] And it is here that *form* finds its function. As Luhmann puts it,

> the function of art is to make the world appear within the world—with an eye toward the ambivalent situation that every time something is made available for observation something else withdraws, that, in other words, the activity of distinguishing and indicating that goes on in the world conceals the world . . . *Yet a work of art is capable of symbolizing the reentry of the world into the world because it appears—just like the world—incapable of emendation.*[88]

The work of art, then, is radically contingent *and*, at the same time, seems to be possessed of its own internal necessity.

To return to the issue of poetry specifically, what this means for a poet like Stevens is that the *less* "poetic" his work is—the less we find the tra-ditional prosodic devices (rhyme, alliteration, and so on) that foreground the difference between perception and communication—the *more* po-etic he is in the specific sense of formally modeling the dynamics of the observable-unobservable that Luhmann describes. Or, better, the paring away of conspicuous "poetic" features in his work can be seen as func-tioning in two different ways. First, it functions in the service of a com-munication in which the motivated refusal to indulge traditional pro-sodic devices is an important element of the poetry's meaning, how it communicates by means of things *not* present (a calculated formal de-cision that signifies against its literary-historical background along the lines of Miles Davis's famous pronouncement that what is important is not the notes you play, but rather the notes you *don't* play). And second, that evacuated perceptual substrate makes Stevens's poetry, paradoxi-cally, *more* poetic by directing our attention (with increasing rigor and without distraction, as it were) to the basic formal function of poetry, now understood in light of the formal dynamics of observation and invisibility described above.

Here again, it's worth remembering the discussion in the previous chapter of Stevens's foregrounding of the "functional core" of English in his poetry (especially his later poetry), the "poetry of grammar," as Hammond puts it, around which Stevens's late "desert music" is built.[89] These stylistic features of Stevens's sentence structure, phrasing, and diction work to "unobscure," as Stevens might say, the fact that the increasingly abstract, "philosophical" bent of his poetry is actually best understood precisely in the terms made available by Luhmann. That is, a poetics of increasingly rigorous refinement and astringent abstraction that moves steadily away from depending on the perceptual and the prosodic (in the traditional sense) and toward forcing us to fix our attention upon the fundamental—and fundamentally paradoxical—aspect of poetry, and of art generally, as Luhmann defines it: the crucial, mutual overdeterminations between the question of form and the paradoxical relations of the visible and invisible, the observable and unobservable, which have typically been handled in literature and philosophy under the rubrics of the Sublime, imagination vs. fancy, and so on.

The paradoxical dynamics of observation and self-reference—which Stevens "solves," as it were, in part by the stylistic means described by Hammond, Gilbert, and others in chapter 1, foregrounding the nonrepresentational and contingent nature of the utterance via rhetoric, grammar, modals, and so on—are very obviously on display in a whole host of Stevens's poems, and achieve a characteristic pitch and resonance for his later poetry at the end of "Esthétique Du Mal," where he recurs once again to an intensely Emersonian *topos*, where "One might have thought of sight, but who could think / Of what it sees, for all the ill it sees?" Stevens's answer to that question in the poem seems to be both "no one" and "anyone at all," in the sense that the finitude of "sight," its contingency, its self-reference, is paradoxically the source of "so many sensuous worlds," as if "the mid-day air, was swarming / With the metaphysical changes that occur," not in the realm of transcendence or the Sublime, but "merely in living as and where we live."[90] And it receives even more technical, topological treatment in "The Idea of Order at Key West," which is very careful to distinguish the first-order observations of "the single artificer" addressed in the poem from the second-order observations (the observations of those observations) by the speaker and his strange companion, "pale" Ramon Fernandez. Stevens is characteristically assiduous as he insists upon the difference between "*her* voice that made / The sky acutest at its vanishing," "the world in which *she* sang," and, on the other hand, the "we" who know that "there never was a world *for her* / Except the one she sang and, singing, made."[91]

This does not mean, of course, that we are dealing here with "concepts," for, as we have already seen, art consists precisely in presenting what cannot be conceptualized but can, nevertheless, be communicated—and communicated, in the case of this poem, by the staging of, and increasingly recursive responses to, the central question of the poem, "Whose spirit is this?" to which the speaker responds (otherwise oddly, I think) that we knew "we should ask this often as she sang."[92] But why not ask "this" just *once*? Because, apparently, it cannot be answered only once—that is, once and for all, a fact the poem recursively builds up through the increasing submission of its key terms (song, sea) to a relentlessly erosive, provisional phalanx of ands, buts, ifs, and yets of the sort highlighted by Maeder, Vendler, and Hammond earlier. Or to put it in Luhmannian terms, the "song" of the "single artificer"—her observation that makes "the sky acutest at its vanishing"—discloses a "spirit" and not a substance: not the binaries of mind/nature, subject/object, imagination/reality, and so on, among which we must choose as either philosophical idealists or realists, but rather a *form*, a *movement* of observation that is irreducible, with no resting place. It is driven by the paradoxical difference-in-identity of observation's constitutive structure (shared by both the speaker and the singer), *and* the difference between first- and second-order observers, a difference that, by definition, takes *time*. Thus, the premium, in the end, not on "song" or "sea," but on a third term, "spirit." And hence, the only answer to the question "Whose spirit is this?" would not be—indeed *could not* be—either "song" or "sea," but might be, oddly enough: "Often."[93]

I put it in this odd way to make it clear that we are not dealing here simply with problems of logic. To the contrary, as Luhmann writes, "the problem [of the paradoxical self-reference of any observation] cannot be solved by logical maneuvering"; but it can "be undertaken more or less skillfully, can have a more or less unblocking effect, can be more or less fruitful."[94] As in art, for example. Indeed, as noted earlier in the context of Derrida and Kant's *als ob*, this is perhaps what Stevens meant when he suggested—rather enigmatically, after all—that the function of the poet "is to help people to live their lives." Such is the spirit, I think, of Stevens's suggestion about the poet's function, earlier in that same passage, that "certainly it is not to lead people out of the confusion in which they find themselves. Nor is it, I think, to comfort them while they follow their readers to and fro."[95] But it is *also* not just a problem of logic in a second and more important sense—a sense that once again depends upon our paying attention to the *disarticulation* of consciousness and communication that I have insisted on in these pages. For, as Luhmann remarks in his "Notes," "the observation of a paradox has a peculiar kind of temporal structure: it makes the present shrink to a point to which no reality any longer corresponds." And yet, because "communication requires more time than experience does"—it is sequential and slower than the movement of consciousness—it "requires a certain period of actuality." "Within this time period," he continues, "the paradox can be made to oscillate." The utterer "wants to convey the fact that he does not mean what he says, although he does not say anything which he does not mean."[96]

Here, it seems to me, we are very close to the core dynamic of Stevens's poetry—especially his most resolutely and opaquely "philosophical" poetry—and its signal effect of confirming the otherness and difference of "external" reality precisely by insisting on its inseparability from the mind and imagination, all of which takes place (to borrow Luhmann's characterization) in a present that has "shrunk to a point," to which "no reality any longer corresponds." Or, to put it in terms of "The Poems of Our Climate," which has been central in these sorts of discussions for a host of critics, "the evilly compounded, vital I"—in Luhmann's terms, the fact that observation is multiple, contingent, and paradoxical in its self-reference—cannot be overcome. But it's a good thing, too. It both creates and partakes of a world that is "imperfect," that "Lies in flawed words and stubborn sounds" because the world is thus riven by paradoxical difference (the self-reference of any observation *and* the difference between first- and second-order observers) that can never add up to the "simplified" "world of white and snowy scents," of "clear water in a brilliant bowl."[97] Why is the unavailability of the world "as such and in its being" (to use Heideggerian language) crucial to the ongoing *maintenance* of the world? Because, as Luhmann explains, the phenomenon of paradoxical self-reference—and the experience of it as an actuality in the disjunction between consciousness and communication, the experience of something that, in a way, is impossible and yet "oscillates" before us— "reveals that the inference from nondescribability to nonexistence is not logically tenable."[98] And this question opens onto another that I cannot pursue adequately in this book (though it is surely of signal interest for Stevens and his critics): the relations, and disrelations, of philosophy and literature in the services of that broader thing called "knowledge."

After this extended detour through systems theory and poetics, and in particular its emphasis on the *disarticulation* of consciousness and communication, we are in a much better position to understand what otherwise must seem an enigmatic prose piece (even for Stevens), his essay "The Irrational Element in Poetry" from 1936, which helps us unlock in another way how Stevens's poetics operates. To establish the larger thematic framework for Stevens's essay, it's useful to return to his review of Marianne Moore's work from a year earlier, "A Poet That Matters," and to remember our discussion earlier of Stevens's defense (as Robert Lehmann put it) of Romanticism. In his essay on Moore, Stevens writes of "the romantic in its other sense"—the sense he wants to defend against the onslaught of T. S. Eliot, Irving Babbitt, and others—that it is a matter of "the living and at the same time the imaginative, the youthful, the delicate" as that which "constitutes the vital element in poetry."[99] Stevens continues, "The imagination does not often delight in the same thing twice. Professor Babbitt says that 'a thing is romantic when, as Aristotle would say, it is wonderful rather than probable,'" but, Stevens counters, "it must also be living. It must always be living. It is in the sense of living intensity, living singularity that it is the vital element in poetry . . . *It is a process of cross-fertilization, an immense process, all arts considered, of hybridization.*"[100]

Here, I think it is easy enough to see that Stevens is insisting on a point for which systems theory (in either Bateson or Luhmann) gives us a more technical vocabulary: namely, that in any system, it is not the discrete *element per se* that is important, but rather *how* such an element interacts with the changing dynamic state of the system itself. The imagination "does not often delight in the same thing twice" simply because the effect of the "thing" on the imagination depends on its structural coupling to a larger system that is fundamentally temporal. And, as Stevens discusses in some detail, that is true whether we are speaking of the movement of consciousness (the psychic system) or of the externality of poetic elements in relation to social systems of communication (literary tropes and how they change and become stale over time, for example). (This is in part why, to use Stevens's famous phrase in "Notes toward a Supreme Fiction," "it must change.") Or, as Luhmann explains in *Social Systems*, "a piece of information that is repeated is no longer information. It retains its meaning [its formal characteristics] in the repetition but loses its value as information. One reads in the paper that the deutsche mark has risen in value. If one reads this a second time in another paper, this activity no longer has value as information . . . although structurally it presents the same selection."[101] This is why, Luhmann suggests—and this will be important for our discussion of "The Irrational Element in Poetry"—it is "unproductive for meanings to circulate as mere self-referentiality or in short-circuited tautologies . . . One can think, 'This rose is a rose is a rose is a rose.' But this use of a recursive path is productive only if it makes itself dependent on specific conditions and does not always ensue."[102] In this light, Stevens's "living intensity" and "living singularity" refer us to an ecological poetics in which the "hybridization" of the "living" and the "imaginative" is achieved by the structural coupling of the two through the medium of poetry, which in turn makes "the living element" of poetry—"true" poetry, as he puts it—radically *dependent* on the externality of the environment outside the consciousness that takes it up in the imagination.

This enables us to understand Stevens's otherwise enigmatic assertion on the very next page of "A Poet That Matters," that "the romantic that falsifies is rot and that is true even though the romantic inevitably falsifies: it falsifies but it does not vitiate. It is an association of the true and the false. It is not the true. It is not the false. It is both. The school of poetry that believes in sticking to the facts would be stoned if it was not sticking to the facts in a world in which there are no facts: or some such thing."[103] The distinction between "falsify" and "vitiate" here directs us toward the necessity of an "association of the true and the false" through "cross-fertilization" and "hybridization," or what systems theory calls, much more simply, the "structural coupling" of mind and world through the medium of language and the process of reducing complexity through *selection* ("sticking to the facts in a world in which there are no facts"). Meaning inheres in the relation between both, but not in a generic or given way, because an element's meaning, its effect on the system (whether psychic or social), depends on the system's state itself. And that, of course, changes, and in a changing environment, as Stevens reminds us time and again in his poetry.

We can now move to that most enigmatic of Stevens's essays, "The Irrational Element in Poetry," and understand why he insists that "what I have in mind when I speak of the irrational element in poetry"—he defines it as "the transaction between reality and the sensibility of the poet from which poetry springs"—is set in explicit contrast to what he calls "the din made by the surrealists and the surrationalists."[104] "All of us understand what is meant by the transposition of an objective reality to a subjective reality," he continues. "The transaction between reality and the sensibility of the poet is precisely that." Now I want to pause here and mark this moment, utterly typical in Stevens, in which the prose of his "philosophical" formulation—in this case, the language of "objective" and "subjective"—is entirely inadequate (for reasons already discussed) to what Stevens's poetics is actually up to. And that necessitates, in turn, a certain degree of detail in our examination of Stevens's poetics.

Let's move with Stevens, then, for the moment, to a more refreshing and indeed wonderful passage early in the essay. He writes,

> I awoke several hours before daylight and as I lay in bed I heard the steps of a cat running over the snow under my window almost inaudibly. The faintness and strangeness of the sound made on me one of those impressions which one so often seizes as pretexts for poetry. I suppose that in such a case one is merely expressing one's sensibility and that the reason why this expression takes the form of poetry is that it takes whatever form one is able to give it. The poet is able to give it the form of poetry because poetry is the medium of his personal sensibility . . . What gives a man his personal sensibility I don't know and it does not matter because no one knows. Poets continue to be born not made and cannot, I am afraid, be predetermined.[105]

Remembering our discussion of dynamic system states earlier, let's follow him as he develops the anecdote a couple of pages later in a very Emersonian direction:

> As a man becomes familiar with his own poetry, it becomes as obsolete for himself as for anyone else . . . We say that we perfect diction. We simply grow tired. Manner is something that has not yet been disengaged adequately. It does not mean style; it means the attitude of the writer, his bearing rather than his point of view. His bearing toward what? Not toward anything in particular, simply his pose. He hears the cat on the snow. The running feet set the rhythm. There is no subject beyond the cat running on the snow in the moonlight . . . Now, just as the choice of subject is unpredictable at the outset, so its development, after it has been chosen, is unpredictable. One is always writing about two things at the same time in poetry and it is this that produces the tension characteristic of poetry. One is the true subject and the other is the poetry of the subject. The difficulty of sticking to the true subject, when it is the poetry of the subject that is paramount in one's mind, need only be mentioned to be understood.[106]

This trope of the poet's "bearing"—-which is not his "point of view," exactly, but rather his "manner" and "attitude," and not his "style"—is quite interesting. Here, Stevens goes out of his way to make the point that whatever this bearing is, it is not the subjectivity or mind of the poet, nor even that as it manifests itself in the poet's distinctive "style," but rather, something like the *form* of an ongoing, recursive relationship between the consciousness of the poet and the world of "fact" to which the poet responds, a form that gives the stability of "manner" and "attitude" to the dynamic, changing state of consciousness as it responds to its world.

Let's remember now the remarks near the end of this passage about the "true subject" (the environmental element that perturbs the psychic system) and "the poetry of the subject" (how that is taken up by the poet's mind—and the fact that how it *is* taken up is a matter of the poet's "bearing"). That this relationship *is* dynamic and recursive is made clear by Stevens's comments about becoming bored with one's own poetry; it no longer has the power to renew and reinvigorate the consciousness of the poet. And this makes clear that the "bearing" of the poet is composed not just of two primary elements but of three, which are structurally coupled: the poet's psychic system in all its biophysical closure and specificity; how the mind of the poet is itself changed and shaped by language, culture, and so forth (and we know that "mind" is not "brain," of course), opening up some pathways of reception or excitement and foreclosing others; and, third, the quite different externality of the environment itself (the cat's footfalls in the snow, the "true subject"), which serves as a trigger or perturbation for the "poetry of the subject," but a trigger or perturbation that depends upon the "bearing" and "attitude" of the poet even as it is demonstrably independent of it. Here again, Stevens is stretching to say what he never is quite able to technically express in his prose: that this cannot be described satisfactorily in terms of any subject/object terminology and the representationalism it entails.

As we will see in some detail later, this "bearing" of Stevens is directly related to what I have called, following Derrida's reading of Paul Celan, the "bearing capacity" or "carrying capacity" of ecopoetics, the ethical responsibility of which lies in the fact that the world is not simply, passively registered as a phenomenon of either the subject (the poet's "point of view") or the object (the "true subject") of the poem, but has to be ongoingly *made*. What is the poet's "bearing," "manner," and "attitude" in the face of this? And what are the contours, processes, and dynamics of that "making"? Why I am going on in such excruciating detail about how this process and "bearing" works? In part, because Stevens himself does—specifically, in his attempts to differentiate what he has in mind from "surrealism" and "surrationalism" *and* from Freudian psychoanalysis. This is why he writes that "with the irrational in a pathological sense we are not concerned . . . nor with any irrationality provoked by prayer, whiskey, fasting, opium, or the hope of publicity."[107] "What interests us," Stevens continues, "is a particular process in the rational mind which we recognize as irrational in the sense that it takes place unaccountably. Or, rather, I should say that what interests us is not so much the Hegelian process as what comes of it."[108]

What Stevens calls the "automaticity" of the irrational element in poetry is thus not to be associated with the automaticity of the chemical reaction of the brain to "whiskey" or "opium"—that would be, quite simply, a biological, psychic phenomenon in Luhmann's sense—but nor is it to be confused with the automaticity of so-called automatic writing, as we find it in the Surrealists. Rather, Stevens writes, "while there is nothing automatic about the poem, nevertheless it has an automatic aspect in the sense that it is what I wanted it to be without knowing before it was written what I wanted it to be, even though I knew before it was written what I wanted to do. If each of us is a biological mechanism, each poet is a poetic mechanism. To the extent that what he produces is mechanical: that is to say, beyond his power to change, it is irrational."[109] Or, as Luhmann puts it, a bit less enigmatically, regarding the distinction between process and product, and what he calls the "internal nexus" of the poem:

> this analysis precludes comprehending an artwork in terms of the relation between a whole and its parts . . . The artwork closes itself off by reusing what is already determined in the work as the other side of further distinctions. The result is a unique, circular accumulation of meaning, which often escapes one's first view (or is only grasped "intuitively") . . . This creates an overall impression of necessity—the work is what it is, even though it is made, individual, and contingent, rather than necessary in an ontological sense. The work of art, one might say, manages to overcome its own contingency.[110]

Stevens's "automaticity" may in this light be viewed as the recursive relationship between the poet's "bearing" and the elements in the environment that provoke in the poet the undertaking of the poem, which in turn takes the shape it does independently from the poet's psychic states (or "automatically") precisely because of the recursive build-up in the poem of self-reference through form that gradually reveals to the poet the "poetry of the subject," which would not have happened without the perturbation of "the true subject." Stevens again: "it has an automatic aspect in the sense that it is what I wanted it to be without knowing before it was written what I wanted it to be, even though I knew before it was written what I wanted to do."

On the next page of the essay, Stevens shifts the discussion to a more ethical register, one that moves away from the individual imagination and toward a nascent question of community: "while it can lie in the temperament of very few of us to write poetry in order to find God, it is probably the purpose of each of us to write poetry to find the good which, in the Platonic sense, is synonymous with God. One writes poetry, then, in order to approach the good in what is harmonious and orderly. Or, simply, one writes poetry out of a delight in the harmonious and orderly."[111] "Harmonious and orderly" here does *not* mean "rational" or "logical," of course—and precisely in the sense of Luhmann's contention that in poetry something that does not make sense can make meaning. And *that* question refers us, in turn, not just to the question of *form* but also, for Stevens, to the question of form's function. Here is Luhmann's version of the stakes (the "good") of what Stevens calls "the harmonious and orderly":

> The word *formal* here does not refer to the distinction, which at first guided modern art, between form and matter or form and content, but to the characteristics of an indicating operation that observes, is if from the corner of its eye, what happens on the other side of form. In this way, the work of art points the observer toward an observation of form . . . However, the social function of art exceeds the mere reconstruction of observational possibilities that are potentially present in the work. Rather it consists in *demonstrating the compelling forces of order in the realm of the possible.*[112]

Later in "The Irrational Element in Poetry," Stevens takes up more explicitly what Luhmann calls "the social function of art" and its formal dimension in his discussion of "the pressure of the contemporaneous" and how art responds to it, but in a nonrepresentational and nonthematic way. In a fascinating—and, for Stevens, rather unusual—passage, he writes, in 1936:

> The pressure of the contemporaneous from the time of the beginning of the World War to the present time has been constant and extreme. No

one can have lived in a happy oblivion. For a long time before the war nothing was more common . . . The period was like a stage-setting that since then has been taken down and tucked away . . . We have a sense of upheaval. We feel threatened. We look from an uncertain present toward a more uncertain future. One feels the desire to collect oneself against all this in poetry as well as in politics. If politics is nearer to each of us because of the pressure of the contemporaneous, poetry, in its way, is no less so and for the same reason . . . The trouble is that the greater the pressure of the contemporaneous, the greater the resistance. Resistance is the opposite of escape. The poet who wishes to contemplate the good in the midst of confusion is like the mystic who wishes to contemplate God in the midst of evil. There can be no thought of escape . . . In poetry, to that extent, the subject is not the contemporaneous, because that is only the nominal subject, but the poetry of the contemporaneous. Resistance to the pressure of ominous and destructive circumstances consists of its conversion, so far as possible, into a different, an explicable, an amenable circumstance.[113]

What this means is that poetry is thus *dependent* on the world of "fact" and "circumstance" that it transforms—and transforms, by the operation of form, in a quite particular way, from the merely contemporaneous to "the poetry of the contemporaneous," toward an "amenable circumstance": in short, toward a kind of order. Here again, what is being described, I think, is the transformation of environmental complexity through the operation of form. Poetry pushes back, in resistance, against contemporaneous events, not by simply making up soothing songs, comforting images, or polemical representations of other contemporaneous states of affairs—all of which are what Stevens would call "escape"—but by using the pressure of events as the environmental engine and trigger to push ever harder, in resistance, to reveal what Luhmann calls "compelling forces of order in the realm of the possible," what Stevens calls "order and harmony."

We have now framed out a way to understand with greater depth Stevens's offhand *gravitas* when he writes,

in poetry, you can do as you please. You can compose poetry in whatever form you like. If it seems a seventeenth-century habit to begin lines with capital letters, you can go in for the liquid transitions of greater simplicity, and so on. It is not that nobody cares. It matters immensely. The slightest sound matters. The most momentary rhythm matters.

> You can do as you please, yet everything matters. You are free, but your
> freedom must be consonant with the freedom of others . . . There is,
> in short, an unwritten rhetoric that is always changing and to which
> the poet must always be turning. That is the book in which he learns
> that the desire for literature is the desire for life. The incessant desire
> for freedom in literature or in any of the arts is a desire for freedom
> in life.[114]

At the core of Stevens's assertion here, I think, is the understanding
that freedom is not the opposite of finitude but is rather a *product of
finitude*—hence Stevens's relentless reminders to stay with "things as
they are," with "reality," and so on. You can do as you wish, but the *mean-
ing* of whatever you do is dependent upon "the freedom of others" and
"an unwritten rhetoric that is always changing." And this is actually
not a representational problem, but a pragmatic one, in which freedom
finds its expression only through a confrontation with finitude. As Luh-
mann puts it,

> if one starts from the assumption . . . that this is always a real process in
> a real environment, which is always subject to limitations coming from
> the environment, what might then be the problem? The problem could
> reside in the question of how a system is able to transform such *limita-
> tions* into *conditions for increasing its own complexity*. The *non-arbitrariness*
> of knowledge would then be nothing other than the evolutionarily-
> controlled *selectivity* of this process of change.[115]

This is why, in Stevens's words, "you can do as you please," yet "every-
thing matters": not "freedom" in the sense of voting or right to assem-
bly, but freedom in the sense of innovating, being free to "do what you
please," though in an environment in which one does not and cannot
operate solipsistically (hence Stevens's observation about "seventeenth
century habit"). And this means that the only source of new formal in-
novations is the pressure of a changing environment (earlier, "the con-
temporaneous") in which any given system finds itself; or, as Gregory
Bateson puts it, "all that is not information, not redundancy, not form
and not restraints—is noise, the only possible source of *new* patterns."[116]
And this is precisely where Stevens directs our attention late in the es-
say when he writes that "the irrational bears the same relation to the ra-
tional that the unknown bears to the known . . . That the unknown as the
source of knowledge, as the object of thought, is part of the dynamics of

the known does not permit of denial. It is the unknown that excites the ardor of scholars, who, in the known alone, would shrivel up with boredom . . . The rational mind, dealing with the known, expects to find it glistening in a familiar ether. What it really finds is the unknown always behind the known, giving it the appearance, at best, of chiaroscuro."[117]

"At best, of chiaroscuro"—what a wonderful way to evoke Stevens's nonrepresentational poetics of environmental resonance. We now have a better way to unpack Richard Poirier's observation—both perceptive and peevish—that the "deconstructionist" idea that "the word is not the thing that it represents" means for Emersonian pragmatists such as Stevens that "the evidence of a gap or an abyss is an invitation simply to get moving and keep moving, to make a transition"—a process of "onwardness" (to use Cavell's term about Emerson) that Stevens dwells upon in "The Irrational Element in Poetry."[118] *Why* this matters is the subject of Stevens's late poem "The Rock," which Poirier returns to in *Poetry and Pragmatism* as a way of reaching back to this Emersonian impulse. It is, Stevens writes, "As if nothingness contained a métier," "an illusion so desired" that it seems to give birth to leaves and lilacs that come to cover the rock, "like a blindness cleaned, / Exclaiming bright sight."[119]

The structuring force of the Emersonian I/eye is clear enough here in the last three lines, and Poirier notes, correctly I think, that this whole section of "The Rock" recalls in its mood the opening paragraphs of Emerson's "Experience." But then, he domesticates Stevens (and Emerson) by asking "to what can this 'métier' refer, if not to a Jamesian will to believe *something*, to believe at least in the work of knowing?"[120] To me, this seems a radical foreshortening, for all the reasons explored in this chapter, of what Poirier himself calls the "performing self," because the larger project of "onwardness" (what Poirier earlier called "superfluity") is brought back under the umbrella of the philosophy of the subject and its consciousness, while the more radical sense of the performative that I am pressing here *involves* consciousness and belief but is not anchored by it or dependent upon it—and that is exactly what Stevens parses (sometimes in excruciating detail) in "The Irrational Element." The reason for Stevens's otherwise odd engagement of Surrealism (of all things!) is to call our attention to the essentially and irreducibly impersonal nature of this process through the *machinalité* of the poem, for which the poet and his belief serve, as it were, not as source and anchor but as only one component in a larger ensemble.

And so—to return to Poirier's quite perceptive invocation of "Experience" in this context—Stevens's answer to Emerson's question at the opening of that essay, "Where do we find ourselves?" would be something like "in the not here and the not yet and the not now": that is to say, in the *environment*, a "nothingness" that can contain a "métier" only because it is brought into being by the ongoing movement of observation (Stevens often simply calls it "desire"), which unavoidably produces—*because of its contingency*—"an impermanence in its permanent cold" (as "The Rock" voices it in the passage above), leading to a renovative and revelatory "blindness cleaned, / Exclaiming bright sight." But make no mistake: this is not simply a matter of a Jamesian "will to believe," as the companion poem "No Possum, No Sop, No Taters" of Stevens reminds us. In that poem, we are told instead that it is "in this bad, that we reach / The last purity of the knowledge of good," as "Snow sparkles like eyesight falling to earth, // Like seeing fallen brightly away." That this is not a matter of consciousness, or will, or belief, but something far more environmental and infrastructural—far more inhuman and posthumanist—is made clear in the closing lines, where the crow rises up, "Bright is the malice in his eye." We join him, Stevens tells us, but "at a distance, in another tree."[121] To put it telescopically, the domain of observation and its work of environing, here troped once more, and canonically so, as the eye (as it will be too in "Thirteen Ways of Looking at a Blackbird") is a far from human, or humanist, phenomenon alone. The crow observes, we observe, but what is also observed is the difference between the two. And why that matters, in not just an epistemological sense but a biological and ecological one, will be the subject of the next chapter.

PART II

From Epistemological to Ecological Poetics

"There Is No World":

Deconstruction, Theoretical Biology, and
the Creative Universe

AS WE HAVE NOTED IN THE previous two chapters, much ink has
been spilled on questions of "epistemology" and "phenomenology" in re-
lation to Stevens's poetry and poetics. In the next two chapters—and in
this one in particular—I will lay the foundations for what would be, in a
different context, an extensive undertaking: to show how the epistemo-
logical and phenomenological questions in Stevens's poetry are actually
better understood if they are reframed in terms of a reconceptualiza-
tion of ecological poetics that is available to us by means of a cross-
conjugation of theoretical biology and poststructuralist thought (my
example will be deconstruction, though it need not be limited to that in
the larger project to which I have just gestured). The emphasis here, as I
have already insisted, is a *nonrepresentationalist* understanding of *poeisis*:
whether we are talking about the *poeisis* of "life" and the evolution of the
biosphere in theoretical biology, or the *poeisis* of worlding and world-
making in deconstruction, or the *poeisis* of Stevens's poetic practice.

Part of my motivation is that deconstruction has been considered
less relevant than other approaches to the kinds of questions around

"life" and ecology that I will be pursuing. Martin Hägglund has noted, for example, that "the revival of 'life' as a central category during the last decade of continental philosophy" has led to the downgrading of deconstruction "in the name of a return to the real, the material, and the biological."[1] At the same time, Vicki Kirby asserts that "there is no doubt that deconstruction is out of favour in critical theory circles" today, asking if deconstruction can "reinvent itself as 'new,' as 'creative,' as different from its former manifestations?"[2] I think the answer to her question is yes, not in spite of but *because of* the fact that in Derrida's work, as Kirby puts it, "a model, or representation, is not a third term in-between the biologist and biology or the writer and the world," but rather "the one who knows, the measuring apparatus and the object to be interpreted are strangely involved."[3]

What Kirby characterizes as the reinvention of deconstruction is part of what I have been trying to do over the past twenty years by bringing deconstruction into conversation with biological and social systems theory. Take, for example, this passage from Humberto Maturana and Francisco Varela, which I quoted in my book *Animal Rites* from 2003, where they offer their own version of what Kirby calls "strange involvement." The nervous system, they argue,

> does not operate according to either of the two extremes: it is neither representational nor solipsistic. It is not solipsistic, because as part of the nervous system's organism, it participates in the interactions of the nervous system with its environment. These interactions continuously trigger in it the structural changes that modulate its dynamics of states . . . Nor it is representational, for in each interaction it is the nervous system's structural state that specifies what perturbations are possible and what changes trigger them.[4]

But this leads to "a formidable snag," as they put it, because "it seems that the only alternative to a view of the nervous system as operating with representations is to deny the surrounding reality."[5] All this indicates, however, is the need (to use Niklas Luhmann's language) to pay attention to not just first-order but also second-order observation, to shift to the observation of observations. Thus, "as observers," they explain,

> we can see a unity in different domains, depending on the distinctions we make. Thus, on the one hand, we can consider a system in that domain where its components operate, in the domain of its internal states

and structural changes . . . On the other hand, we can consider a unity that also interacts with it . . . Neither of these two possible descriptions is a problem per se: both are necessary to complete our understanding of a unity. It is the observer who correlates them from his outside perspective . . . The problem begins when we unknowingly go from one realm to another and demand that the correspondences we establish between them (because we see these two realms simultaneously) be in fact a part of the operation of the unity.[6]

Methodologically speaking, this leads to the conclusion that

contrary to a common implicit or explicit belief, scientific explanations . . . constitutively do not and cannot operate as phenomenic reductions or give rise to them. This nonreductionist relation between the phenomenon to be explained and the mechanism that generates it is operationally the case because the actual result of a process, and the operations in the process that give rise to it in a generative relation, *intrinsically take place in independent and nonintersecting phenomenal domains.* The situation is the reverse of reductionism . . . [T]his permits us to see, particularly in the domain of biology, that there are phenomena like language, mind, or consciousness that require an interplay of bodies as a generative structure but do not take place in any of them. In this sense, science and the understanding of science lead us away from transcendental dualism."[7]

And also lead us away, it should be emphasized, from the *representationalism* that we have already seen dismantled, in philosophical terms, by Richard Rorty in chapter 2.

Deconstruction has traditionally been thought of as inimical to the idea of "nature," and as suspicious of biology and ecological concepts in general. What Michael Marder calls "deconstruction's allergy to ecology" stems in no small part from the holism and organicism that has typically characterized the concepts of nature and ecology as a site of "the persistence of *logos*" in the familiar forms of presence, gathering, harmony, the proper, the given, plenitude, origin, nonsupplementarity, and so on.[8] Here, however—and I've made a similar point elsewhere about Derrida's wary view of the concepts of "communication" and "information" in his work at mid-career—what is problematic is not the concept of ecology *tout court*, but rather the traditional ways (what we might call "first-order" ways) of thinking about it. I'll provide an alternative to that view here, extending considerably some of the formulations I introduced in my earlier book, *Before the Law*, regarding how a deconstructive rethinking of these concepts can be brought into a robust articulation with contemporary ecological and biological thought. For both deconstruction and contemporary theoretical biology, our attention needs to be focused squarely on the problems of temporalized complexity, the co-implication of observer and observed, and the contingent relationship between organism and environment. To put it slightly otherwise, we find a fundamental *nonpresence* and radical supplementarity or self-supplementarity at the heart of the evolution of the biosphere—there is no "there" there, in short—and it is this open-ended, nonteleological (though purposive) self-surpassing that theoretical biologist Stuart Kauffman calls "creative," and that Derrida's early work associates with the idea of "play."[9] This fundamental nonpresence is actually *crucial*, as we'll see in chapter 4, to the ethical implications Derrida derives in the second set of seminars on *The Beast and the Sovereign* from this remarkable passage, centered on his reading of Paul Celan and Martin Heidegger (though we need to hear the sense of "world" here that Heidegger inherited in part from biologist Jakob von Uexküll). Pedagogically tuned to the setting, Derrida Socratically offers three theses, with a sustained meditation on the third as the seminars unfold:

> 1. Incontestably, animals and humans inhabit the same world, the same objective world even if they do not have the same experience of the objectivity of the object. 2. Incontestably, animals and humans do not inhabit the same world, for the human world will never be purely and simply identical to the world of animals. 3. In spite of this identity and this difference, neither animals of different species, nor humans of different cultures, nor any animal or human individual inhabit the same world as another . . . and the difference between one world and another will remain always unbridgeable, because the community of the world is always constructed, simulated by a set of stabilizing apparatuses . . . nowhere and never given in nature. Between my world . . . and any other world there is first the space and time of an infinite difference, an interruption that is incommensurable with all attempts to make a passage, a bridge, an isthmus, all attempts at communication, translation, trope, and transfer that the desire for a world . . . will try to pose, impose, propose, stabilize. There is no world, there are only islands.[10]

We'll return to this important passage in a different key in chapter 4, but for now, we can say that one of the reasons "there is no world" is that "life" or "nature"—rather than being a site of fullness, positivity, and identity (that is to say, nonsupplementarity)—is importantly in a relationship of *différance*, asynchronicity, and "spacing" to itself because of the fundamental circularity and recursivity that takes place in an ever changing environment for biological life forms—the fundamental "repetition with difference" familiar from poststructuralist philosophy but radicalized and, as it were, three-dimensionalized, by theoretical biology. And this enables, in turn, what I will call a "topological" rather than "topographical" way of thinking the ecological. As Ana Soto and Giuseppe Longo note, "biological systems are characterized by the simultaneous co-existence of opposites as exemplified by change and stability, the incomplete separation between internal and external (topology), and before and after (time), the notions of extended present, memory and anticipation."[11] The issues here are both ontological and epistemological, and they lead inexorably to an ongoing deconstruction of the ontological/epistemological divide—a deconstruction that poetry can handle better than philosophy, as we saw Gregory Bateson suggest in chapter 2.

What I mean by "topological" is that the issues involved here are not just "ecological" in the straightforward sense. To be sure, both the ecological and topological senses of the evolution of the biosphere push back against the "central dogma" that has dominated the conversation about life in the biosphere for the last fifty years. That dogma, famously formalized by Francis Crick and institutionalized by molecular biology and figures such as Richard Dawkins, holds that in evolutionary heredity, inheritance that has evolutionary significance is limited to the "vertical" transmission of DNA sequences; that the only variations that are heritable in organisms take place in DNA sequences; and that variations in organisms do not occur as a result of somatic changes or environmental pressures, but only take place by means of random mutations in DNA sequences.[12] Now, as Russell Winslow and Denis Noble (among others) have noted, well-known biological phenomena, such as "horizontal inheritance," epigenetic inheritance, niche construction, "adaptability drivers," and so on, make it clear that the understanding "in which identities are fundamentally tied to family lineages of vertical inheritance must be replaced by something far more ecological."[13] In the so-called "Baldwin effect" of niche construction, for example, an organism moving to a new niche "can change the course of evolution even with no mutations whatsoever," as biologist Denis Noble points out, resulting in "an evolution of the genome by combinatorial selection, not selection of new random mutations."[14] Niche construction and its effect on evolution only dramatize the fact that "construction," not "adaptation," is *le mot juste* in this situation. As none other than Richard Lewontin argues, "the claim that the environment of an organism is causally independent of the organism, and that changes in the environment are autonomous and independent of changes in the species itself, is clearly wrong. It is bad biology, and every ecologist and evolutionary biologist knows it is bad biology."[15]

More radically still, as Winslow notes, "insofar as the organisms niche-construct, they inscribe themselves into the environment phenotypically; they carve the history of their *capabilities* into the hieroglyphic cave-walls of organismic space and time." And this means that "spaces are not substances, they are not *present* things . . . insofar as the ecosystem contains the trace of former, past activity and already gestures toward a future."[16] This is anything but a generic process, of course—and not just because of the gap between what G. Evelyn Hutchinson called "the ecological theater and the evolutionary play"—and it mitigates any kind of holistic or topographical concept of ecology (even though we may search for, and find, underlying regularities in how that process takes shape).[17] Part of the reason that holism in any familiar sense is out of the question is that in such topological forms of "mereological" relations, the relationship between the part and the whole is radically changed, and so are the qualitatively different forms of causality that obtain at different levels. We typically think of causation in the scientific domain as bottom-up (as we do in the "central dogma," where the lines of causality run from the gene to the physical characteristics, biomorphology, and so on of the organism). But in the dynamic, self-organizing, autopoietic forms of life in the biosphere, we find a much more complex relationship between component (or element) and system, because causality often operates in top-down fashion as well. As Alicia Juarrero notes, these "mereological" relationships (part-to-whole or whole-to-part) have "bedeviled philosophers of science for centuries,"[18] but we now see that "the unpleasant whiff of paradox" that "remains in any mention of recursive causality" in living systems is unavoidable, and indeed productive.[19] We find in autopoietic biological systems what she calls a "decoupling in the locus of control: the components' behaviors suddenly originate in and are under the control, regulation, and modulation of the emergent properties of the macro level, *as such*," which in turn "*loosens the one-to-one strict determinism from micro to macro levels*."[20] In contrast to physical systems that show emergent self-organization—dust devils, tornadoes, Bénard cells, and so on—where "external agents or circumstances are responsible for the conditions within which physical self-organization takes place," in autopoietic systems, those conditions and constraints are introduced and maintained *by the system itself*, resulting in a strong "downward causation" in which systemic closure becomes "a closure of constraint production, not just a closure of processes."[21]

This means—and here I think a strong return to deconstruction is unavoidable—that (as Juarrero notes, following Stuart Kauffman), "it is impossible to predict emergent properties even in principle because the 'categories necessary to frame them do not exist until after the fact.'"[22] Is this uncertainty epistemological or ontological? Juarrero asks. "Does emergence therefore simply come down to an *epistemological* ignorance, to our human inability to exhaustively list every *ceteris paribus* and disjunctive condition (even though such an exhaustive set of conditions in fact exists and there is a 1:1 correlation between each fully specified set of conditions and corresponding emergent property)?"[23] And here is where I think the epistemology/ontology divide cannot be maintained. Indeed, if everything we have said of biological organisms is also true of *us*, it is *all the more the case* with us, and for the reasons Juarrero notes: the more complex the autopoietic life form, the more we find a "dynamic decoupling" of the causative relationships between the micro- and macro-levels. Or, as she puts it:

> System and environment co-evolve over time in such a way that the identification between macro-property and specific configuration becomes irrelevant; as we go up the evolutionary ladder, the go of things issues more and more from higher and higher levels and according to criteria established at progressively emergent levels. Just as living things are autonomous and self-directed in a way that physical dissipative structures are not, sentient, conscious, and self-conscious being are even more autonomous and self-directed.[24]

But here, I think, is where we need an astringent dose of deconstruction, specifically, Derrida's critique of the "auto-" of autonomy, auto-affection, autobiography, and the like—in short, his critique of intentionality and related concepts such as "agency."[25] It's not that autonomy and self-directedness don't increase, as Juarrero suggests, with the increasing decoupling of micro- and macro-structures and the growing importance of downward causality. They do. It's just that the picture that intentionality and autonomy *gives to itself* of its situation is unavoidably partial, reductive, and blind to its full infrastructural conditions of possibility for emergence (or what we have already called its "ecological" embeddedness). Or, to remember Maturana's claim above: "there are phenomena like language, mind, or consciousness that require an interplay of bodies as a generative structure but do not take place in any of them." Or, as Maturana and Varela put it in *Autopoiesis and Cognition*:

> the domain of discourse is a closed domain, and it is not possible to step outside of it through discourse. Because the domain of discourse is a closed domain it is possible to make the following ontological statement: *the logic of the* description *is the logic of the* describing *(living) system (and his cognitive domain)*.
>
> This logic demands a substratum for the occurrence of the discourse. We cannot talk about this substratum in absolute terms, however, because we would have to describe it . . . Thus, although this substratum is required for epistemological reasons, nothing can be said about it other than what is meant in the ontological statement above.[26]

What this means—more radically still—is that when intentionality *does* attempt to give itself a nonreductive or complete picture of this situation, it is unavoidably subject to the phenomenon of recursivity that is at the core of both deconstruction and theoretical biology. And it is also "blind" to the self-reference of its own description. As Vicki Kirby reminds us, in deconstruction, "the purported gap that secures and separates the analytical instrument from the subject who uses it and the object scrutinized, is confounded," and this means that we are always already in "an ecology that is so intricately enmeshed and all-encompassing that even those expressions (of itself) that appear circumscribed, isolated, and autonomous, are 'themselves' generated by this generality."[27]

All of the foregoing should make clear what I am *not* doing here. I am not engaging in the kind of argument that is all too familiar from approaches such as "literary Darwinism," "neuroaesthetics," "cognitive cultural studies" or "cognitive poetics," all of which, as Carsten Strathausen puts it, presume "to understand all aspects of human culture, including art and politics, in biological terms as part of our evolutionary heritage, often in the process embracing an oversimplified and reductionist version of Darwinian theory."[28] Unlike the position I am developing here, "biologism calls on art for the sole purpose to verify what it already knows. It fails or refuses to acknowledge the fact that the concepts we use codetermine the objects we analyze."[29] In short, the position I am developing here is the *opposite* of reductionism, and I am happy to say that it is increasingly shared by exciting and inspiring new work in theoretical biology. Or, as Denis Noble puts it, regarding the posthumanist sense of "observation" that I am invoking here, "a proton (a hydrogen ion) views a cell much as we view the universe. And that is also how a single cell views us. Universes within universes within universes—and beyond what we can see and know about, who knows? 'Know' is the right word here. We have no idea what, if anything, could lie beyond what we see and observe. That should inspire humility."[30] And yet, this is not a generic, generalizable observation—as if there were just one type of thing called "observing"—precisely because of the qualitatively different kinds of causation and constraint in different physical and biological phenomena, as discussed above.

The relationship between deconstruction and the life sciences has been taken up in the past, of course, by figures such as Anthony Wilden and, more recently, Christopher Johnson, in his book *System and Writing in the Philosophy of Jacques Derrida*. Johnson provides a useful overview of the interdisciplinary matrix out of which the crosstalk between deconstruction and the life sciences emerged. As he notes, during the 1960s, we find an epistemic shift "occurring within structuralism—or between structuralism and 'post-structuralism'—with respect to the linguistic analogy, involving a change of emphasis from 'language' to the more specific notion of 'writing.'"[31] This shift coincided in France with the Nobel Prize–winning work of theoretical biologists François Jacob, Jacques Monot, and André Lwoff on the role of RNA in the transmission of genetic information, and opened the door for the reconceptualization of "writing" in terms of code and program that Derrida famously explores in *Of Grammatology*, whose first chapter, "The End of the Book and the Beginning of Writing," begins with a section called "The Program."[32] The first chapter of Jacob's influential book *The Logic of Life*, from 1965, is also called "The Programme," and in it he argues that "heredity is described today in terms of information, messages, and code," and thus (and here we find a clear through-line to Derrida's reading of Saussure, Husserl, and, especially, Austin) "the intention of a psyche has been replaced by the translation of a message. The living being does indeed represent the execution of a plan, but not one conceived in any mind."[33] It is in this sense that *Of Grammatology* announces a "primary writing" that "*comprehends* language" as we usually think of it, in the same way that the "contemporary biologist speaks of writing and *pro-gram* in relation to the most elementary processes of information within the living cell. And finally," Derrida continues,

whether it has essential limits or not, the entire field covered by the cy-
bernetic *program* will be the field of writing . . . Even before being de-
termined as human (with all the distinctive characteristics that have al-
ways been attributed to man and the entire system of significations that
they imply) or nonhuman, the *grammè*—or the *grapheme*—would thus
name the element. An element without simplicity.[34]

As we know, this claim leads directly to Derrida's assertion years
later—one that makes clear the theoretical underpinnings of his later,
well-known work on "the question of the animal"—that "the elaboration
of a new concept of the *trace* had to be extended to the entire field of
the living, *or rather to the life/death relation*, beyond the anthropological
limits of 'spoken' language."[35] Or, as he puts it in the interview "Eating
Well," "if one reinscribes language in a network of possibilities that do
not merely encompass it but mark it irreducibly from the inside, every-
thing changes. I am thinking in particular of the mark in general, of the
trace, iterability, of *différance*. These possibilities or necessities, without
which there would be no language, *are themselves not only human* . . .
And what I am proposing should allow us to take into account scientific
knowledge about the complexity of 'animal languages,' genetic coding,
all forms of marking."[36]

But here I want to come back to an important point easily missed in
Of Grammatology and amplify it. Namely: why does Derrida assert that
the *grammè* is "an element *without simplicity*"? Rather than launching
into a long discussion of Derrida's early work at this juncture, I will rely
here, for the uninitiated, on Matthias Fritsch's able summary of "decon-
struction 'in a nutshell'" (as he puts it). For deconstruction (and I hope
the resonances with theoretical biology will already be clear),

the object is not seen as preexisting its context but as owing itself to the
environment of its emergence and being . . . But the context is not itself
exhaustively analyzable, as if we could list all of its elements in a com-
plete list . . . [T]he context is inexhaustible, not because the list would
be too long to itemize, but rather for the more essential reason that the
context is itself undergoing change as it constitutes the elements of
which it is made up . . . Further, and for the same reason, the depen-
dence on a constitutive context is not fully determining for an element,
for it can be recontextualized; an entity can, indeed cannot but, shift
from context to context.

It is these two moments of differentiation and recontextualizability (or iterability) that Derrida sought to capture economically with the neologism *différance*. The term is to encompass difference and deferral—that is, situation in context but without final determinability, anticipation of future environments (for not anything goes), but also exposure to the open-ended future the elements in an ongoing system cannot know. And despite having first developed it in the context of structuralist accounts of language and culture, it is the notion of *différance* that Derrida sees as "co-extensive" with mortal life.[37]

A few crucial points follow from this. First, *time* is thus constitutive of the problem of the system/environment relationship for Derrida as it is for systems theory (a point that Martin Hägglund has made well in his book-length study of Derrida), which is why Derrida writes that the play of *différance* designates "the unity of chance and necessity in calculations without end," precisely in the sense that we will see described by Stuart Kauffman on the terrain of chemistry and biology.[38] Or, to combine the terms of systems theory and deconstruction, the formal element of a system can never be characterized by any kind of basal simplicity because its meaning depends upon the real-time dynamic state of the system in which the element functions—what Derrida would call the moment of the element's "performativity" or "iteration." Indeed, one of the ironies of our story is that Derrida, like Monod before him (who emerged as a foundational figure for molecular biology), became associated with the obsession with "code," "text," and so on that would encourage the more reductive tendencies of the neo-Darwinian synthesis, even though Derrida had made it clear from the beginning that code was always only half the story—not just in *Of Grammatology* but also in his work on "general" versus "restricted" economy in *Writing and Difference*, which references Bataille's *The Accursed Share, Vol. 1*, who in turn references Vernadsky's *The Biosphere* (one of the founding texts of ecological thought).[39] As biologist Denis Noble points out, even for Jacob and Monod themselves, "code" was only part of a much bigger picture. The concept of the genetic "programme" may have been borrowed from the computer program, and "in principle, the code is independent of the machine that implements it," but when we ask, "where, then, does the full algorithmic logic of a programme lie?" the answer "is in the cell or organism as a whole, not just in the genome."[40] As Jacob wrote in *La logique du vivant* in 1970, "the incessant execution of a programme is inseparable from its realisation."[41]

Or, as Noble notes—in a passage utterly consonant with Derrida's sense of the "programme" in *Of Grammatology*—"there is no meaning in the nucleic acid sequences themselves. Meaning arises as a consequence of the contextual logic within which they are interpreted within a living organism."[42]

This helps bring into focus, as Christopher Johnson puts it, that "Derrida's appropriation of this vocabulary is profoundly *un*structuralist," and has "a greater affinity with the metamorphic and adaptational ('open-system') models found in systems theory."[43] But I would make an even stronger claim here: namely, that Derrida gives us a theory of something like the relationship of the genetic (or systemic, formally code-bound) and the epigenetic factors (the environmental or contextual setting in which the code is deployed) that we will see developed on the biological side, beginning in the late 1950s, by Conrad Waddington and Stuart Kauffman, among others. In the 1960s, Derrida was formalizing and ramifying a theory of the relationship between the genetic, the epigenetic, and the ecological that was being pioneered at the same time (1957) by Waddington, but which is only now being fully articulated after fifty years of hegemonic rule by neo-Darwinian reductionism, with its over-emphasis on the genetic level of code or "script" alone.[44]

To put it this way is to enable a more robust understanding of the second point that follows from our examination of "deconstruction 'in a nutshell'" above—what I have elsewhere called the question of "double finitude" that attends both human and nonhuman life, and that is in turn subtended by the genetic/epigenetic form of iterability theorized in the 1960s by Derrida: our finitude not just as embodied and vulnerable beings who are dependent on our environments and who need care (finitude number one), but also as ones who, to enter into communicative relations and social bonds with others *at all* (human or nonhuman), are by necessity subjected to the "not me" and "not ours" of semiotic systems characterized by *différance* and the trace that, as Derrida puts it, must "be extended to the entire field of the living, or rather to the life/death relation, beyond the anthropological limits of 'spoken' language."[45] It's not just human beings, in other words, who are subjected to the finitude of *différance* and the trace—*any* creature that engages in communicative, semiotic behaviors is; and that means that this second form of finitude is not held in reserve for a "human" who can thereby be ontologically separated decisively from other forms of life.

Third, and crucially, this enables us, in turn, to understand the importance of what I have elsewhere called the "second-order" turn of systems theory (which, in my view, formalizes the problem more clearly than deconstruction), showing us that—contrary to the understanding of autopoietic systems as solipsistic—the operational closure of systems and the self-reference based upon it arise as a practical and adaptive necessity precisely because systems are *not* closed: that is, precisely because they find themselves in an environment of overwhelmingly and exponentially greater complexity than is possible for any single system. To put it another way, systems have to operate selectively and "blindly" (as Niklas Luhmann puts it) not because they are closed, but precisely because they *aren't*, and the asymmetrical distribution of complexity across the system/environment difference is what *forces* the strategy of self-referential closure and autopoiesis.[46] Indeed, as we saw in chapter 2, the "second-order" turn, as I have argued elsewhere,[47] is to realize that the more systems build up their own internal complexity through recursive self-reference and closure, the *more* linked they are to changes in their environments to which they become more and more sensitive, but in relation to which they may also have more "management strategies" by building up their own internal complexity (both ontogenetically and phylogenetically). This is why the system/environment relationship is more multidimensional and complex for a bonobo hunting for food in the forest than for an amoeba swimming up a gradient of sugar solution on a microscope slide.

As Johnson points out, a crucial causal principle for open systems is one framed by one of the founding figures of systems theory, biologist Ludwig Bertalanffy: the principle of "equifinality," which makes possible the recursive feedback loops through which autopoiesis occurs. As Bertalanffy writes,

> in any closed system, the final state is unequivocally determined by the initial conditions . . . If either the initial conditions or the process is altered, the final state will also be changed. This is not so in open systems. Here, the same final state may be reached from different initial conditions and in different ways. This is what is called equifinality, and it has a significant meaning for the phenomena of biological regulation.[48]

We find a path-breaking example of the principle of equifinality in the work of Kauffman's mentor Conrad Waddington, whose famous model of the "chreode" (or "developmental landscape") models the sort of relationship between biological system and its environment that we are interested in here. As Noble notes in an article in the *Journal of*

Experimental Biology, Waddington was able to demonstrate, in a classic experiment, "the inheritance of a characteristic acquired in a population in response to an environmental stimulus." August Weismann had unsuccessfully attempted to demonstrate this in 1890—a failure that, along with his assumption that genetic mutation was random, laid the foundations for the neo-Darwinian "Modern Synthesis" that we have already touched upon.[49] Waddington realized that the developmental plasticity of organisms (in his case, fruit flies) could be affected by environmental factors that interceded at different points along the developmental timeline. He used the term "canalized" for this type of environmental influence, and he "represented the developmental process as a series of 'decisions' that could be represented as a series of 'valleys' and 'forks' in a developmental landscape," what Waddington dubbed a "chreode."[50] As Noble explains,

> He knew from his developmental studies that embryo fruit flies could be persuaded to show different thorax and wing structures, simply by changing the environmental temperature or by a chemical stimulus. In his landscape diagram, this could be represented as a small manipulation in slope that would lead to one channel in the landscape being favoured over another, so that the adult could show a different phenotype starting from the same genotype. The next step in his experiment was to select for and breed from the animals that displayed the new characteristic. Exposed to the same environmental stimulus, these gave rise to progeny with an even higher proportion of adults displaying the new character. After a relatively small number of generations, he found that he could then breed from the animals and obtain robust inheritance of the new character even without applying the environmental stimulus. The characteristic had therefore become locked into the genetics of the animal. He called this process genetic assimilation. What he had succeeded in showing was that an acquired characteristic could first be inherited as what we would now call "soft" inheritance, and that it could then be assimilated into becoming standard "hard" genetic inheritance. Today, we call "soft" inheritance epigenetic inheritance, and of course, we know many more mechanisms by which the same genome can be controlled to produce different epigenetic effects.[51]

We thus end up with the fundamental evolutionary and developmental unit being—as Gregory Bateson would put it a decade and a half after the publication of Waddington's book *The Strategy of the Genes* (1957)—not organism-as-printout of a genetic code, nor even organism-as-printout varied in its successive copies by random genetic mutations, but rather what Bateson calls "flexible organism-in-its-environment" (with "flexible" here denoting not just behavioral flexibility but the very plasticity that Waddington had exploited in his experiment)—all versus the neo-Darwinian identification of the "unit of survival" as "the breeding individual or the family line."[52] This reconceptualization is captured quite well in Noble's modification of Waddington's own image, because it emphasizes an aspect that will become crucial to Kauffman's own work, namely, the "functional *networks*"—that is, the real-time dynamic, material processes—that interact with environmental influences in specific ways to produce the developmental landscape, which can be varied by altering either the organism in question or the environmental factors that influence it.[53] As we shall see in a moment, this is precisely where Stuart Kauffman's work on emergence, self-organization, and complexity picks up the story—and picks it up in a way that is, for Kauffman, consonant with Bateson's insistence that the redefinition of the fundamental unit of evolution has ethical, not just scientific, consequences. As Bateson writes, "you have at each step to include the completed pathways outside the protoplasmic aggregate, be it DNA-in-the-cell, or cell-in-the-body, or body-in-the-environment . . . Formerly we talked about the breeding individual or the family line or the taxon, and so on. Now each step of the hierarchy is to be thought of as a system, instead of a chunk cut off and visualized as *against* the surrounding matrix."[54]

We are now ready to trace the broader ramifications of these principles in Kauffman's work, which will in turn enable us to understand that the more radical and profound way of thinking ecology is *not* "everything is connected" and not "nothing is connected," but rather "some things are connected and some things aren't—and in highly specific ways." (Indeed, this is what we find in Waddington's and Kauffman's focus on the quite specific, radically contingent system/environment interactions that result in the emergence of what Kauffman calls "order for free," but only under some conditions and not others, just as, in epigenetics, the plasticity of a certain material, genetic substrate will result developmentally in some expressions and not others, but only under quite specific conditions and interactions—hence Noble's modification of Waddington's developmental landscape, above). And crucial here, as we shall see, is what I am prepared to call Kauffman's "deconstructive" assertion that all such designations are unavoidably retroactive attributions. As Kauffman argues, because "we cannot prestate the relevant functional variables" that will end up being indispensable for further evolutionary states, and because causal consequences "pass from organism to world and back to the organism," there is "no noncircular way to define the 'niche' of the organism separately from the organism. But that niche is the boundary condition on selection. The 'niche' is only revealed *after* the *fact*, by what succeeds in evolution."[55]

Having already touched on the radical implications of this seemingly straightforward point noted by Alicia Juarrero (among others), I now focus on Kauffman's recent book *Humanity in a Creative Universe* (2017), and in particular its third and fourth chapters, to illustrate the importance of the point a bit more. In this text, Kauffman—cofounder of the famed Santa Fe Institute and a former MacArthur Fellow—ranges from organic chemistry and biology to economics, quantum mechanics, and much else, but what I am most interested in here is the central claim of the book: namely, that there are no "entailing laws" that predetermine the evolution of the biosphere (hence the "creative universe" of the book's title). As Kauffman notes, "Newton's laws yield classical physics, causally closed, and an entirely 'entailed' view of the becoming of reality," a view that was turbo-charged by what Kauffman calls "the birth of reductive materialism": Laplace's claim that a "demon" who knew all of the positions and momenta of the particles in the universe could calculate the entire past and future of the universe based on Newton's differential equations.[56] But in 1898, Henri Poincaré introduced an important crack in the edifice of reductive materialism by showing that there is no analytical solution for the "three body problem" that Newton had worried about (in the form of the Sun, Earth, and Venus). Poincaré introduced what would become known in chaos theory as "sensitivity to initial conditions" by showing that "two 'infinitely close' initial positions and momenta can follow trajectories that veer apart, becoming 'exponentially' more distant with time," meaning that "determinism no longer implies predictability for we cannot measure initial conditions to infinite accuracy."[57]

In the section of Kauffman's book that I am interested in, he assumes, almost exclusively, classical chemistry and physics, and "the point is not to show that Newton's laws do not often work (they do) . . . but to begin to demolish the hegemony of reductive materialism and its grip on our scientific minds."[58] The central thrust of this section of the book, which forces us to rethink not just the evolution of the biosphere but the entire concept of "ecology," is that "at least part of why the universe has become complex is due to an easy-to-understand, but not well-recognized,

'antientropic' process that does not vitiate the second law [of thermody-
namics]." He continues:

> Briefly, as more complex things and linked processes are created, and
> can combine with one another in ever more new ways to make yet more
> complex amalgams of things and processes, the space of possible things
> and linked processes becomes vastly larger and the universe has not had
> time to make all the possibilities . . . There is an indefinitely expand-
> ing, ever more open space of possibilities ever more sparsely sampled,
> as the complexity of things and linked processes increases . . . [T]here
> is a deep sense in which the universe becomes complex in its explora-
> tion of these ever more sparsely sampled spaces of what is next possible
> because *"it can."*[59]

One of the more compelling examples Kauffman gives of this prin-
ciple obtains at the level of organic chemistry, before we even get to the
domain of autopoietic organisms, or what he calls "Kantian wholes,"
where we would more likely expect to find such forms of complexity. In
a core passage of the book, he writes, "Proteins are linear strings of amino
acids bound together by peptide bonds. There are twenty types of amino
acids in evolved biology. A typical protein is perhaps 300 amino acids
long, and some are several thousand amino acids long." He continues:

> Now, how many possible proteins are there with 200 amino acids? Well,
> there are 20 choices for each of the 200 positions, so 20^{200} or 10^{260} possi-
> ble proteins with the length of 200 amino acids. This is a tiny subset of
> the molecular species of CHNOPS [Carbon, Hydrogen, Nitrogen, Ox-
> ygen, Phosphorus, Sulfur] with 100,000 atoms per molecule. Now the
> universe is 13.7 billion years old and has about 10^{80} particles. The fastest
> time scale in the universe is the Planck time scale of 10^{-43} seconds. If
> the universe were doing nothing but using all 10^{80} particles in parallel
> to make proteins the length of 200 amino acids, each in a single Planck
> moment, it would take 10^{39} repetitions of the history of the universe to
> make all the possible proteins the length of 200 amino acids just *once!* . . .
> [A]s we consider proteins the length of 200 amino acids and all possi-
> ble CHNOPS molecules with 100,000 atoms or less per molecule,
> it is obvious that the universe *will never make them all.* History enters
> when the space of what is possible is vastly larger than what can actually
> happen . . . A next point simple and clear: Consider all the CHNOPS

molecules that can be made with 1, with 2, with 3, with 4, with n, with 100,000 atoms per molecule. Call the space of possible molecules with n atoms of CHNOPS the phase space for CHNOPS molecules of n atoms. That phase space increases enormously as n increases. Consequently, in the lifetime of the universe, as n increases, that phase space will be sampled ever more sparsely.[60]

As Kauffman shows, this "nonergodic" principle obtains even more radically and obviously at the level of the biosphere, in which "its becoming cannot be prestated, is not 'governed' by entailing laws, in which what becomes constitutes ever-new Actuals that are 'enabling constraints' that do not cause, but enable, ever-new, typically unprestatable, Adjacent Possible opportunities into which the evolving biosphere becomes."[61] When we reach the level of what he calls "Kantian wholes," or autopoietic organisms, this process is (not surprisingly) even more striking.[62] If we think about the concept of biological function, for example, it is clear that "in classical physics there are only 'happenings.' The ball rolls down the hill, bumps a rock, veers," and so on. But in biology we have to distinguish function from mere physical happenings. "The function of the heart is to pump blood," Kauffman notes, but the heart "causally also makes heart sounds, jiggles water in the pericardial sac," and so on.[63] Classical physics will not help us here, because "the *function* of the part is its causal consequences that help sustain the whole"; "function" is causal, in other words, but *causal in a qualitatively different way from classical physics.*[64] As Kauffman notes, another nail in the coffin for the reductionist approach is that "this capacity to define a function as a subset of causal consequences that can be improved in evolution further separates biology from physics, which cannot make the distinction among all causal consequences into a subset which are functions."[65] As Kauffman baldly puts it, "Dawkins wrote *The Selfish Gene* (1976) as if DNA replicators were the heart of biology, and the organism merely a 'vehicle' for the self gene in evolution. I completely disagree. Organisms are autopoietic self-creating wholes that achieve functional sufficiency, often improvable, as the biosphere becomes . . . [I]t is the functional closure/sufficiencies of organisms as Kantian wholes, not the genes they carry along, which is the heart of life and its evolution."[66]

Having established the importance of the concept of biological function, Kauffman hypothesizes that "we cannot prestate the evolution of new functions in the biosphere, hence cannot prestate the ever-changing phase space of biological evolution which includes precisely the functions of organisms and their myriad parts and processes evolving in their worlds. But these ever-new functions constitute the ever-changing *phase space* of biological evolution." And this means (logically enough) that "we can have *no entailing laws* at all for biological evolution."[67] He offers a nice, compact example of this process in his discussion of Darwinian "pre-adaptations" or "exaptations"—the emergence of new, possibly useful, traits through random genetic mutation (staying within the neo-Darwinian orthodoxy for the moment). All that needs to happen in an autopoietic biological entity—an *E. coli* bacterium, let's say—is that it "*finds a use that enhances the fitness of that bacterium in its local world.* Then, if there is heritable variation for that screwdriver, natural selection acting, not at the level of the screwdriver, but at the level of the Kantian whole cell in its world, will probably select a modified *E. coli* with a *new use* or function. Three major comments are critical," Kauffman continues:

> (1) We cannot prestate this new use or function, which after selection, becomes part of the evolving biosphere and feeds into the future evolution of the biosphere. (2) This "finding of a new use" *is* "the arrival of the fitter," never solved by Darwin. Darwin could not have solved this issue, for the "arrival of the fitter" is typically unprestatable in its new functionality. (3) While we cannot prestate what selection will select, there are still "winners and losers." Selection does act, but we typically, in the real evolving biosphere, cannot prestate what selection will select, such as new functionalities.[68]

Kauffman's especially winning example of this process—where a side-effect generated by random genetic mutation can become a functional asset under different environmental conditions, as Darwin himself surmised—is the emergence of the swim bladder in fish. The Darwinian exaptation whereby some early versions of fish had lungs, enabling them to bounce from puddle to puddle, led in time to the biological *function* of a ratio of air and water in fish that now live wholly in water that allows neutral buoyancy in the water column. Did this change the future evolution of the biosphere? Kauffman asks:

> Yes, and in two vastly different ways. First, new daughter species of fish with swim bladders and new proteins evolved. But second, *once* the swim bladder exists, it constitutes a new Actual condition in the evolving biosphere. The swim bladder now constitutes a new, empty but Adjacent

Possible niche, or opportunity for evolution. For example, a species of worm or bacteria could evolve to live, say exclusively, in the swim bladder. The Adjacent-Possible opportunities for evolution, given the new swim bladder, do not include all possibilities. For example, a *T. Rex* or giraffe could not evolve to live in the swim bladder.[69]

One of the key theoretical points here—and one that articulates *directly* with deconstruction, in my view—arises when Kauffman asks, "do we think that selection, in any way at all, 'acted' to achieve the swim bladder as *constituting a new adjacent-possible empty niche* in which a worm or a bacterial species might evolve to live? No."[70] Further, he adds—and again I would point out how resonant this is with the fine print of the deconstructive apparatus—"does the swim bladder, once it has come to exist, *cause* the worm or bacterial species to evolve to live in it? *No*. The swim bladder *enables, but does not cause, the bacterial or worm species to evolve to live in it*. Instead, quantum random mutations to the DNA of the bacterium or worm yield variations in screwdrivers that may be selected at the level of the whole organism by which the worm or bacterial species evolves to live in the swim bladder."[71] And what this means—to return now to Derrida—is that "code," in Derrida's understanding, is, as Johnson puts it, "therefore constituted *in process* rather than in anticipation. Despite the suggestion of precedence implied . . . in Derrida's articulation of the word programme (*pro-gramme*), the gram, the trace, the inscription are never absolutely primary. There is instead a kind of *precipitation* towards sense that is ignorant of its future,"[72] so that "the system is not pulled into the future by a mysterious first (and last) principle, but is pushed *a tergo* by what is handed down, selected and recombined, from its ancestral past. This philosophy is, in essence, a philosophy of *evolution*."[73] And that is why—again to quote Kauffman—"there is, therefore, no noncircular way to define the 'niche' of the organism separately from the organism. But that niche is the boundary condition on selection. The 'niche' is only revealed *after* the *fact*, by what succeeds in evolution."[74]

It is hard to imagine a clearer articulation, in robust naturalistic, biological terms, of what Derrida calls "the becoming-space of time and the becoming-time of space," the "will have been" of that which is "to come," unprestatable and unanticipatable, with Darwin's "pre-adaptations" being precisely the material substrate, the trace, on which retentions of the past and protentions of the future are inscribed. As Martin Hägglund explains:

Given that every temporal moment ceases to be as soon as it comes to be, it must be inscribed in a trace in order to be at all. This is the *becoming-space of time*. The trace is necessarily spatial, since spatiality is characterized by the ability to remain in spite of temporal succession. The spatiality of the trace is thus a condition for the synthesis of time, since it enables the past to be retained for the future. The spatiality of the trace, however, is itself temporal. Without temporalization a trace could not remain across time and relate the past to the future . . . In order to remain—even for a moment—a trace cannot have any integrity as such but is already marked by its own becoming past and becoming related to the future. Accordingly, the persistence of the trace cannot be the persistence of something that is exempt from the negativity of time. Rather, the trace is always in relation to an unpredictable future that gives it both the chance to remain and to be effaced.[75]

Equally important (and I think this helps to underscore and clarify an aspect of Kauffman's argument that is often only implicit) is what Hägglund calls the fundamental "negativity" of time, "which undermines *both* the idea of a discrete moment *and* the idea of an absolute continuity. Only if something is *no longer*—that is, only if there is negativity—can there be a difference between before and after. This negativity must be at work in presence itself for there to be succession. If the moment is not negated in being succeeded by another moment, their relation is not one of temporal succession but of spatial co-existence."[76] The combination of this negativity of time with what Hägglund calls the "arche-materiality" of the trace makes Kauffman's nonentailed evolution of the biosphere thinkable. "Precisely because every temporal moment negates itself," Hägglund writes, "the duration of time can never be given in itself but depends on the material support of spatial inscription" in the form of the trace; "without the later inscription nothing could persist and there would be no movement or passage of time."[77]

We find here, in fact, the site of a *double* inscription: not just on the material substrate of the living being (whether we think of Waddington's "soft" and "hard" inheritance or the pre-adaptation of the swim bladder) but also in the dynamic contingency of the organism/environment relationship in which that ontogenetic inscription happens, which can make the "same" inscription function differently, in terms of adaptation, at different points in time. As Bateson points out in his discussion of "iconic genotypic signals," it is common to find what he calls "a secondary statistical iconicism" in the animal kingdom of the following type:

Labroides dimidiatus, a small Indo-Pacific wrasse, which lives on the ec-toparasites of other fishes, is strikingly colored and moves or "dances" in a way which is easily recognized. No doubt these characteristics at-tract other fish and are part of a signaling system which leads the other fish to permit the approaches of the cleaner. But there is a mimic of this species of *Labroides*, a saber-toothed blenny (*Aspirdontus taeniatus*), whose similar coloring and movement permit the mimic to approach—and bite off pieces of the fins of other fishes.

Clearly the coloring and movements of the mimic are iconic and "represent" the cleaner. But what of the coloring and movements of the latter? All that is primarily required is that the cleaner be conspicuous and distinctive. It is not required that it represent something else. But when we consider the statistical aspects of the system, it becomes clear that if the blennies become too numerous, the distinctive features of the wrasses will become iconic warnings and their hosts will avoid them.[78]

If theoretical biology reminds us of this fact of double inscription, de-construction reminds us that there is no evolution without the negativity of time and its inscription in the arche-materiality of the trace, figured on a larger biological canvas as the dynamic complexity of the organ-ism/environment relationship. No negativity of time, no evolution; but also: no materiality of inscription in the trace, no evolution.

I will end this chapter by amplifying a couple of additional theoretical points before stepping back onto more thematic terrain that will prepare us for the next chapter. First, as Kauffman notes, he and others (such as Longo, Soto, Noble, and Juarrero) seek "what might be called *formal cause* laws of organization that are independent of the specific matter and energy involved,"[79] but the really interesting question here, he notes, is whether such constraints and laws might *themselves* evolve.[80] In my view, it is hard to imagine why not, particularly if we are talking about the biosphere. If that's the case, then it means, as he puts it, that "our specific laws are *foundationless!*"[81] This is, I think, an important moment in Kauffman's book, and one that is different in character from William Rasch's related observation that "complexity can never be fully reduced to an underlying simplicity since simplicity, like complexity, is a con-struct of observation that could always be other than it is. Contingency, the ability to alter perspectives, acts as a reservoir of complexity within all simplicity."[82] In Kauffman's account of why this is so, the accent falls on the "foundationless" nature of the "formal cause laws" at work in the evolution of the biosphere—not just the nonentailed nature of its evolution—because the laws themselves are subject to evolution: that is to say, they are, strictly speaking, contingent. For Hägglund and Rasch, in contrast, the fundamental point here is less ontological than logical.[83]

But I will step back from both of these for a moment and note that *either* orientation fundamentally changes how we think about our relationship to the rest of existence. As Peter Sloterdijk notes—and this is to glance briefly in the direction of my final chapter—what we find here is a "pluralistic ontology" that will eventuate in the historical shift across disciplines from "globes" to "foams" (as he puts it in his massive *Spheres* trilogy) as the fundamental paradigm, one "prefigured by modern biology and metabiology" and announced at its outset by none other than Jakob von Uexküll, whose concept of "world" or *umwelt* reaches forward, as we have already suggested, through Heidegger to the Derrida of "there is no world" with which we opened this chapter.[84] Sloterdijk quotes Uexküll:

> It was an error to think that the human world provided a shared stage for all life forms. Each life form has a special stage no less real than the special state of humans . . . Through this insight we gain an entirely new view of the universe: it consists not of a single soap bubble that we have blown up beyond our horizon into the infinite, but of countless millions of narrowly bounded soap bubbles that overlap and intersect everywhere.[85]

As Sloterdijk glosses this passage, this aggregate of "countless" soap bubbles can "no longer be envisaged as the monocosmos of metaphysics," held together by "a logos common to all." That gives way, instead, to "a polycosmic agglomeration," in which "sentient existence in sense-structured environments is already developed at the level of animal intelligence."[86] Here, we find Sloterdijk's more architectonic version of Derrida's assertion in *The Animal That Therefore I Am* that, when it comes to the difference or border separating human from other forms of life, the interest is "not in effacing the limit, but in multiplying its figures, in complicating, thickening, delinearizing, folding, and dividing the line precisely by making it increase and multiply."[87] Or, as Sloterdijk, puts it, in what we have called this new topological rather than topographical ecology, "humans, for their part, after the end of the centric delirium (anthropo-, ethno-, ego-, and logo-), will perhaps develop slightly more appropriate notions of their existence in a milieu of ontological foams."[88] In the next chapter, I shall turn to one such example: Wallace Stevens's birds.

CHAPTER 4

"Never Again Would Birds' Song Be the Same"

ONE OF MY FAVORITE EPISODES IN Jacques Derrida's first set of seminars on *The Beast and the Sovereign* is devoted to poetry; it takes place in the ninth session, when he pauses (and there *is* the distinct sense of something like a pause, as Derrida says, "It is time, then, that we had a real discussion . . . And then next week I'll pick up the course of the course again")[1] to read D. H. Lawrence's poem "Snake" in the context of a whole nest of questions: sovereignty (a bit of a surprise), but also Levinas's ethics of "the face," the relation of original sin to violence, of friendship to hospitality, and much else besides. Interestingly enough—and this may be because the session is more "real discussion" than lecture—Derrida's reading of the poem remains largely on the thematic level, which seems a bit strange, especially in a poem about an encounter between a human and a nonhuman animal. Why? Because part of the lesson of Derrida's work is that in such a *mise en scène*, the question of the nonhuman (which may be rendered in terms of "the animal" but also in many other ways, as the technical, the dead, the spectral, and so on) obtains on not just one level but two.

To recall our discussion from chapter 3, what binds the human addresser and the animal addressee is not just their shared finitude as

embodied beings, their shared mortality (what Derrida calls the "not be-
ing able" and "non-power" that subverts the supposed autonomy, the
"auto-," of the "autobiographical animal," of "what calls itself man"). In
fact, humans and animals are bound by another, different kind of "auto-"
that deconstructs the supposed opposition of the "auto-" of human "au-
tonomy" (typically associated with the ability to "respond," as Derrida puts
it) and the "auto-" of the "automaticity" of the animal (typically associ-
ated with its programmed instinctive behavior, the fact that it is bound
only to "react"). This deeper and more complicated form of the "auto-" is
what Derrida calls the *"machinalité"* of any semiotic system that enables
two beings to interact in any kind of communicative behavior whatso-
ever.[2] It's not just a question of our relations *to* nonhuman forms of life,
in other words; it's also a question of a more profound and, as it were, non-
representational *form* of relation that obtains in our address to the non-
human other, one that has to do with the means by which "relations"
themselves—to nonhuman others, between nonhuman others, or to
ourselves—may take place *at all*. So, what we share, in our "being-with"
the animal, is a *second* form of finitude that obtains in our subjection to
any semiotic system whatsoever that makes possible "our" concepts, "our"
recognition and articulation of our "nonhuman relations" in the first place.

Whatever those relations are, then, they involve a scene of address (to
stay with the terms of the seminar session on "The Snake" for a moment
more) that no party unilaterally controls or masters, because that scene of
address and the form of relation that makes it possible was on the scene,
as it were, before either party in the transaction (whether in the form of
an explicitly shared semiotic code, or in the form of evolutionary and "in-
stinctive" behaviors that drive and configure an interaction in ways only
partly accessible to either participant, human or animal). This grows
even more complicated, of course, when the beings in question inhabit
different phenomenological worlds, bound together by the *machinalité*
of a recursive loop, a semiotic form, that can braid together different
life worlds in a third space irreducible to that of either party—the very
space, that is to say, of "relation." This means, then, that the "animality"
in question in that relation isn't just a matter of our relation *to* that ani-
mality (either the animality of the nonhuman other or the animality of
ourselves); it is also, and more complexly, a matter of the "animality" of
the form of relation itself. We are talking, in other words, not just about
a *thematics* of address, but also about a *technics* of address.

This is what Derrida has in mind, I think, in an enigmatic moment
late in the opening essay of *The Animal That Therefore I Am*, where he

quotes a footnote in his *Of Spirit* regarding "the gnawing, ruminant, and silent voracity" of what he calls "an animal-machine of reading and rewriting," one that would cross out and put under erasure terms in Heidegger's corpus such as "Being," "spirit," and so on.[3] Why "animal"? Because it is associated in Heidegger's discourse (and in Western philosophy generally), not with "responding" but with "reacting," with automaticity. "This animal-machine," he continues, "has a family resemblance to the virus," being "neither animal nor nonanimal, neither organic nor inorganic, neither living nor dead."[4] This hyphenated (non-)existence, this neither/nor quality of the "quasi-animal" would thus "no longer have to relate itself to being *as such* (something Heidegger thinks the animal is incapable of)," because it would (in advance, as it were) "take into account the need to strike out 'being.'" But does doing so, Derrida asks, mean that this "animal-machine" is "something completely other than a species of animal?"[5] Clearly, the answer is yes, because this "animal-machine" is not a biological entity, but rather a kind of materialized technicity, the trace-structure that, as Derrida puts it, traverses "the life/death relation." And that is why it "takes into account" (and the associations of "account" with both numericity and seriality are very much to the point here) of "the need to strike out 'being.'" As we have already seen in chapter 3, that trace-structure can be redescribed in terms of contemporary theoretical biology, which enables us to articulate quite precisely what Stuart Kauffman calls the "creativity" and "re-enchantment" at work in the biosphere. And that enchantment, in turn, is registered in more familiar terms in poetry's long-standing fascination with birds' song. Both birds and bards sing, and the question is, how do we describe an ecopoetics that binds them together in a nonrepresentational way?

Now, as we all know, birds are central to the Anglo-American poetic tradition (and beyond that): Shelley's skylark, Keats's nightingale, Poe's raven, Hopkins's windhover, the list goes on and on. One of the better known entries in the bird/bard sweepstakes is the poem by Robert Frost that gives my chapter its title, "Never Again Would Birds' Song Be the Same":

> He would declare and could himself believe
> That the birds there in all the garden round
> From having heard the daylong voice of Eve
> Had added to their own an oversound,
> Her tone of meaning but without the words.

Admittedly an eloquence so soft
Could only have had an influence on birds
When call or laughter carried it aloft.
Be that as may be, she was in their song.
Moreover her voice upon their voices crossed
Had now persisted in the woods so long
That probably it never would be lost.
Never again would birds' song be the same.
And to do that to birds was why she came.[6]

Now the first thing everyone will notice about the poem is that it is a sonnet—more specifically, an Elizabethan or Shakespearean sonnet, so called because it ends in a rhymed couplet. The second piece of literary historical heavy artillery that Frost rolls out in this poem is the pastoral mode—Virgilian, if we believe John Hollander. And the third is the "mythopoetic" invocation (to use Hollander's phrase) of Adam, Eve, and the Garden of Eden.[7]

But here we find something interesting—two things actually. The first is the poem's insistence that "an eloquence so soft" could only have had this effect on birds' song "when call or laughter carried it aloft." In short, this is emphatically *not*, it seems, a mythopoetics of the biblical Fall and how one might understand the relationship between Eve's song and bird song within its purview. And this leads us, in short order, to Derrida's entire discussion of—and rejection of—what he calls the various "sacrificial symbolic economies" at the core of "carnophallogocentrism" and the Abrahamic religions that secure the transcendence of the "properly" human, "what *calls itself* man," as he puts it, by means of sacrificing the animal and the animality of the human.[8] This poem, in other words, is not about the realization of Original Sin in the Garden of Eden, and how such a realization elevates the human and its song above the rest of creation via sacrificial expiation. But nor it is, I think, a mythopoetic affirmation of the holistic oneness of creation, human and nonhuman, *before* the biblical Fall, when the Garden was still a place of "call or laughter," not sin and guilt.

The issue here is not simply, as the psychoanalytically inclined among us would point out, that any human registration of the so-called "fact" of nature is always already radically denaturalized because the symbolic and imaginary realms that make the presence of nature manifest to us in their different ways are anything but "natural." Or as Slavoj Žižek put it, now more than twenty-five years ago, "the fact that man is a speaking being means precisely that he is, so to speak, constitutively 'derailed,'" an "open wound of the world," as Hegel put it, that "excludes man forever from the circular movement of life," so that "all attempts to regain a new balance between man and nature" can only be a form of fetishistic disavowal.[9] It is rather that everything Žižek says does not apply—simply, purely, decisively (as Derrida might say)—to human beings, because we aren't the only "speaking beings" in the sense intended here (as we'll see later in this chapter), even as we cannot say in any neat and simplistic way which nonhuman forms of life fall under the purview of this assertion and which do not.

A desire to split the difference between the two mythopoetic stances noted above—prelapsarian holism and immanence, on the one hand, or postlapsarian transcendence, on the other—is at work in some of the earlier criticism on Frost's poem. I have no intention, of course, of exhaustively surveying the literature on this poem or its place in Frost's corpus, but let's take, for example, this snippet from Robert Kern's essay on "Frost and Modernism," which finds in the poem a focus on

a substratum of speech that can apparently cross over from human beings to birds and be reproduced by them in a way that thereafter becomes meaningful to human ears, or at least perceptible as "song." This crossing over can take place, however, only because it is not meaning but sound that the birds pick up and convey. In Frost's conception, one which plays an interesting variation on traditional notions of linguistic origins, a language of spoken words is preceded or underlain by a language of sounds without words, and like most notions of an original or ideal language, this one is both *prior* to actual speech, and so free of the problems of signification, and somehow communicative nevertheless.[10]

Or let's linger over Hollander's observation that the animating myth of the poem is

that of the imprinting of consciousness onto nature . . . Hereafter, the poem says, nature would exist as a meaningful communicant . . . to be listened to because human meaning would always be in it . . . "Her tone of meaning, but without the words" . . . He meant the delicate but crucial modulations of phrase-stress pattern, contrastive stress, the rhetorical suprasegmentals, that not only make oral communication what it is, but which a practitioner of classical accentual-syllabic verse must be aware of. It is the music of English verse in which syntax plays a necessarily important role. "Just so many sentence sounds belong to man as just so many vocal runs belong to one kind of bird," he writes to Sidney Cox in 1914. "We come into the world with them and create none of them. What we feel as creation is only selection and grouping. We summon them from Heaven knows where under excitement with the audile imagination." The sound of sense: the music of speech, but of speech being watched, in its transcribed form, within a diagramming and punctuating and annotating grid of metrical pattern. To this degree, we all still dwell in the Romantic world of the ear . . . the ear's larger, undomesticated vastnesses, those regions in which real poetry, rather than cultivated verse, is to be found, the realm of all the human and natural utterance, from cries of pain to shouts of discovery: the sounds of language and of the wind in trees.[11]

Before I place these observations alongside contemporary ornithological theory on birds' song, let me stress two points: first, we have here the larger assertion of a shared form of "meaning" among and between human and nonhuman beings that is emphatically *not* reducible to language per se (and I've written a good bit on this about work stretching back to at least Gregory Bateson's writings on mammalian and cetacean communication, for example).[12] As we have already discussed, it is far from fanciful—in either contemporary philosophy or contemporary biology—to entertain the possibility of a shared form of meaning between human and nonhuman beings. But second—and this is crucial because it defeats any attempt one might make to offer a reductionist account based on an overextension and misunderstanding of point one—while Frost writes to Sidney Cox that "just so many sentence sounds belong to man as just so many vocal runs belong to one kind of bird," it is also emphatically and obviously the case with this poem, as Hollander shrewdly observes, that we have here "the music of speech, *but of speech being watched, in its transcribed form.*" And this, in its emphasis on the poem's self-reference, short-circuits Hollander's own backsliding elision of "the sounds of language and the wind in the trees," and his too-rapid distinction between "real poetry" and "cultivated verse."

For that is one of the strangest things about this poem: its "cultivation." And here I draw attention to what an earlier type of literary criticism would call, disparagingly, the poem's excessively and quite explicitly foregrounded "rhetorical" quality, what we might call its "equivocal" (rather than "univocal") poetics. This is already intuited in the differentiation between "sound," "song," "speech," and "speech observed" in Hollander's gloss (these are obviously four very different things). And it is also and most obviously at work in the rhetorical surface of Frost's poem from the first line, the heavily modal and conditional "He would declare and could himself believe" (as if he—and it's not even clear who "he" is, an unnamed contemporary speaker or Adam?—"could," but also might *not*, believe a prior declaration about the nature of what he's hearing in the birds' song in the garden). The main force of the line, I suggest, is to foreground, and in an unmistakably self-conscious way, its own grammatical and rhetorical performance, establishing thereby even more distance between the event and the emotions generated by the event than might otherwise already obtain. "He would" (but then again he might not, under other circumstances) "declare" (and thus perhaps the need to "declare" instead of simply acknowledging) something that he *later*, "himself," might or might not believe (and that is a very, very odd insertion, as if to say "for me, but perhaps but not for everyone").

Frost goes out of his way to foreground (however *sotto voce*) the fact that whatever is going on here is exactly the opposite of an unmediated, unconditional affirmation of the birds' song and what it means in all its intoxicating beauty and power. But, "be that as it may" (to borrow Frost's own phrasing), this same rhetorical conditionality threads its way throughout the poem in "admittedly," "could only," "moreover," and "probably," consistently exerting a kind of disruptive and denaturalizing rhetoricity on the poem as it unfolds, so that by the time we get to the last line, we are forced to choke down the provisionality of "why she came" to do something to birds' song that, in fact, has only a "probable" chance of success. The entire *raison d'être* of Eve's being is to do something that, well, depends. I hope you find all of this as weird as I do.

As we'll see later in this chapter, we find exactly the same sort of thing in one of Wallace Stevens's most important bird poems, the late masterpiece "Not Ideas about the Thing but the Thing Itself," which we can only begin to discuss by first noting that the title is *already* a permutation of William Carlos Williams's famous shibboleth "no ideas but in things" from book 1 of his long poem *Paterson*, the sensibility of which Stevens had famously engaged in a notorious review of Williams, one of the most important short prose pieces in all of Stevens.[13] In other words, to put it bluntly, this poem that is supposedly about "not ideas" but "the thing itself" is in fact, right out of the gate, about "ideas about the thing" in the form of an allusive intertextuality in which Stevens's differentiation of his own form of "romanticism" from that of Williams is invested. And as we'll see below in greater detail, we find in Stevens's poem the same kind of weak and equivocal poetics, the same kind of obsessively fore-grounded rhetoricity, that we find in Frost's poem as the poet's way of responding to the event of hearing birds' song.

To fully burn in a sense of the corrosive force of this heightened fore-grounding of rhetoricity and performativity in these heard bird poems by Frost and Stevens, we may contrast them to the opening of Robert Morgan's remarkable poem "Mockingbird." Morgan's poem piles on the figuration—specifically, piles on the metaphors—while giving almost no room at all to the merely grammatical and rhetorical elements that take front and center (and at key moments) in the poems of Frost and Stevens that we've touched on here. Morgan launches the poem in classic fashion: the poet being inspired, even thrilled, by the sound of the mockingbird arriving in the fading light:

> While the bee sleeps in the southern night
> and weeds weigh under dowries of dew,
> above the distant honkey tonk of falls in
> the July dark, before the katydids, when
> the only frost is lunar, a voice that
> raises the hackles on mountains and chills
> the barometric spine, that radios through
> many channels in the crab orchard and from
> maples above the road. What madrigalist
> watering the night with polyphony.
> You could see orchestras and oratorios
> in the polyglot dark, not so much a
> mocking of the many-voiced populations
> as a gathering to unlikely congregation
> of all song, an anthology including
> rooster and cricket broadcast from an ounce
> of hot flesh through its briar tongue and filling
> the hollows and thickets and dry ditches of
> the river valley, and soaking under eaves
> to the inner ear's accelerator,
> circling quick into sleep and bombarding
> the ledges of dream.[14]

This description will probably resonate with anyone who has heard the mockingbird do its thing, especially in the spring months, and in the

ornithological literature the mockingbird is indeed, as Jennifer Acker-
man reports in her best-selling book *The Genius of Birds*, a superstar poly-
phonic madrigalist. Darwin found them everywhere in South America
during his voyage on the *Beagle*, and declared their song "far superior to
that of any other bird in the country."[15] But here's the interesting thing
(and interesting in light of our discussion of Frost's and Stevens's rheto-
ricity and intertextuality): as Ackerman notes, "mockingbirds have been
maligned as mere thieves who pilfer tunes and miss the main musical
point of their stolen songs," which in some cases have been reported to
consist of thirty-nine bird songs and fifty bird calls, as well as the sounds
of frogs, crickets, car alarms, squeaky pumps, and barking dogs (among
others).[16] But though "calls are typically short, simple, succinct, and in-
nate," while "songs are generally longer, more complex, and learned,"
there is "no neat division between call and song, and there are plenty of
exceptions."[17]

Part of the reason this is so, as David Wills notes in a fascinating chap-
ter of his book *Inanimation* called "Meditations for the Birds," is that
even birds with a repertoire far smaller than that of the mockingbird may
sing both accented or unaccented versions of a song, one to patrol terri-
tory and one to attract mates (the two functions of bird song taken to be
axiological in the ornithological literature). There's lots of disagreement
about what constitutes a "different" song, and even a middle-of-the-road
songbird like the cardinal is said by one authority to possess eight to twelve
songs and by another to be capable of "innumerable" different tunes. And
this fact, when crossed with the factors of territory vs. mating and accented
vs. unaccented, leads to a whole series of other questions. Is a song, Wills
asks, "a verse, or rather a refrain? Are the birds making music, or simply
mimicking, parroting or aping themselves? Is their song a call and re-
sponse, a chant, or simply a repetition? Is it a theme and variation, in-
deed an improvisation, or rather a mechanical repetition, or indeed re-
production? Those questions might also be tantamount to asking what
life is in it," he writes, and, moreover, to asking after the extent to which
we are in the presence of a genuine "response" expressed by the birds'
song, or merely a mechanical and instinctive "reaction."[18] At which point,
of course, we are right back to the terrain from Derrida we explored in
chapter 3, and with which we began here: how the mechanicity and tech-
nicity of the trace, upon which communication is dependent, destabilizes
and deconstructs the opposition between "responding" and merely "re-
acting" that has underwritten the hierarchical ontology of "the" human
over "the" animal. In light of which, one might say, provisionally, that

the excessive rhetoricity of the poems by Frost and Stevens, which foreground the inescapably performative and iterative nature of meaning (which is not, as we know, limited to the domain of the human), stages the bond between human beings and animals, their shared finitude, *but in a posthumanist and nonrepresentational way*: not by the poets *refusing*, as it were, to be "human" (refusing, that is, to be "expressive," "responsive," and not merely rhetorical) but rather by their foregrounding (through the inescapably performative, rhetorical, and iterative nature of the utterance) the *impossibility* of being "human," if by "human" we mean something indexed to a secure cordoning off of the difference between genuinely "responding" and merely "reacting."

It is interesting that all of the above—the uncertain relation between call and song, between reaction and response, and thence between "human" and "animal"—are at the core of the current ornithological literature on birds' song itself. As Ackerman points out, "many people assume that birdsongs are genetically encoded," but "birds go through the same process of vocal learning that people do—they listen to adult exemplars, they experiment, and they practice, honing their skills like children learning a musical instrument."[19] And just as with a human being practicing an instrument to build muscle memory, "it takes practice, trial and error, hearing your mistakes and correcting them," and repeating that process "often enough to reinforce the brain pathways that created the memory in the first place."[20] As Ackerman notes, "mockingbirds are really, really good at this . . . Sonograms comparing a prototype song and the mockingbird's copy show that the imitator sings nuthatch and thrush and whip-poor-will with almost perfect fidelity to the original script." Moreover, she writes—and I find this a startling discovery—"scientists found that when a mockingbird sings a cardinal's song, it actually mimics the muscular patterns of the cardinal."[21]

We find here a kind of literalization and materialization of the very technicity, automaticity, and mechanicity that is on display ("at issue" might be a better way to put it) in perhaps the greatest heard bird poem in all of Stevens: "Of Mere Being," whose "gold-feathered bird" alludes (as every critic has noticed)[22] to Yeats's mechanical singing bird of "hammered gold and gold-enamelling" in "Sailing to Byzantium." As with Stevens's "Not Ideas about the Thing but the Thing Itself," it's worth lingering for a moment over the title. The word "mere" may suggest the sense of "only" or "simply," of course (as it is usually taken), and as such is apparently deflationary if not pejorative. But it may also mean "essential" or "very"—the very being of Being, as it were, but a kind of Being that is the real thing only because it is "merely" what it is. This is not just a case, however, of Being's essence turned inside out, subordinated to becoming; rather, as we're about to see, it is something much more radical, foreign, and strange, because radically denaturalized by its technicity and rhetoricity.[23]

Stevens's poem shares Yeats's rejection of naturalism, to be sure. But it also, and equally important for our purposes, shares its paradoxical "becoming space of time" (to use Derrida's formulation). Stevens's palm "beyond the last thought," standing "at the edge of space," is also part of the strange loop of temporality of "what is past, or passing, or to come" in Yeats's poem that can only be revealed, it seems, in and through the "artifice of eternity" (in Yeats's memorable words), by something that is not temporal but technical, whose technicity, in fact, enables and makes manifest temporality itself. We find here a quintessential example of the relationship between materialization and temporality whose Derridean name is the "trace." As Martin Hägglund explains it,

> the classical distinction between space and time is the distinction between simultaneity and succession. The spatial can remain the same, since the simultaneity of space allows for one point to co-exist with another. In contrast, the temporal can never remain the same . . . By the same token, however, it is clear that time is impossible without space. Time is nothing but negation, so in order to be anything it has to be spatialized . . . The very concept of duration presupposes that something remains across an interval of time and only that which is spatial can remain. Inversely, without temporalization it would be impossible for a point to *remain* the same as itself or to exist *at the same time* as another point. The simultaneity of space is itself a temporal notion. Accordingly, for one point to be simultaneous with another point there must be an originary *becoming-time of space* that relates them to one another. The structure of the trace—as the co-implication of time and space—is therefore the condition of everything that is temporal. Everything that is subjected to succession is subjected to the trace, whether it is alive or not.[24]

Yeats's poem, having rejected the "birds in the trees" early on as a part of "Whatever is begotten, born, and dies"—a land that is "no country for old men"—opts in its regal last two stanzas for "the artifice of eternity" as an antidote, and associates *that* with the figure of sovereignty, the "drowsy emperor." But the question for Stevens—remembering the "-reign" of both "sovereign" and "foreign," and its etymological associations with both "out of doors" and "outside"—is, you might say, how to make the "foreign" *truly* "sovereign," how to make it, that is, truly "outside" (just as the sovereign, we remember from Derrida's seminar, is outside the law and, for that very reason, can secure it). And here, in these poems, it seems that what is sovereign, foreign, and truly outside is neither the organic nor the mechanical, neither the "dying generations" nor the "artifice of eternity," but rather their radical co-implication, which has a kind of dizzying and galvanizing effect on one's mode of attention. Or as Hägglund characterizes it, drawing together the themes of mortality, technicity, and temporality that animate the poem, time is best thought of in terms of "survival" (following Derrida's French neologism *sur-vivance*, which designates something that is neither life nor death, pure and simple): a survival that "does not hinge on the emergence of life" and its continuation, but rather marks "a continuity between the non-living and the living in terms of the arch-materiality of time. The latter is implicit not only in our understanding of the temporality of living processes but also in our understanding of the disintegration of inanimate matter."[25]

This is a useful context for understanding what Henry Staten has called the "strong naturalist view," which holds that life emerges from matter organized in particular ways (and not others) while rejecting the idea that "life is somehow hidden in matter and just waiting to manifest itself."[26] "Life," in other words, is one possible outcome of the recursive concatenation of material processes that obey the logic of the trace, but it is certainly not the only, much less the "expected," one. As such, this position, as Hägglund puts it, allows "for a conceptual distinction between life and matter that takes into account the Darwinian explanation of how the living evolved out of the non-living, while asserting a distinguishing characteristic of life that does not make any concessions to vitalism."[27] To put it this way is to realize, as we saw in some detail in chapter 3, that "life" or "nature," rather than being a site of fullness, positivity, identity, and nonsupplementarity, is importantly in a relationship of *différance*, asynchronicity, and "spacing" to itself. It is to realize that the material processes—some organic and biological, and some not—that give rise to particular forms of life move at different speeds, with different effects, from the inhuman pace of evolutionary mutation and adaptation to the "fast dynamics" of learning and communication that rewire the neurophysiological plasticity of particular kinds of organisms.

Let me emphasize that this is a far cry from a "merely philosophical" matter. Indeed, it's what we find in birds' song itself, where these trace dynamics are registered not just ontogenetically but phylogenetically, as a site of double inscription and materialization: not just in the vocal learning that rewires the brain's plasticity, but also in how that learning and that rewiring are performatively manifest at particular moments, in particular contexts, for which the axiological functions of mating and territory are only the tip of the iceberg. Ackerman reports, for example, on a crested lark in Germany that learned how to imitate four different whistled signals that a shepherd used to work his herding dogs. "So faithful were the imitations." she writes, "that the dogs instantly obeyed the bird's whistled commands, which included 'Run ahead!' 'Fast!' 'Halt!' and 'Come Here!'" Even more remarkably, the calls spread to other larks in the area, creating what Ackerman calls "a little pocket of local 'catchphrases' (and quite possibly some very winded sheepdogs)." Ackerman calls this instance of ontogenetic plasticity "a fine example of cultural transmission,"[28] but we also find such plasticity *phylogenetically*, in the relationship between the genetic and epigenetic factors at work in birds' song and the contingency of their iterative relationship at various points in the animal's development. A zebra finch, for example, grows up hearing all sorts of songs of different species in the surrounding environment, but it only learns the song of its own species—a case of genetic predisposition. But "baby birds raised without any exposure to a tutor song sing abnormally, usually a very stunted, simplified version of the species song." And the same obtains for human upbringing as well, the result of a weak feedback loop between genetic predisposition, neurophysiological plasticity, and environment.[29]

But most interesting—and here we enter into the domain of epigenetics—is that the effects of this feedback loop are nonlinear. As ornithologist Sarah London from the University of Chicago notes, "a tutor's song actually alters a young bird's brain in a way that affects his future ability to learn." As Ackerman summarizes it, London's research shows that young birds with a tutor learn just fine until the age of sixty-five days, but after that, the ability to learn diminishes rapidly, and the song remains fixed for life. Birds isolated from a tutor early on, however, can go on learning well after the sixty-five-day mark. "The experience of hearing another bird singing," Ackerman writes, "apparently alters the song-learning genes of the learning bird through 'epigenetic' effects; in this case, says London, through the actions of histones—proteins that coat DNA and allow genes to be turned on or off."[30]

What this means, then—to flesh out the argument pursued in chap-
ter 3—is that "the living" is the site of a *triple* inscription: not just on the
material substrate of the living being (as in, for example, the rewiring of
the bird's neurophysiological plasticity that results in the difference be-
tween its genetically predisposed song and those it can learn); and not
just in the dynamic contingency of the organism/environment relation-
ship in which that ontogenetic inscription happens, which can make the
"same" inscription function differently at different points in time (as in
the actualization of innate vs. learned songs in their accented vs. unac-
cented forms, depending on time of year, breeding pressures, and much
else besides); but also in *how* those prior two inscriptions are taken up
in processes of "cultural transmission" that are themselves dependent on
ontogenetic and phylogenetic contingencies (and not just by human au-
ditors, as we saw earlier in Ackerman's example of the crested lark and
the herding dogs in southern Germany). To put it this way, then, is to
realize something we focused on in the previous chapter, that "episte-
mological" isn't the *opposite* of "ontological" but *means* "ontological"; and
"ontological," in turn, *means* "environmental" but *means* "environmen-
tal" in this very specific sense: you can't take embodiment seriously, of
whatever form of life, without also taking epistemological questions se-
riously, because if epistemology is precisely the study of how we know
things, then those modes of knowledge and experience of the world de-
pend directly on the embodied "enaction" (to use Maturana and Varela's
phrase)[31] that is a product of the recursive loop between an organism's
neurophysiological wetware and how it gets rewired by external interac-
tions, environmental factors, semiotic systems, cultural inheritances, tool
use, and much else besides. And it is also to realize, as I argued in *Before
the Law*, that the rejection of "biologistic continuism" such as we find in
Derrida's work actually makes possible a *more* robust, naturalistic account
of the processes that give rise to phenomenological domains that cannot
be reduced to the biological—or, more radically still, to the organic—
alone.[32] We could say, as I argued in chapter 3, that Derrida gives us a
theory of something like the relationship of the genetic factors (the sys-
temic, infrastructural, and formally code-bound) and the epigenetic fac-
tors (the environmental or contextual setting—what Derrida calls the
"pragmatic aspect"—in which the code is deployed) at work in any form
of expression[33]—a fact foregrounded in the rhetoricity and technicity of
these poems by Frost and Stevens, but not in a way that marks as it the
private and ontologically defining reserve of the human alone.

*

I now turn in greater detail to the work of Wallace Stevens and its obsession with birds, and I might as well (as Derrida has done with his own animals)[34] start with an inventory: grackles, warblers, doves, swans, robins, nightingales, jays, owls, peacocks, a "big bird" with a "bony appetite," a bird "with the coppery, keen claws," a "parakeet of parakeets," some very famous pigeons, ganders, what is called simply a "red bird," lots of cocks and one cockatoo, a "widow's bird," and one very famous blackbird that summons thirteen ways of looking.[35] Birds are all over the place in Stevens's poetry, from beginning to end. They are so ubiquitous that only two works into the *Collected Poems* we get an "Invective Against Swans," and the final poems in *The Palm at the End of the Mind* and *The Collected Poems* ("Of Mere Being" and "Not Ideas about the Thing but the Thing Itself," respectively) leave us to contemplate for eternity, as it were, two of the most striking instances of the bird in Stevens's entire corpus. Birds, birds, birds. And plenty of cousins, too—bees, angels, cicadas, and a whole host of other winged things.

To begin to unpack this topos in Stevens's poetry and its relationship to the broader contours of his poetics, we have to understand that at the core of his poetics as it develops over the course of his career is a two-stage progression. First, as Simon Critchley has characterized it, Stevens's poetry enables us to recast "what is arguably the fundamental concern of philosophy, namely the relation between thought and things or mind and world, the concern that becomes, in the early modern period, the basic problem of epistemology." Stevens's poetry does so in "a way that lets us cast it away. Stevens's verse shows us a way of overcoming epistemology."[36] We have already touched on this theme in the Stevens criticism, but I add here that the even deeper question becomes, for Stevens, how to do this nondialectically, as it were (how not to be Whitman, if you like, which Stevens had not yet figured out in a poem such as "Sunday Morning"). And this nondialectical and nonrepresentational challenge leads to the *second* important progression in Stevens's poetics, his contention that "the theory / Of poetry is the theory of life, / As it is, in the intricate evasions of as."[37] This is so, as Critchley characterizes it, because it is "performed in the specific poem insofar as that poem concerns itself with some real particular, with some object, thing or fact," which means that "things as they are" (to use Stevens's phrase from "The Man with the Blue Guitar") "only are in the act that says they are."[38] Thus, for Stevens, poetry "reveals the idea of order which we imaginatively impose on reality . . . The fact of the world is a *factum*: a deed, an act, an artifice."[39]

Here, Critchley's idea of the "deed" and "act" draws (although he does not say so) on Derrida's concept of the performative, and we should remember here, too, the performative character of "belief" and "professing" that Derrida discusses in a range of texts, especially given Stevens's well-known doctrine of "final belief" in a "Supreme Fiction," which, as he puts it, "you know to be a fiction, there being nothing else."[40] From Derrida's point of view, Stevens's "final belief" will turn out to be not so final after all, we might say, since "a profession of faith, a commitment, a promise" calls "not upon discourses of knowledge but upon performative discourses that produce the event of which they speak."[41] For Derrida as for Stevens, then, that "act of sworn faith" morphs into something no less serious, "in the strong sense of the word, an *engagement*, a commitment," as Derrida characterizes it,[42] and as Stevens puts it, "on that yes the future world depends."[43]

Stevens's traffic in the *factum* of the poetic deed or act takes forms both minimal and maximal. As for the former, take the strange ending of the wonderful poem "The Man on the Dump," in which we are led—after a series of seven very odd, oblique questions, to a final question and a final answer: "Where was it one first heard of the truth? The the."[44] But what kind of answer is that, strange even for Stevens? There's not just *one* kind of weirdness going on at the end of this poem, there are *two*: one semantic (which is already weird enough, given the nature of the definite article itself), and one nonsemantic and acoustic. After all, is "the the" a repetition of the same "the"? And acoustically, do we read/hear "thuh *thee*?" "Thee *thuh*?" "*Thee thee*?" "Thuh thuh?" How do we know? How *could* we know? This undecidability and unanticipatability of this barest iterated mark becomes, in terms of the poem's own self-referential communication, all the more crucial because, after all, "the the" is given as the answer and antidote to the stale images and generic meanings decided in advance, as it were, all of which are signified by the dump itself. But "Between that disgust and this," between the things on the dump and "those that will be"—"azaleas and so on"—"One feels the purifying change. One rejects / The trash."[45] But the change can be "purifying," it seems, only because it is, like the iterability and performativity of "the the," empty (purged of the given, as it were) and, for that very reason, unanticipatable, unknowable in advance. Stevens is describing a *process*, not a thing—an opening, however brief, between the trash that is there and the trash that will be. And so (for reasons we'll discuss in a moment), it's important that "the purifying change" happens only in the dynamic moment of the gap "*between* that disgust and this."

We are now in a better position to understand how the poem that immediately follows "The Man on the Dump" in *The Collected Poems*, "On the Road Home," stages this complex interweaving of temporality and contingency in its own way, proceeding quite systematically to insist on the inseparability of the said and the *being* said (its performativity)—"It was when I said"; "You . . . you said"—leading up to the poem's enigmatic pivot at midpoint, "We were two figures in a wood. / We said we stood alone."[46] The poem goes on in this vein for another three stanzas—which begin, in turn, "It was when I said," "It was when you said," and "It was at that time"—but here I emphasize Stevens's undeniable insistence on the performative *factum* of "saying." I mean, when you think about it, how odd it is to say, "we *said* we stood alone."

I am dwelling on this rhetorical slackness, which is also a kind of heightened artifice that Stevens repeatedly insists upon in the poem, to underscore that the poem doesn't just foreground the contingency of the fact that "there is no such thing as the truth," that "there are many truths, / But they are not parts of a truth." And it doesn't just tell us that it is precisely this fact that reveals the *thereness* and *quidditas* of the world to us—that makes the grapes fatter, makes the fox run out of his hole. It also, and most important, insists on its *own* contingent performativity—"it was when I said," "it was at that time"—to prevent everything we just said from flipping over into its own form of philosophical idealism in the form of relativism: that is, "the only universal truth is that there is no universal truth." Stevens's antirepresentationalist poetics here makes available to us a logic that is "heterogeneous" to idealism, as Derrida puts it, one that "entails the necessity of thinking *at once* both the rule and the event, concept and singularity," marking "the impossibility of idealization as such."[47] And, thus, what looks like—and in a way *is*—a rather Emersonian commitment at the end of stanza 4 of "On the Road Home" gets routed through the iterability of the trace, of speech become writing through the performative *factum* of the poem ("It was when I said"), leading to the conclusion that "The world must be measured by eye."[48]

This eye—a rewriting not only of the (Emersonian) "I," but also of the semantically contingent and empty pronoun "I" of "I said"—is at the center of Stevens's poetic universe, and this same eye pops up in a key bird moment (one of the most famous of all in Stevens) halfway through "Notes Toward a Supreme Fiction," where an "Eye without lid, mind without any dream," is the figural space in which we find "the first leaf is the tale/

Of leaves" and "the sparrow is a bird // Of stone, that never changes."[49] The general sense here is "if you've seen one, you've seen them all," and how to escape that deadening dilemma is referred in turn to the nature of the one doing the seeing. By the logic of the poetics I'm articulating here, the eye needs a lid simply because what Derrida calls the *augenblick* (or "blink") figures a hiatus or "spacing" that holds the sound of one's own voice, like one's own reflection in the mirror, at a distance of a before and an after that divides the "I" from itself, so that Emerson's "transparent eye-ball" can say (and make sense in saying), "I am nothing, I see all." And in that space of a "between"—"between that disgust and this," as Stevens puts it in "The Man on the Dump"— the "mind" can have its "dream," imagination can enact its "purifying change."[50]

Stevens in his mature poetry is almost obsessed with this dynamic, and it often takes the form of what you might call the *augenblick* of the before and after, as in "Thirteen Ways of Looking at a Blackbird," where the speaker does not know whether to prefer "The blackbird whistling / Or just after."[51] This "just after" captivates Stevens in all sorts of important heard bird poems—"Autumn Refrain" is one example, "Not Ideas about the Thing but the Thing Itself" is another—but I note in closing out "On the Road Home" that, for these very reasons, Stevens's insistence that "The world must be *measured* by eye" is precisely right, since "measuring" is only a particularly schematic instance of what is always already true of the "spacing" of iteration and the movement of protention and retention that it generates, creating the strange loop of temporality, of the "before" and "just after," that Stevens very much insists on with the repeated "It was when" in "On the Road Home."

This inheritance and then radical reworking of the Emersoninan "I"/ eye has been noted by many critics—it is the most familiar story of the Emerson/Stevens lineage transmitted to us by critics such as Harold Bloom—but none explains how Stevens does this through a logic that is "heterogeneous" to idealism (as Derrida characterizes it). I have presented so far the deconstructive version of what that heterogeneous logic looks like, but let me now briefly redescribe it in the more naturalistic and pragmatic terms of biological systems theory to more fully contextualize how Stevens's intense interest in the "epistemological" problems attending the relation between mind and reality eventuates, as Critchley put it earlier, in "overcoming epistemology."

Epistemology is often understood, these days, as a branch of what Graham Harman and other object-oriented ontologists call "correlationism," but this charge doesn't apply to systems theory for a few reasons.

First of all, for systems theory, the question is not epistemological but *pragmatic*. As both Niklas Luhmann and Humberto Maturana make clear, the veracity of the systems-theoretical analysis is not about epistemological adequation to some pregiven state of ontological affairs (whether realist *or* idealist), but is rather based on its *functional* specificity. In other words, what we think of as "fact" is here rewritten precisely as "*factum*." As we saw in the previous two chapters, contrary to the understanding of autopoietic systems as solipsistic, the operational closure of systems and the self-reference based upon it arise as a practical and adaptive necessity precisely because systems are *not* closed—that is, precisely because they find themselves in an environment of overwhelmingly and exponentially greater complexity than is possible for any single system. This means that systems are characterized by a kind of *finitude* that can be formalized as a complexity differential; they maintain themselves and achieve their autopoiesis against all odds, in a very real sense. To put it another way, systems have to operate selectively and "blindly" (as Luhmann puts it) not because they are closed, but precisely because they *are not*, and the asymmetrical distribution of complexity across the system/environment threshold is what *forces* the strategy of self-referential closure.[52] Indeed, the "second-order" turn that we touched on in chapter 3 is, as I have argued elsewhere,[53] to realize that the more systems build up their own internal complexity through recursive self-reference and closure, the *more* linked they are to changes in their environments to which they become more and more sensitive, which is why a bat or a dolphin—or a bird!—can register a higher degree of environmental complexity than an amoeba that responds only to gradients of light or dark, higher or lower sugar concentrations, and so on, even though both are autopoietic systems. As Luhmann puts it in one of his more Zen-like moments, "Only complexity can reduce complexity."[54]

It ought to be obvious by now that this is not at all about "correlationism" as it us usually described—the idea that "being exists only as a correlate between mind and world"—and not least of all because "mind" is no more a constitutive element for systems theory (as we saw in chapter 3) than it is for deconstruction.[55] Quite the contrary, it is about systems *not* being free to just think whatever they will at their whim about objects and things. To put it another way, there is nothing to stop you on *epistemological* grounds from thinking that humors or ethers exist; indeed, the history of philosophy and of science makes that abundantly clear. But there is plenty to stop you on *pragmatic* grounds, even if, as Bruno Latour reminds us, bad ideas can work well enough under the right constraints for long periods of time. As Richard Rorty quite elegantly puts it, "what shows us that life is not a dream, that our beliefs are in touch with reality, is the *causal*, non-intentional, non-representational, links between us and the rest of the universe."[56] The pragmatist, he continues, "believes, as strongly as does any realist, that there are objects which are *causally* independent of human beliefs and desires."[57] She "recognizes relations of *justification* holding between beliefs and desires, and relations of *causation* holding between those beliefs and desires and other items in the universe, but no relations of *representation*."[58] And these facts—no relations of representation, and plenty to stop you on pragmatic grounds— turn out to be true (or, one should say, more precisely, "useful") for Stevens in the domain of poetry, which is why he moves away from an "idealist" rendering of mind and imagination toward one that ceaselessly foregrounds how the paradoxes attendant upon "overcoming epistemology" are actually pragmatically *productive* of a meaningful relationship between mind and world. Or, as Stevens puts it in a poem we will examine in some detail, "You know then that it is not the reason / That makes us happy or unhappy." No, it is something less "reasonable," less logical (remembering here Gregory Bateson's biologization of the Liar's Paradox from chapter 1), and, for that very reason, more *meaningful*.

Now, what does all this have to do with birds? you might rightly ask at this point. Well, we should remember that birds figure crucially at the end of "The Man on the Dump" (the "crow's voice," the nightingale, the "peevish birds," the "blatter of grackles")[59] and in ways that will direct us unavoidably to the bird poems that end both *The Palm at the End of the Mind* and *The Collected Poems*. In these very last poems, Stevens is resisting what he was not yet able to resist—beautifully, of course—at the end of the early long poem "Sunday Morning," where "casual flocks of pigeons" sink "Downward to darkness, on extended wings."[60] But the birds in late Stevens reveal those pigeons to be a little too beautiful, and a little (as it were) too dialectical, as Stevens will reveal in one of his final poems, "Of Mere Being," which begins, "The palm at the end of the mind, / Beyond the last thought, rises / In the bronze decor."[61] The intertextual difference here between "decor" (used in the original typescript and restored in *The Palm at the End of the Mind*) and "distance" (used in the poem's publication in *Opus Posthumous* in 1957 and then corrected in later editions) stages in miniature the prosthetic entanglement of the given and the made that is figured more obviously in the conjugation of flesh and metal that suffuses the poem, most obviously in the "gold-feathered bird," singing as it sits in the palm tree "without human meaning, / Without human feeling." As noted above, the allusion to Yeats's bird in "Sailing to Byzantium" shares not only that poem's rejection of naturalism, of representationalism and mimesis, but also its staging of the "becoming-space of time," its intrication of "what is past, or passing, or to come" with the "artifice of eternity" (as Yeats puts it) that is available only through the contingent and fleeting *factum* of the poem.

I'll come back to these questions later in this chapter, but I underscore here how Stevens's poem also rivets our attention on a quite peculiar logic of hearing and seeing—hearing *as* seeing—and how the particular modes of attention being invoked here have more to do with birds, and with "animal studies," than one might think. As Derrida writes in a fascinating and somewhat out-of-the-way passage on Aristotle in "The Principle of Reason,"

> Opening the eyes to know, closing them—or at least listening—in order to know how to learn and learn how to know: here we have a first sketch of the rational animal . . . I shall run the risk of extending my figuration a little farther, in Aristotle's company. In his *De Anima* (421b) he distinguishes between man and those animals that have hard, dry eyes, the animals lacking eyelids, that sort of sheath or tegumental membrane that serves to protect the eye and permits it, at regular intervals, to close itself off in the darkness of inward thought or sleep. What is terrifying about an animal with hard eyes and a dry glance is that it always sees. Man can lower the sheath, adjust the diaphragm, narrow his sight, the better to hear, remember, and learn.[62]

But, he continues, it is "not a matter of distinguishing here between sight and nonsight, but rather between two ways of thinking sight and light, as well as between two conceptions of listening and voice. But it is true that a caricature of representational man . . . would readily endow him with hard eyes permanently open to a nature that he is to dominate . . . by fixing it in front of himself, or by swooping down on it like a bird of prey."[63]

As I have been arguing throughout, Stevens is anything but "representational man," and in light of Derrida's reading of Aristotle here, these lines take on a new resonance, for he writes that when you hear the bird's song, "You know then that it is not the reason / That makes us happy or unhappy. / The bird sings. Its feathers shine."[64] That is to say, we "learn how to know," beyond "reason," not just by opening the eyes and closing them—by blinking and blindness, in short, by contingency (with Derrida)—but also (with Stevens) by listening to the "after" of the bird's song ("The blackbird whistling / Or just after") found, oddly enough, in the shining of the feathers, "two ways of thinking sight and light," "listening and voice" (as Derrida puts it): a strange but altogether poetic logic that is redoubled in the gaudy alliteration of the last line, where we see/ hear again, "The bird's fire-fangled feathers dangle down." Here, it's not just that the voice, the song, is on the side of the bird rather than the human (but paradoxically only through the human *factum* of the poem itself). It is also that the bird's song—the very example, after all, of the barest iteration—is as dependent on the *machinalité* of iteration and trace as ours is: a point nailed down firmly by the poem's allusion to Yeats's bird of "hammered gold and gold enamelling," its own gaudy alliteration and chiasmus flashing before our eyes.

We're now in a better position to understand more fully not just Stevens's fascination with birds and bird *song*, but also its stakes, for we are back (as Derrida's discussion of Aristotle a moment ago reminds us) to the question of sovereignty by way of its zoological avatars, "response" vs. "reaction," thought vs. instinct, and, eventually, "human" vs. "animal." And now we can return one last time to the relationship between "foreign" (as in the bird's "foreign song") and "sovereign" (as in *The Beast and the Sovereign*) that I bookmarked earlier. For as David Ferrell Krell notes, the second session of Derrida's last seminar on *The Beast and the Sovereign*, focused on Defoe's *Robinson Crusoe*, begins with the words, "I am alone" (itself a characteristic, even defining, note for Stevens's poetry, that "affair of places rather than people"). Do such expressions, Krell writes, "communicate something like boredom, or does their melancholy run deeper? As for boredom, can beasts be bored? Can a sovereign king or queen be bored? Better said, can a sovereign be anything but bored? Recall the entire literature on the need to amuse the sovereign, who needs beasts and birds, if only mechanical ones, 'to keep a drowsy emperor awake.'"[65] The message here, in so many words—and it is one that Stevens would take to heart in his later work—is that when it comes to privileging an idealist concept of the sovereign power of the imagination (as Stevens had done in many of his early poems), you should be careful what you wish for.

If the essence of sovereignty is what Derrida in his late work calls "ipseity" and the "self-same,"[66] then surely, as he notes in the first volume of *The Beast and the Sovereign*, its most canonical figure is the phallus. But, as he points out in his quite funny commentary late in that seminar, the phallus was originally in Greece and Rome a kind of "marionette" used for various ceremonies, a "prosthetic representation" made of springs, cables, and fabric, "detached from the body proper," a "rigid automat" that would be cranked up to erect posture "by reaction to the orders that operate it." And "just as the erection itself is or seems to be . . . automatic, independent of will and even of desire," the phallus that "is machinelike or mechanical, already in itself prosthetic," quite aptly figures not sovereignty but the inability to isolate "response" from "reaction," reason and desire from automaticity and instinct, human from animal, and even, for that matter, the organic from the mechanical or technical. And thus, Derrida asks, is the phallus "proper to man or else, already cut from man, is it a 'something,' a thing, an a-human, inhuman *what*, which is, moreover, scarcely more masculine than feminine? Neither animal nor human?"[67]

If we transpose Derrida's reading of the phallus here onto the "gold-feathered bird" and its "foreign song" in "Of Mere Being" as itself a figure for the deconstruction of the sovereign power of the imagination so associated with Stevens's entire poetic project, then we are in a better position to make sense of the "new knowledge of reality" in the last piece in *The Collected Poems*, "Not Ideas about the Thing but the Thing Itself," which handles this same logic in a manner closer to what we might call the rhetorical "weakness" or "slackness" of "On the Road Home." In this crowning poem, one cannot miss how Stevens's insistence at poem's end on the "new knowledge of reality" from exposure to the "outside" is, as it were, "blinking" from the very beginning of the poem, at sunrise. Here, we find not the crow of the "cock" of the imagination's sovereignty recorded in "Depression Before Spring" (where "The cock crows. / But no queen rises"),[68] but rather the scrawniness of the bird's cry that is matched, weakness for weakness, you might say, by the scrawniness of the poem and its heavily mediated immediacy—its (im-)mediacy—by the phalanx of prepositions Stevens walks us through: "at," "in," "of," "from," and, most crucially, "by" and "like": a weakness and (im-)mediacy only redoubled by the fact that it is not a sound in his mind but *like* a sound in his mind or, more forcefully still (because weaker still), it *seemed* like a sound in his mind. And we need, moreover, to be told (again, oddly enough) that "he *knew* that he heard it." This makes us wonder, with the speaker of the poem, where it came from, this sound, this "new knowledge of reality" that is only "*like* a new knowledge of reality," this "C" that precedes, that is thus also a "pre-C," that comes before the Apollonian "colossal sun" which is "still far away." The poem only tells us—oddly, modally—that "It would have been outside."

Here, we find a key moment in the complex articulation of Stevens's ecological poetics, but Stevens shows us that "ecology" in literature is not always where you think it is. For Stevens, it is not a matter of "representing" and, as it were, cheering for "nature," but rather one of showing how "nature" must be replaced by that better term "environment," in the sense that we sketched earlier, for this very simple reason: the term "environment" reminds us that what counts as "nature" is always, as we have noted earlier, a product of the contingent and selective practices deployed in the embodied "enaction" of an observing system. In biological terms, as we saw in chapter 3, this realization reaches back to Jakob von Uexküll's theories of human and animal *umwelten* and forward to ecological (though not, importantly, organicist) work in the philosophy of mind and consciousness by thinkers such as Alva Noë, who argues that "the locus of consciousness is the dynamic life of the whole, environmentally plugged-in person or animal."[69] As his work shows, recent research in the biology of consciousness makes it clear that these questions do not neatly break along lines of human vs. animal, inside vs. outside, brain vs. world, or even, for that matter, organic vs. inorganic. Mind is not brain, in other words, precisely *because* it is ecological, a recursive loop between the "inside" of the system, including its biological wetware, and the "outside" of things like semiotic systems, technologies, and cultural practices (among many others).[70] As Noë puts it, "it is not the case that all animals have a common external environment," because "to each different form of animal life there is a distinct, corresponding, ecological domain or habitat," which means, in short, that "all animals live in structured worlds."[71]

From here it is but a short step to the question Derrida raises early in the second volume of *The Beast and the Sovereign*, against the backdrop reminder that "sovereignty cannot be shared, it is indivisible. The sovereign is alone (sovereign) or is not."[72] That question (which is framed by Derrida's entire engagement of Heidegger on this issue) is, "what do beasts and men have in common?" And in reply, Derrida offers this remarkable passage that we discussed briefly in chapter 3, made up of a movement through three theses, finished off with a meditation on the last:

> 1. Incontestably, animals and humans inhabit the same world, the same objective world even if they do not have the same experience of the objectivity of the object. 2. Incontestably, animals and humans do not inhabit the same world, for the human world will never be purely and simply identical to the world of animals. 3. In spite of this identity and this difference, neither animals of different species, nor humans of different cultures, nor any animal or human individual inhabit the same world as another, however close and similar these living individuals may

be (be they humans or animals), and the difference between one world and another will remain always unbridgeable, because the community of the world is always constructed, simulated by a set of stabilizing apparatuses, more or less stable, then, and never natural, language in the broad sense, codes of traces being designed, among all living beings, to construct a unity of the world that is always deconstructible, nowhere and never given in nature. Between my world, the "my world," what I will call "my world"—and there is no other for me, as any other world is part of it—between my world and any other world there is first the space and time of an infinite difference, an interruption that is incommensurable with all attempts to make a passage, a bridge, an isthmus, all attempts at communication, translation, trope, and transfer that the desire for a world or the want of a world, the being wanting a world will try to pose, impose, propose, stabilize. There is no world, there are only islands.[73]

Now it is the first thesis that is usually taken to be "ecological," but my point here is that by the second-order logic we have been developing thus far, it is actually the *third* thesis that is the most radically ecological, in a fashion related to (but ultimately different from) the suggestion by my colleague Timothy Morton that ecological thinking begins precisely where "nature" ends, precisely after "the end of the world."[74]

To show why, we must track Derrida as he moves rapidly in the next moment of the seminar to a line taken from Paul Celan's poetry that echoes throughout the second seminar: "the world is gone, I must carry you." The world is gone, as you will already have guessed, for precisely the reasons marshaled in Derrida's third thesis, above. Contrary to Heidegger's assertion that humans are worlding and worldly while the stone is "without world" and the animal "has a world in the mode of not having," humans *do not*, Derrida suggests, have a world in Heidegger's sense. Rather, as I've argued elsewhere, "having a world in the mode of not having" is as good a definition of *Dasein* as we are likely to get.[75] Why? Because, for "all animals who live in structured worlds" (to recall Noë's phrase) the thing that makes the world available to us—the "map that is not the territory" in systems-theoretical terms, the *grille* and *gramme* of semiotic code or program in deconstruction, the language or "song" that in Stevens's "The Idea of Order at Key West" "makes the sky acutest at its vanishing," the "blind spot" of the contingent self-reference of observation in Luhmann that dictates that "reality is what one does not perceive when one perceives it"[76]—is also and at the same time what makes the world *unavailable* to us. And this fact—that "the world is gone," not just for nonhuman life but also for human beings, thus linking human and non-human life in their shared finitude—is precisely where ethics and eco-logical responsibility begin. As Derrida puts it in a later session that year, picking up the thread:

> We could move for a long time, in thought and reading, between *Fort und Da, Da und Fort*, between these two undistancing distancings . . . these two *theres*, between Heidegger and Celan, between on the one hand the *Da* of *Dasein* . . . and on the other hand Celan's *fort* in "Die Welt ist fort, ich muss dich tragen": the world is far, the world has gone, in the absence or distance of the world, I must, I owe it to you, I owe it to myself to carry you, without world, without the foundation or grounding of anything in the world, without any foundational or fun-damental mediation, one on one, like wearing mourning or bearing a child, basically where ethics begins.[77]

Here, I think—"the world is far, the world has gone," "it would have been outside," "it seemed like a sound in his mind"—we can locate the particular kind of ecological poetics that we find in Stevens, especially in his later work, a poetics that makes his poetry quite different from the more conspicuously ecological work of a Gary Snyder or a Robinson Jef-fers. In these poems, it's as if Stevens insists on a scene of address, a *mise en scène*, that in so many words says to the reader: "*you*: it's on you, you are the one who has to look, listen, receive, think—not the TV, not the cell phone, not the computer, not the iPad: *you*. I am alone. With you." Hence the significance, in the hypermediated landscape we all share, of what I have characterized as not just the quietness and calmness of Ste-vens's poetics, but its "weakness," especially in the sparse and spartan late poems. In that light, this weakness is part of its strength; indeed, it is key to what we might call (remembering Derrida on Celan) the "carrying capacity" or "carrying ecology" of Stevens's poetry. Stevens's poems put us on an island where we discover, "I am alone. The world is gone and I'll have to carry you." Or, as Stevens puts it in "On the Road Home," "We were two figures in a wood. / We said we stood alone."[78]

*

With this movement between "*Fort und Da*," the question of what is near and what is far—which hinges crucially on the question of what and where is *here*—we move to a particular conception of ecology that we might, drawing on the work of Michel Serres, call *topological* rather than *topographical*. The terminology of folds, knots, and paths that we often find in Serres's work is drawn from mathematical topology and its opposition to geometry—an opposition that, for Serres, is not just logical but also ethical. As Steven Brown summarizes it, while geometry "rests upon clear notions of identity and distinction, topology, and the mathematics which underpins it, is concerned with transformation and connection."[79] Or, as Serres himself analogizes it in a series of conversations with Bruno Latour,

> if you take a handkerchief and spread it out in order to iron it, you can see in it certain fixed distances and proximities. If you sketch a circle in one area, you can mark out nearby points and measure far-off distances. Then take the same handkerchief and crumple it, by putting it in your pocket. Two distant points suddenly are close, even superimposed. If further, you tear it in certain places, two points that were close can become very distant.[80]

As Paul Harris points out, "topology poses problems of spatial relations through questions such as: 'What is closed? What is open? What is a connective path? What is a tear? What are the continuous and the discontinuous? What is a threshold, a limit?'"[81] Now, without getting into an extended investigation of the lines of relation and difference between this sense of the topological and the very large amount of Derrida's writing on what he calls "spatialization" and "the becoming-space of time,"[82] I simply note here how these questions animate the very large amount of space given, in the second set of seminars on *The Beast and the Sovereign*, to questions such as the following: "does solitude *distance* one from others? What am I saying when I say 'I am alone'?" Derrida responds that "to begin to reply to these questions or even to elaborate them as questions, we would need to begin by agreeing as to what *coming closer* or *distancing* mean," by acknowledging that "the proxim*ity* of the close is not, for its part, necessarily close."[83]

Derrida and Serres draw our attention to the fact that we find a fundamentally different underlying *logic* at work in thinking topological relations, one that folds and twists, if you like, the observation made famous by Gregory Bateson (borrowed from Korzybski), that "the map is not the territory."[84] This topological reorientation helps us understand more fully much of what is going on with Stevens's birds—where they're coming from, you might say—and even helps shed light on how we are to understand the peculiar nature of the trees in which they roost, as with "The palm at the end of the mind, / Beyond the last thought" in "Of Mere Being," which "stands on the edge of space."[85] We might ask, in tune with Derrida's investigations of "world" and the "-imity" of "proximity," what does it mean to mark "the end of the mind"? and is that not itself an act of mind, and thus not at the "end" of the mind? To put it topologically and not topographically, how is something that is the most distant also something that is closest?[86] And we might ask, moreover, since when does space have an "edge"?

One of Serres's answers to this question is figured in the topological process of the baker's kneading of dough, "a certain folding of half a plane of dough over the other half, repeated indefinitely according to a simple rule," which "produces a design precisely comparable to the flight of the fly or wasp," an implicating and explicating movement—literally a "folding" and "unfolding" (*pli*) of space and time.[87] This movement also characterizes the formal operations of Serres's chief topological figure, Hermes: the "free mediator" (as Latour calls him) "who wanders through this folded time, establishing connections between what look at first glance like distant and unrelated phenomena (as in, for example, the connections between La Fontaine's fables and information theory in Serres's book *The Parasite*). Hermes leads us to "the spaces situated between things that are already marked out—spaces of *interference* . . . This god or these angels pass through folded time, making millions of connections."[88]

What this means, Serres writes, is that "*the semiotic is above all a topology*." And in language proper, Harris points out, "topological relations are most visibly expressed in prepositions. Topology in general and prepositions in particular share concerns with modes of linkage, and are therefore intrinsic to figuring the space-between."[89] Here, I think, we find a useful template for understanding the peculiar poetic space that Stevens builds in poems such as "Of Mere Being," and we might well be reminded of our discussion earlier of Stevens's "weak" poetics in poems like "On the Road Home" and, especially, "Not Ideas about the Thing but the Thing Itself," with its succession of prepositions—"at," "in," "of," "from," and, most crucially, "by" and "like"—but also its figuration (one of the most famous in all of Stevens) of what we could call, following Serres, this Hermes figure of the bird whose song comes "from outside," delivering something "like a new knowledge of reality."[90] As Serres observes of the Hermes operator, "as soon as this intermediary comes to rest on a spot, he sometimes finds himself far off but also sometimes very close to foreignness."[91] "The messenger," he concludes, "always brings strange news; if not, he's nothing but a parrot."[92]

Now, as it happens, a parrot *does* figure centrally in the second set of seminars on *The Beast and the Sovereign*—specifically, Poll the Parrot in Defoe's *Robinson Crusoe*. Here's the passage from Defoe's novel that fascinates Derrida:

> For I was very weary, and fell asleep: But judge you, if you can, that read my story, what a Surprize I must be in, when I was wak'd out of my Sleep by a Voice calling me by my Name several times, *Robin, Robin, Robin Crusoe,* poor *Robin Crusoe,* where are you *Robin Crusoe?* Where are you? Where have you been?[93]

Crusoe "thought I dream'd that some Body spoke to me," Defoe continues. "But as the Voice continu'd to repeat *Robin Crusoe, Robin Crusoe,* at last I began to wake more perfectly," and "no sooner were my Eyes open, but I saw my *Poll* sitting on the Top of the Hedge; and immediately I knew that it was he that spoke to me; for just in such bemoaning Language had I used to talk to him, and teach him; and he had learn'd it so perfectly, that he would sit upon my finger, and lay his Bill close to my Face, and cry *Poor* Robin Crusoe, *Where are you? Where have you been? How come you here?*"[94]

What we find in this passage, Derrida writes, is a rather "uncanny" moment that remains, nonetheless, "a circular auto-appellation, because it comes from a sort of living mechanism that he has produced, that he assembled himself, like a *quasi*-technical or prosthetic apparatus, by training the parrot to speak mechanically so as to send his words and name back to him, repeating them blindly."[95] As Derrida notes, this circular movement of the self-same and the self-named is, for all that, unavoidable; "one could say of every autobiography, every autobiographical fiction . . . that it presents itself through this linguistic and prosthetic apparatus," which "speaks of him without him . . . without the author himself needing to do anything else, not even be alive."[96] But that means that this auto-appellation proceeds—and can only proceed—by means of the hetero-appellation of a prosthetic and technical apparatus, what Michael Naas calls (making much of the pun) "a sort of originary Poly-semy or Poly-graphy that expropriates right from the start what we might believe to be a, spontaneous, self-naming voice"—a polygraphy marked by the deformation of "Robinson" to "Robin" in the bird's enunciation.[97] But

Derrida's point, of course, is that this generalized exappropriation could only ever be controlled or mastered—could only ever be turned into a perfectly "circular auto-appellation"—in the realm of fantasy. That is to say, on a "desert island," as it were, where Crusoe explicitly figures his place in relation to the lands and creatures around him, as Krell notes, in terms of sovereignty: "Then to see how like a King I din'd too all alone," Defoe writes, "attended by my Servants, *Poll*, as if he had been my Favourite, was the only Person permitted to talk to me."[98]

While I cannot pursue here the entire topos of sovereignty that Derrida explores in such rich detail in both sets of seminars, I conclude by noting that this discussion of "circular auto-appellation" marks both an important point of convergence and an important point of difference between Serres's and Derrida's topological rendering of ecological thought—specifically, with regard to the role of the performative, in the more radical and biological sense of embodied enaction. Serres, like Derrida, "strives for a more radical rethinking of subject and object," in which "we have to think of sensation (and cognition) as neither directed outwards from the recesses of our bodies, nor as flowing into us from the outside world, but rather as an ever ramifying and branching network that blooms into life in the middle of worldly engagements."[99] The point of these itineraries, as Harris puts it, is "to weave together the fabric of knowledge into a 'pattern that connects' (as Bateson called it) humans to the world."[100] As the invocation of Bateson here suggests, one advantage of the systems-theoretical rearticulation of this relationship is to provide, as we have already seen in chapter 3, a more robust "environmental" account of these itineraries than we are likely to receive from Derrida: to underscore that these itineraries are always a matter of *specific, embodied forms of life*, which have their own autopoietic system/environment relationship in ways that are far from generic. "Knowing things," as Serres puts it, "requires one first of all to place oneself between them. Not only in front in order to see them, but in the midst of their mixture, on the *paths* that unite them."[101]

Derrida's rendering of these "paths" and "itineraries," however, emphasizes not just our finitude (the particular, nongeneric forms of our embodied being, and the vulnerability and mortality to which it subjects us) but also, and most important, how autopoietic self-reference constitutes *the finitude of our finitude*, its nonappropriability—which Derrida often in the seminars treats under the rubric of (auto-)immunity. As he writes in a dense and fascinating passage, everything that can happen to the *autos* [of autoaffection, of autobiography, of autonomy, and so on] is indissociable from what happens *in the world* through the prosthetization of an ipseity which at once divides that ipseity, dislocates it, and inscribes it outside itself *in the world*, the world being precisely what cannot be reduced here, any more than one can reduce *tekhne* or reduce it to a pure *physis*. The question, then, is indeed that of the world . . . and what I want to say is that there is no ipseity without this prostheticity in the world, with all the chances and all the threats that it constitutes for ipseity, which can in this way be constructed but also, and by the same token, indissociably, be destroyed.[102]

Where Derrida is reaching with such formulations, I think, is in the direction of the "ecological" that we explored in chapter 3—"the question, then, is indeed that of the world": an understanding that moves us out of what might sometimes seem in his work a rather thin epistemological treatment of such questions. In Serres, however—and Latour presses him on this point repeatedly in the *Conversations*—it is never really clear where and how the reality of these topological paths and itineraries is to be located or defined; sometimes Serres speaks as if *we* do it, and sometimes as if we merely find ourselves in the midst of a topological space that has its own antecedent reality, whose topological quality does not depend upon our activity (as his recourse to the mathematical grounding of topology often suggests).

Now, from the pragmatist point of view I have already invoked, one might well say—and sometimes Serres himself *does* say, in so many words—"who cares, since both realist and idealist forms of this charge are, from the standpoint of an anti-representationalist philosophy, both unprovable and empty?"[103] Or as Michael Naas puts the Derridean version of this rejoinder, "there is thus no solipsism that needs to be overcome by putting worlds together or by demonstrating that we in fact belong from the beginning to a shared or common world," because it is "only through the self's detour through the world as originary prosthesis—that the self, that any ipseity or identity, is first constituted."[104] As we have seen, however, Derrida is decisive on this point in a way that Serres is not; indeed, the nonappropriability of finitude, the *finitude of finitude*, depends upon it. It is only *because* "the world is gone" that the ethical responsibility of "I'll have to carry you" is possible—a responsibility that, in turn, we can only take on performatively, not constatively. Or, to put it another way, what is "near" and what is "far," what is close to us, concerns us, and what does not, is something that is *made*, not given—by mathematics or anything else—for the reasons we explored in detail in chapter 3 regarding such biological phenomena as "downward causation," "constraint," and so on.

Here again, a systems-theoretical redescription of Derrida's point will help it seem less counterintuitive to those who are not deconstructively inclined. As Maturana and Varela put it, "we do not see what we do not see," and this is so not only for epistemological reasons but also for ecological and biological ones.[105] As Hans-Georg Moeller points out, such a perspective makes impossible any kind of transcendental agency or intentionality with regard to the determination of what "world" is. For systems theory, because "an ecosystem has no center . . . the very condition of seeing something is not to see everything. The ability to observe, paradoxically, also implies limitations, and thus inabilities, of observation. The partial blindness that comes with evolution also implies a certain ethical and pragmatic blindness. Since it is impossible to see everything, it is also impossible to see what is good for all."[106]

This returns us, then, to the quintessentially Derridean point that I have taken up in some detail elsewhere around Derrida's thinking of conditional and unconditional hospitality: that ethics is, in this sense, a matter of doing the impossible. (And in this connection, it is perhaps not surprising that the central scene of ethical responsibility in the second set of seminars—"The world is gone. I'll have to carry you"—is staged in terms of an uncanny hauntology: "I'll have to carry you" as in "wearing mourning or bearing a child," marking our responsibility to those spectral ones who are not here, either already departed or not yet arrived, those whose alterity can never be done justice, and indeed structurally so.)[107] We have to choose, we have to act, and yet we do so without grounds, without foundations, without, precisely, "world"—without what we care about, and what we should do about it, being *given* to us by nature.[108]

It is exactly here, however, as we touched upon earlier, that Derrida locates a special role for art and poetry, one *predicated* on the fact that "the world is gone." As he puts it in the tenth and last session, "if *Die Welt ist fort*, if we think we must carry the other," then either we "carry the other out of the world" and "share at least this knowledge without phantasm that there is no longer a world," or else we must turn to what he calls the "second hypothesis": that I must "do things so as to make *as if* there were just a world, and to make the world come into the world," to "make the gift or present of this *as if* come up poetically."[109] As we saw in chapter 2, unlike Kant's version of the "as if" (the *als ob*) in the form of a "regulative idea" of the world that considers phenomena "as if they were the arrangements made by a supreme reason of which our reason is a faint copy,"[110] this "poetic" "as if" does not deny or repress its fictive nature, but acknowledges and embraces the fact that "the community of world," as Derrida puts it, "is always constructed, simulated by a set of stabilizing apparatuses."[111] If there is to be a "world," a "shared world," in other words, *we* must make it, without any taking for granted of who or what this "we" might be.[112]

Here—as you will have already guessed—we are very close indeed to Wallace Stevens's well-known doctrine of the "Supreme Fiction" as the chief duty of poetry. "The final belief," he writes, "is to believe in a fiction, which you know to be a fiction, there being nothing else. The exquisite truth is to know that it is a fiction and that you believe in it willingly."[113] For Stevens, as for Derrida, however, the point is not so much epistemological as it is pragmatic and ethical. Or as Stevens put it in *The Necessary Angel*, meditating on the "social obligation" of the poet,

> What is his function? Certainly it is not to lead people out of the confusion in which they find themselves. Nor is it, I think, to comfort them . . .
> I think that his function is to make his imagination theirs and that he fulfills himself only as he sees his imagination become the light in the minds of others. His role, in short, is to help people to live their lives.[114]

PART III

"Farewell to an Idea": Some Later Long Poems

CHAPTER 5

Scapes and Spheres

IN THIS CHAPTER AND THE NEXT, I will describe the general trajectory of Stevens's long poems as a fundamental transformation of the idea of "dwelling" (in the ecological sense of the term) into what Stanley Cavell calls, in his writings on Emerson, a process of "onwardness" and "abandonment." Here, dwelling becomes movement, a moving out or moving on (often, literally, walking), but only to return us to what Cavell sometimes calls a "transfigured" sense of the "ordinary" (the latter, a term he borrows from Wittgenstein) as a kind of answer to the problem of "reality" that Stevens poses insistently in his later poetry. Here, the story that Peter Sloterdijk tells in his massive *Spheres* project about "*homo habilitans*" and his changing modes of dwelling and "immunitary" protection provides a useful architecture for mapping the evolution of Stevens's poetics from "the death of the gods" to the crafting of a "Supreme Fiction" as a kind of substitute religion, and finally to the transfiguration of dwelling as "onwardness" that we find in "An Ordinary Evening in New Haven."[1]

Sloterdijk's scheme in *Spheres* is useful because it architectonically maps the dynamics of paradoxical self-reference, the paradoxical identity-in-difference of "inside" and "outside," "imagination" and "reality," and so on that is sometimes difficult to grasp in the verbal abstractions of second-order systems theory; it enables a kind of three-dimensional visualization of the framework I am using to map the development of Stevens's poetics. The point here is not just logical, but existential—even, for Sloterdijk, ontological. As Timothy Campbell summarizes it,

> Sloterdijk will put forward the modern figure of *homo habilitans*, who, in suffering the loss of transcendental and cosmic insurance, is made homeless . . . Such a space had been projected as a safe outside that suddenly has now become not only unreachable but profoundly indifferent to future existence. Why is the loss of protection offered by a transcendental homeland here understood as an outside that was formerly man's own? According to Sloterdijk, the loss of protection occurs when Humboldt, along with Martin Behaim, Johannes Schöner, Peter Apian, and others, mapping the cosmos, take up a second order observation "on their planet." This allows them to admit that external spaces are nothing other than extensions of a uterine-social, domestic fantasy established regionally.[2]

We thus have a framework to connect the tropological and formal architecture of Stevens's poetics with its thematics of "the death of the gods" (and the "Supreme Fiction" that follows), "which was first announced," Sloterdijk writes, "in a morphological obituary: 'The orb is dead.'" In the event of which, he continues, "the previously epicentric points are forced either to choose themselves as the center of all relationships or, beyond the familiar obsession with the central point, to surrender to the masterless game of decentered streams of events. The first option gives rise to modern systems theories, while the second possibility has so far been the prerequisite for a contemporary, post-monospheric philosophy."[3]

Stevens's poetry, as it develops from "Sunday Morning" to "Notes Toward a Supreme Fiction" to "An Ordinary Evening in New Haven," explores increasingly sophisticated poetic strategies for dealing with this "postmonospheric" challenge—what "Sunday Morning" calls "this dividing and indifferent blue,"[4] an outside suddenly and utterly foreign, ahumanly contentless, you might say. Stevens captures the particularly posthumanist character of this newly foreign space in exquisite detail in "Two or Three Ideas," when he writes of "the end of gods,"

> [t]o see the gods dispelled in mid-air and dissolve like clouds is one of the great human experiences. It is not as if they had gone over the horizon to disappear for a time; nor as if they had been overcome by other gods of greater power and profounder knowledge. It is simply that they

came to nothing . . . It left us feeling dispossessed and alone in a soli-
tude, like children without parents, in a home that seemed deserted, in
which the amical rooms and halls had taken on a look of hardness and
emptiness. What was most extraordinary is that they left no memen-
toes behind, no thrones, no mystic rings, no texts either of the soil or of
the soul. It was as if they had never inhabited the earth.[5]

As we shall see, these are the terms—of immunitary protection lost, of
legacies abandoned or obsolesced—taken up by Stevens in "The Auro-
ras of Autumn," with its repeated refrain of "farewell to an idea" and its
central tropes of house, cabin, and dwelling, all of which the poem finds
burned away by the radical outside—sometimes exhilarating, sometimes
threatening—whose signal is the aurora borealis in the night sky.[6]

The relevance of the *Spheres* architecture for my reading of Stevens is
made clear early in the introduction to volume 1, *Bubbles*, where Sloter-
dijk provides us with a passage that we can use to link Stevens's musings
on "the death of the gods" earlier with the immunitary regime of insur-
ance that occupied Stevens's everyday, working life (and about which
Stevens wrote, as we'll see later):

> What makes the Modern Age special is that after the turn to the Co-
> pernican world, the sky as an immune system was suddenly useless.
> Modernity is characterized by the technical production of its immuni-
> ties and the increasing removal of its safety structures from the tradi-
> tional theological and cosmological narratives. Industrial-scale civiliza-
> tion, the welfare state, the world market and the media sphere: all these
> large-scale projects aim, in a shelless time, for an imitation of the now
> impossible, imaginary spheric security.[7]

Stevens obviously found the poetic challenges he faced in such a situ-
ation more daunting than the pragmatic ones he dealt with on a daily
basis in his work for Hartford Accident & Indemnity. Indeed, I sug-
gest that wherever we find the trope of sky and the heavens in Stevens,
we will often find the logic identified by Sloterdijk: a logic, announced
full-throatedly by Stevens, of a sky no longer assuredly a "heaven" but
instead what will become the lair of the "serpent," "form gulping after
formlessness" at the opening of "The Auroras of Autumn." Sloterdijk re-
prises in his own theoretical architecture the arc that we can trace from
Emerson's confidence, in "Nature," that we exist nestled in a continu-
ous sphere of spheres, the "shell" that Emerson identifies in the orphic

chants at the end of that essay, to the vertiginous skepticism ("Where do we find ourselves?") that opens "Experience," and finally to Emerson's understanding in the late essay "Fate" of the "blessed Unity" and "beautiful Necessity" of what hems in our freedom.[8] Sloterdijk asks whether it is possible to provide a "competent contemporary reply" to the question, "where are we if we are in the world?" His answer is that "humans are the beings that establish globes and look out into horizons. Living in spheres means creating the dimension in which humans can be contained. Spheres are immune-systemically effective space creations for ecstatic beings that are operated upon by the outside."[9]

Here, we can circle back to the beginning of Stevens's career and situate the interiors and exteriors of *Harmonium* in a new and more grave light. "Disillusionment of Ten O'Clock" obviously remarks on an immunitary domestic interior now turned autoimmune, where the drunken sailor is banished from the land of white nightgowns, taking all that is "strange" and colorful with him.[10] And "The complacencies of the peignoir" in "Sunday Morning" may be read with the aid of Harold Bloom's suggestion that there, the poet's voice, in response to the doubts and reservations of the central female personage in the poem, "has no visionary argument with which to assuage her but relies instead upon the pungency of the earth in contrast with the unknown darkness of the surrounding space."[11] Or, to put it in the terms I have been developing throughout, the "earth" of "Sunday Morning" is still "nature" and not yet "environment."

At the other end of the spectrum, as it were (to stitch together the emerging terms of this chapter and the previous one) we can now see that Stevens's famous blackbird from "Thirteen Ways" is a messenger from another realm, all right—as birds often are in the tradition and in Stevens's own poetry (as we have seen with the great late poems "Of Mere Being" and "Not Ideas about the Thing but the Thing Itself"). But the blackbird of the earlier poem radicalizes, and prepares us for, the news from a particular *kind* of outside (it would be wrong, emphatically, to call it "nature" in the framework into which I am recruiting Sloterdijk here). Indeed—as Sloterdijk writes of "the loss of the firmament and cosmic *clôture* [(en-)closure]" recorded in Alexander von Humboldt's "openly anachronistic" *Cosmos*[12]—we find here a view of the planet "from without," one that refuses "to admit that the outer spaces are merely extensions of a regionally confined, herd-like, domestic, and socio-uterine imagination." In this radically new and estranging context, human beings now know "that they are contained or lost—which now amounts to virtually the same thing—somewhere in the boundless." It begins to dawn on them that "they cannot rely on anything as much as the homogeneous indifference of the infinite space. Here, the 'comfortable component' has been eliminated. The outside expands, ignoring the postulate of proximity in the humane spheres, as a foreign entity in its own right; its first and only principle seems to be its lack of interest in humanity."[13]

It's this realization, inhuman and ahuman, whose "shadow" crosses "Thirteen Ways of Looking at a Blackbird" in sections VI, IX and, especially, XI. In this context, section XI seems and feels all the more astringent and shocking—clinical, even—when Stevens writes, of riding above Connecticut "in a glass coach" (a canonical example, after all, of Sloterdijk's immunitary protective sphere for *homo habilitans*), that he is pierced by fear when he mistakes "The shadow of his equipage / For blackbirds."[14] We find here what Sloterdijk calls "a radically altered sense of human localization. The earth now becomes the planet to which one returns; the outside is the general From-where of all possible returns."[15] In this new context, he continues, "the view from outside results not from a transcendence of the noetic soul into the extra- and supra-terrestrial, but rather from the development of the physical-technical, aero- and astronautical imagination (whose literary and cartographical manifestations, furthermore, were always ahead of the technological ones)."[16] As Timothy Campbell notes, a central icon for Sloterdijk's *homo habilitans* is astronaut Neil Armstrong, who can only experience the radical outside of space by being ensphered in his spacesuit, which allows him to venture away from the "domesticated space" of the *oikos*, the spacecraft in which he breathes.[17] Most important for "Thirteen Ways" is Sloterdijk's observation that "modern notions of flying replaced the ancient and medieval ones of 'ascending'; the airport earth (where one starts and lands) replaced the ascension earth (from which one propels oneself and never returns)."[18] Indeed, as Christopher Schaberg notes in *The Textual Life of Airports: Reading the Culture of Flight*, "Stevens's multiple registers of the blackbird sets up an airborne schema, a soaring experiment in perspective coincidental with the emergence of human flight," and "offers an analytic framework for thinking about the intersections between birdlife and technological flight."[19]

It's worth remembering in this context that multiple senses are conveyed by the enigmatic figure of the blackbird in this, one of Stevens's best known (if perhaps least understood) poems. Joseph Riddel, for example, notes that several of the poem's presentations of the blackbird "acquaint one with death's ever-presence,"[20] while Bloom sees the bird as "Stevens' first thinker of the First Idea," one that "mixes in every-where, including the union of a man and a woman."[21] But a way to join these senses of the blackbird in Stevens's poem—and to draw out "the intersections between birdlife and technological flight" in the specifically posthumanist sense that I have developed in chapters 3 and 4, in par-ticular—is simply to say that Stevens's poem is a kind of anatomy of the problem of observation, and that the problem of observation (and the "worlds" that emerge therefrom) is not exclusively a *human* problem in a universe whose ahumanness (startlingly revealed in the "death of the orb" world that Sloterdijk describes) links us anew and more systemi-cally, ineluctably, to nonhuman life. And this is indexed, iconically, at the opening of the poem in the "eye" of the blackbird as "the only thing moving." The radical contingency of observation, which allows it to be revelatory, is what blackbirds and poets have in common, and that is why the blackbird "mixes in everywhere," as Bloom puts it, but can also be associated with death *qua* finitude. In this light, I think we can throw into relief what is so unsatisfactory (if so beautiful!) in the final lines of "Sunday Morning," where the "casual flocks of pigeons" sink "Downward to darkness, on extended wings."[22] As Vilém Flusser has noted, "for our ancestors, the bird was the link between animal and angel. It is not an angel yet, because it is still subjected to the Earth's attraction," like "a hand linked to the body of the Earth by an invisible arm." The angel, by counterpoint, is "a hand free of a body: the myth of the spirit-dove. An angel is a being that apprehends, comprehends, conceives, and modifies 'freely': pure spirit. A hand free of a body is pure spirit. The bird's flight is its model."[23] The pigeons at the end of "Sunday Morning" are thus, it needs to be said, a little too angelic, as if the angels simply reversed their trajectory and itinerary but maintained, as it were, the same flight path.

But "Thirteen Ways" reminds us, too, in its cubist audacity, that we are not our ancestors anymore, and it prepares us (more technically, as it were) for that cousin of the bird—the serpent—that inhabits this more radical outside in "The Auroras of Autumn," a poem that works through various possibilities of that outside's domestication via an inventory of tropes (Plato's cave, the indigenous, the legacies of "cabin" and "ances-tral theme," and so on), only to affirm the power of this radical outside, this "form gulping after formlessness," this "contrivance of the spectre of the spheres."[24] As Bloom points out, Stevens here attempts to "defy" the auroras, "to show that the auroras are 'nothing' unless and until they are 'contained' by being imagined in his mind," but instead, "having pre-pared himself for this great battle of the mind against the sky, he opens the door of his house, his entire consciousness, to find that the whole sky is on fire, as the auroras triumphantly quell his challenge and reduce him to fear."[25] Now we are in a better position to look back and account for the pronounced torque and traction of one of *Harmonium*'s greatest short poems, "Domination of Black," where the polar senses of immunitary interior and radical outside that we have been discussing collide with particular force: not just the interior, but the interiority of the interior, you might say, that opens the poem: the hearth, "At night, by the fire" (this will be reprised in the middle sections of "Auroras" and its dwellings), and, at the other end of the spectrum, "the cry of the peacocks" that carries the same message as Stevens's blackbird, haunting the falsely secure domain through which the immunitary sphere hurtles: "I saw how the planets gathered," and "I saw how the night came," and "I felt afraid" (this, too, is reprised in "Auroras," in section VI, where fear grips the speaker in the realization of the fragility, and combustibility, of the domestic interior, itself a trope for cultural legacy).

But what is of equal interest is to track Stevens's growing understanding of how all this reshapes his poetic approach, and not just in his explicit doctrines and pronouncements, such as the Supreme Fiction, that are calculated to address thematically what is, in fact, a challenge in poetic strategy. The mature poetics takes up this posthumanist challenge as a problem in its own right, and not just as a theme—indeed, takes it up conspicuously as a problem of *form*, as in the great late poem "The Planet on the Table," and its desire that the poems "bear / Some lineament or character" of "the planet of which they were a part."[26] Let me emphasize again, in the larger context of "ecocriticism," that this is not a matter of the poems *representing* "the planet of which they were a part"—an understanding that is carried here in the precision of Stevens's diction ("lineament," "character," "affluence"—all "only half-perceived"). Here, it's worth remembering Luhmann's point that "art can no longer be understood as an imitation of something that presumably exists along with and outside of art . . . To the extent that imitation is still possible, it now imitates the world's invisibility, a nature that can no longer be apprehended as a whole, and must therefore be represented by emphasizing its curves, its 'lines of beauty.' Art activates distinctions that operate in a 'connexionist' manner."[27] And this is a matter of *form*. Or as Luhmann puts it (invoking Husserl's well-known concept of "horizon"), each act of individuation "refers to other possibilities within a horizon of possible determinations"; hence, "meaning always requires an 'appresentation' (again, I am using Husserl's terms) or concomitant making-present of other possibilities in a concrete act." This is how individuation creates "worlds." Thus—and this is the important point for understanding Stevens's paradoxical navigations of the problem of "reality"—"the real and the possible are thus not separate spheres . . . Instead the space of potentialities, the totality of references, and the horizon-like quality of all meaning form an enlivening or meaning-producing moment in everything that is specific, in every identity."[28]

At this precise point, Luhmann parts ways (as does Derrida) with Husserl—specifically with Husserl's contention that intentionality is the anchor for this entire meaning-making process; and he also raises the question, which we explored in some detail in chapter 4, of whether this entire description of "meaning" and "horizon" might apply to (at least some) nonhuman animals as well.[29] For Derrida, as we have seen, these two questions are intimately connected, as his critique of the alignment of "responding" and "reacting" with the dualism "human" and "animal" makes clear. And I will argue below that Stevens takes very seriously the possibility that this shared *form* of meaning may serve as a bridge between the human and nonhuman world: a fact that is dramatized in an especially powerful way in his bird poems.

For now, however, I simply suggest that Luhmann's characterization is especially illuminating for Stevens's later poems, nowhere more so, perhaps, than in the opening flourish of "Notes Toward a Supreme Fiction," which announces, "You must become an ignorant man again / And see the sun again with an ignorant eye / And see it clearly in the idea of it."[30] Here, I think Stevens quite nimbly and precisely distinguishes the various dimensions of the horizonal *cum* spherological project that we have already discussed: seeing the sun "with an ignorant eye" nonetheless means seeing it within a horizon of meaning, "in the idea of it," and the infrastructure that makes this meaning possible is not the product of an "inventing mind" (as the poem puts it) or an intention (as Stevens reminds us in "The Irrational Element in Poetry"). It is rather a question, to use Luhmann's terminology, of "localization": that is to say, how do we generate new horizons through new localizations of the relationship between the actual and possible against the cultural legacy and backdrop of the announcement in "Notes" that "the death of one god is the death of all"?[31]

Or take "A Primitive Like an Orb," which says of "The essential poem at the centre of things" that "It is and it / Is not and, therefore, is," the central poem here becoming the world, and "the world, the central poem, each one the mate / Of the other."[32] Indeed, the "giant" of that poem—

like "the central man" and other associated personae in Stevens's poetry (that "abstraction given head")[33]—is above all, in Sloterdijk's terms, a globe builder. And the emphasis here, precisely for the reasons Luhmann describes, is—as it is in Emerson, and as it is in James[34]—less on the built than on the process of building itself, which is why Stevens writes that "The central poem is the poem of the whole, / The poem of the *compo-sition* of the whole,"[35] and that "the giant" is thus "ever changing, living in change."[36] This is not simply because new images and tropes, once invented, immediately begin to become stale, part of the "images" that are in the heap in "The Man on the Dump," part of the domain of what Emerson called "conformity"; it is certainly that, but it is also something more than that, something that Stevens's poetry rivets our attention on time and again: to put it technically, that the radical contingency of self-referential and "blind" observation is a reservoir of complexity for what we call "world," for that contingency means that the world could always be otherwise, indeed *will* always be otherwise.

We can trace the itinerary I've just described in Stevens's mature po-etry by going back to yet another figure of the "giant" and the "central," this time not in "Notes" but in section V of "Credences of Summer," which, according to Vendler, proposes a kind of "Hegelian" solution to the fundamental problem of the poem: "the difficult relation between the moment of satisfaction and 'the waste and sad time stretching be-fore and after.'"[37] As Vendler observes, no long poem in the Stevens corpus so firmly plants the speaker in the present moment of a particu-lar landscape, and here, as in "The Auroras of Autumn" that will follow, "Stevens calls the present internal moment 'this,' and everything outside it in space and time 'that,' and the purpose of these two seasonal pas-torals of inner weather is to find a relation between 'this' and 'that.'"[38] Now, given our earlier discussion of the questions of form, meaning, and the topology of the outside in relation to self-referential observation, I think we know what to do with the spatial aspects of this question of "this" and "that." But what interests me equally here is the *temporal* as-pect, the question of "the waste and sad time stretching before and af-ter," as Stevens puts it.

On this point, Hegel, as it happens, is invoked by Luhmann, too, in a lecture on the concept of meaning, where he notes that in the *Ency-clopedia of the Philosophical Sciences*, Hegel uses "the distinction between being and not-being in order to speak of time." As Luhmann notes, from the beginning of the treatise, Hegel "runs into the problem that time apparently is something that is and, at the same time, something that is not, which is to say, something that is no longer or something that is not yet."[39] "You know what I mean when I say 'now' now," he continues, "namely, precisely the moment when I say it." In contrast to this "indexical expression" of "now," we have available a different sense of "now" when we change it into a noun. "Now," Luhmann writes, "we have 'the now,' which apparently possesses a quality that can exist and actually exists continuously, and has existed and will exist at all times."[40] "In consequence," he continues, "we all of a sudden tend to see behind the distinction, behind the treatment of the 'now,' the difference between speaking and writing"; that "time is the whole that is divided into a se-ries of nows or points in time, seems to be, in terms of our schema, an effect of writing."[41] This means—as those who cut their teeth on decon-struction's critique of speech as presence (in particular in Husserl's work) will already have guessed—that the theoretical challenge then becomes one of *form*: of formalizing a concept of form, you might say. The prob-lem becomes "whether we can find a concept or an order within which the entity we call 'meaning' does not depend on shifting the burden by referring to a subject or another carrier of meaning . . . but to find an or-der within which it is possible to formulate a sufficiently formal concept of meaning."[42]

I believe that Stevens was passionately interested in this problem— as the lines quoted earlier from "The Planet on the Table" suggest (but many, many other poems could be cited here)—and in ways not com-pletely explained by J. Hillis Miller's approach to the problem that we discussed in an earlier chapter, where Stevens is thought to oscillate at an increasingly rapid rate between the two poles of "reality" and "imagi-nation," refusing to domesticate their difference by means of a dialectical resolution. I suggest that Stevens's approach to the problem identified by Luhmann is, in fact, "ecological," in this sense: that there is probably no more straightforwardly accurate description of Stevens's entire poetic project than to say that he desired in his poems a kind of meaning that was neither wholly the product of the mind or imagination nor wholly the product of the world to which the poet responds—its seasons, its forms of order, and so on. This has important implications in Stevens's work for the possibility of an inhuman or ahuman form of meaning that, nonetheless, does not exclude or prevent human ways of meaning. These two questions are conjoined at a key moment late in "Notes To-ward a Supreme Fiction," where Stevens writes, "He imposes orders as he thinks of them, / As the fox and the snake do," then observes by way of response, "But to impose is not to discover":[43]

Not to impose, not to have reasoned at all,
Out of nothing to have come on major weather,

It is possible, possible, possible. It must
Be possible[44]

I will come back to this braiding of the questions of the form of meaning and the nonhuman world in a moment, but for now I simply note how, in light of Luhmann's work on the "actual" and the "possible," the conjugation of the relationship between being and not-being and "now" and "*the* now" in "Credences" helps us understand not only what I called earlier the "strange loop" of temporality that is central to Stevens's poems—"the blackbird singing, or just after," the "C" that is also a preceding "pre-C" in "Not Ideas about the Thing but the Thing Itself"—but also the possibility, so captivating in Stevens, of a system/environment relationship and a mode of meaning that is avowed to be not totally knowable to the speaker or *simply* a product of his imagination or intention. We might say, a mode of meaning that is part of an environment that *includes* the "mind" and "imagination" of the poet but is not exhausted or fully captured by that mind. In this light, we can go back to the beginning of "Credences" and see how "the physical pine. The metaphysical pine" are bound by the prostheticity of observation: "the hottest fire of sight" that enables us to see "the barrenness / Of the fertile thing that can attain no more."[45] From this vantage point, "the physical pine. The metaphysical pine" may be paired with the ending of "The Man on the Dump," with "The the,"[46] and with the ending of the nearby poem "Add This to Rhetoric": "Add this. It is to add."[47] What are we to do with such lines? One option is to see that both mark the difference between "now" and "*the* now," between the temporal contingency of performativity and the form in and through which that performativity takes place—and takes place not just *now* but in any "now," marked as the imperative vs. intransitive mood at the end of "Add This to Rhetoric" ("add this *now*; it is *always* 'to add'"). The intrication, in other words, of the infrastructure of iterability and the temporality of its performativity. Or as the opening of "Add This to Rhetoric" puts it, "It is posed and it is posed. / But in nature it merely grows."[48]

These are precisely the moments in Stevens's mature poetry that mark a transition, in Sloterdijk's terms, from a poetics of "globes" to a poetics of "foams." As he writes, "When everything has become the center, there is no longer any valid center . . . In foam worlds, the individual bubbles are not absorbed into a single, integrative hyper-orb, as in the metaphysical conception of the world, but rather drawn together to form irregular hills."[49] To put it another way, the world of foams is not a world holistically organized around a center-periphery relationship (which is simply a three-dimensional version of the "wheel" in Derrida's discussion of sovereignty and the *oikos* in both *Rogues* and *The Beast and the Sovereign, Vol. 2*);[50] rather, it is organized by the "horizontal" iteration (to combine the terms of Luhmann and Derrida) of a *formal* principle of organization, whereby iterability creates the "tensegrity," if you will, that makes the whole aggregate hang together as a detotalized totality (to borrow Adorno's phrase). But the point I stress here is that such a poetics is by definition more *ecological* than a spherological poetry of globes precisely because of its foregrounding of the contingent autopoiesis and self-reference that testifies at every moment to a system's (or observer's) entanglement and finitude in an overwhelmingly complex environment, which directs us in turn toward the "second-order" understanding that as systems build up their own internal complexity by means of their own recursive reentry of the system/environment distinction into the system itself, they actually become *more* attuned and *more* linked, through this recursive closure, to the environments in which they find themselves and with which they work to find resonance. "It is posed and it is posed" in an *environment*, whereas in "nature" it "merely grows."

Here—against the backdrop of Sloterdijk's contention that "foams, heaps, sponges, clouds and vortexes serve as the first amorphological metaphors"[51]—it is useful to contrast Stevens's "Anecdote of the Jar," that most globological of poems, with later poems such as "The Man on the Dump" (and, beyond that, "The Poems of Our Climate" and "Connoisseur of Chaos," among others). All these are recursively self-referential in the way that all poems are, but the later poems subject the globological ordering of the landscape by the round glass jar—"It took dominion everywhere," "It made the slovenly wilderness / Surround that hill"—to what we might call the foaming action of a second-order observation of how form provides certain "connexionist" possibilities for further meaning, but only at the expense of excluding others and being "blind" to them. The jar, we might say, takes its first-order observations all too seriously, but the jar itself will in time, Stevens suggests in these later poems, end up as one of the things on "the dump," precisely because of its lack of perspective, if you will, on its own observations.

As I noted earlier, Stevens's major critics tend to disagree about just what is going on in "The Man on the Dump," particularly in the last stanza. But I think Bloom's reading is especially perceptive when he argues, against the readings of both A. Walton Litz and Vendler, that

> "The the" is not a specific experience or a present moment, not oneself in any anti-Transcendental sense, and not a poetry of the irreducible minimum. "The the" is any object whatsoever, outside the self, which is in the process of being taken up again into language. Or, ironically, "The the" is a necessarily failed fresh attempt to avoid figuration.[52]

Bloom's reading shares much with Poirier's discussion of linguistic skepticism and the "superfluous" in his genealogy connecting Emerson and Stevens (as discussed earlier), and as such it marks the critical climate of its moment. But, as with Poirier's reading, we need to more rigorously describe what Bloom is sniffing out here by means of Luhmann's schema (the "reentry" of the inside/outside relation, his discussion of meaning and form as a horizon without a fixed outside, his analysis of "now" versus "*the* now," and so on). And pursuing this more thorough (if more technically daunting) theorization of the relationship of "The the" and "the truth" in the final stanza of "The Man on the Dump" allows us to excavate more deeply, I think, the connections that previous critics have noticed between what I'm calling the foamological "heaping" or "piling" of images we witness in "The Man on the Dump" and how the recursive, repeated "the the"–ing of the later poems exerts an erosive critical force upon the more globological poetics of *Harmonium*.

Bloom, for example, notes, regarding "The Man on the Dump," the poem's "mad apotropaic litany played upon the sacred word of *Harmonium*, which is 'dew,'" where it served as "a synecdoche for everything in nature that still could be thought of as pure or refreshing, or rather for something that has not yet come into nature." But from this point forward, "the reader of *Harmonium* is now asked by Stevens to undergo the Emersonian wildness of attaining freedom" by encountering, in so many words, the transition that Emerson had made from "Nature" to "Experience," which forces us to confront—embrace—that "what dissolves here is the fiction of the dew" as Stevens lampoons "the floweriest flowers dewed with the dewiest dew."[53] What dissolves, in short, is "nature." As I have already indicated, that "Emersonian wildness" is an "onwardness" and "abandonment" driven by the iterative and recursive framing and reframing processes described by both Derrida and Luhmann—what Emerson called "circling"—and the process is, crucially, both nondialectical and nonlogical (and, as we have seen, paradoxical to its very core).

From this vantage point, we can see how such a process is totally embedded in a world it reveals but does not and could not ever represent or master. Like Bloom, Riddel notes the "deeply rooted Emersonian impulse" in "The Man on the Dump" to be "free of 'the old descriptions of the world,'" but he points out that the poem "lacks at least one coordinate of 'The American Scholar': belief in the greater coherence of things and selves."[54] This is exactly right, I think—not only because of the functional differentiation of modernity and the contingency of observation that goes with it (in Luhmann's terms), but also for reasons that Emerson himself was already exploring in essays such as "Experience" and "Fate." On this terrain, Riddel argues, the late poem "Connoisseur of Chaos" is "the major text," and "it proceeds through three stanzas of non-proof to a poetic conclusion that satisfies connoisseurs but not logicians."[55] But the point is not, as Riddel has it, that "rejecting truth in propositions, he [the poet] discovers instead the felt order of nature";[56] it is rather that the "felt order of nature" is now understood to reveal itself only through provisional acts of individuation and observation, the constant and provisional positing and then rapid abandonment of tropes, images, concepts—"jars," in short—that order the world for a moment, then occlude it. Stevens works this process in the poem quite conspicuously through a schema of first-order vs. second-order observation. First order, second stanza: I see what I see and what I see and say is all:

> If all the green of spring was blue, and it is;
> If all the flowers of South Africa were bright
> On the tables of Connecticut, and they are;
> If English lived without tea in Ceylon, and they do.[57]

Second order, third stanza: "We cannot go back to that. / The squirming facts exceed the squamous mind."[58] To put this in the more ecological terms of Luhmann's rendering of the system/environment relationship, the problem of meaning is here referred to the problem of *complexity*. Stevens's "major man" or "central man" or "giant" (or, here, the "bishop" of "bishops' books") "does not," as Luhmann puts it, "have the 'requisite variety'—that is, the possibility to assume as many states . . . as the external world." And that means that "complexity amounts to selective pressure"—the pressure, in Stevens's terms, to find order out of chaos.[59] Luhmann's formulation of the problem has the additional advantage of helping us understand why Stevens's Supreme Fiction must be "abstract" and "must change," and it helps us see that the provisional nature of ordering selections and ordered elements in the medium of meaning constitutes not a failure but precisely what is needed to "keep the ball rolling," as it were, allowing Stevens's "squamous mind" to handle irreducible environmental complexity ("the squirming facts") by deploying the medium of language and the form of meaning (a qualitative shift in ordering principles from "final" to provisional that is registered in the movement from the simple alliteration of "bishops' books" to the more complexly self-referential double alliteration of "squirming" and "squamous").

The provisionality of such forms is clearly emphasized by Stevens here, as in so many other poems, when we are told:

> A great disorder is an order. Now, A
> And B are not like statuary, posed
> For a vista in the Louvre. They are things chalked
> On the sidewalk so that the pensive man may see.[60]

"Things chalked on the sidewalk" are subject, of course, unlike statuary (or the statue of General DuPuy in "Notes"),[61] to erasure, in both the mundane and the Derridean sense of that term. And we find the same sort of process in the nearby representative late piece "The Poems of Our Climate," which subjects its own globological jar—"a bowl of white, / Cold, a cold porcelain, low and round" (like the jar "round upon the ground," "gray and bare" in "Anecdote of the Jar")[62]—to the same sort of erosive, recursive action of "The evilly compounded, vital I," "the never-resting mind," "So that one would want to escape, come back / To what had been so long composed."[63] We should note here Stevens's insistence on a recursive itinerary, and we should note, too, with more effort, the echo of "landscape" in "escape," as if to underscore what Cavell, reading Emerson, calls the poetics of "aversion," where one turns away, *goes* away (as Emerson says in "Self-Reliance," "when my genius calls me") only to return to "what had been so long composed."[64] Here we find a reprise, too, of the opening of the second section of Emerson's "Nature," but this process of "scaping" is subjected in Stevens to the relentless framing and reframing in the terms we've borrowed from Luhmann, in and through which individuation is worlding in a process of "enaction."

Derrida and J. Hillis Miller will help me make the point in a different vocabulary in Derrida's discussion of Miller's reading of Gerard Manley Hopkins's immersion in the words "scape" and "inscape." As Derrida notes, Hopkins discovered one day in a dictionary "with glee" the word "*scape*, which (as it turns out) is another form of *skep* or *skip*, meaning 'basket' or 'cage.'"[65] Now, one cannot fail to notice, first of all, that we have here yet another avatar of Sloterdijk's sphere. And, as Sloterdijk notes in *Bubbles*, Heidegger uses the curious neologism "inhood" early on in *Being and Time* to express "the fact that the subject or Dasein can only be *there* if contained, surrounded, encompassed, disclosed, breathed-upon, resounded-through, attuned and addressed. Before a Dasein assumes the character of being-in-the-world, it already has the constitution of being-in."[66] Here again, we find an itinerary I have emphasized before in these pages: a direct through-line from Uexküll to Heidegger to the contemporary biology of cognition and perception, with Emerson and Stevens (and now Hopkins) as "literary" stops along the way. As Miller explains, for Hopkins, "inscape" holds and "encloses an inner principle of life," and it is the "inner pressure of instress [another neologism of Hopkins's], permeating nature" that is "the true source of inscape, and brought into the open by it." But most important here is that inscape is "the outer manifestation or 'scape' of an inner energy or activity—not external pattern which is pleasing to the eye as design."[67]

Here, Hopkins gives us a more theological version of Emerson's project in the last three sections of "Nature," but the larger point is that this "inner energy or activity—not external pattern which is pleasing to the eye" may be readily redescribed for our ecological poetics in terms of contemporary theoretical biology and its account of perception and cognition, just as the term "world" was in Derrida's second seminar on *The Beast and the Sovereign*—and this is precisely the point emphasized by Derrida's contention that "inscape can in no way be reduced to the meaning or the thought-out content of poetry, even if it requires them."[68] The "outer manifestation or 'scape' of an inner energy or activity" is precisely how the contemporary theoretical biology of consciousness describes the autopoiesis of perception and cognition, and how it operates to "bring forth a world," as we have seen in earlier chapters. So we can see a clear trajectory here that can, I think, be neatly summarized: from "inscape" as an expression of "instress" in Hopkins, an "inner energy and activity," to Emerson's "eye/I" complex that focuses our attention more squarely on the paradoxical nature of the observation ("I am nothing; I see all")[69] that expresses that "inner energy or activity" and makes a "scape" of it, to Stevens's movement from spheres and globes (or jars) to foams, which is—crucially—framed as an *activity*, an ongoing, recursive, iterative process that emphasizes not just the paradoxical dynamics of observation, but also the difference between first- and second-order observations, the "squirming facts" vs. the "squamous mind." To put it another way, with the biology of cognition, and in Stevens's poetics, we move "from being to doing." This "scaping" activity in Stevens's later poetry exists not as a foray out into the world to either discover or impose some sort of final order, but rather as a way to draw poetic resources from the fact that the environment is always already exponentially more complex than the system that ventures out into it. But why "escape" at all? The answer is commonsensical enough, if we believe Bateson and Luhmann. As Bateson puts it, "all that is not information, not redundancy, not form and not restraints—is noise, the only possible source of *new* patterns."[70]

This helps us to articulate the *raision d'être* for the foaming, heaping, recursive provisionality we find in Stevens's late poetics, and it is part of the reason, I think, that most readers find "The Auroras of Autumn" a more successful poem than its companion, "Credences of Summer." "Credences," like "Sunday Morning," attempts what we might call a dialectical "solution" to the problem posed by the poem, but as Vendler puts it, "the result is happier in *The Auroras of Autumn*, where elegy and description are kept in a dissolving equilibrium, and present and past remain in a fluid focus."[71] In "Credences," the relation between Vendler's "this" and "that," between Luhmann's "now" and "*the* now," is carried, and in all registers, by the poem's framing of the question, as Vendler notes, in terms of the One and the Many, "one man" vs. "a race": the question of whether (as Stevens puts it) "the other days enrich the one?"[72] The poem implores of itself, "Let's see the very thing and nothing else. / Let's see it with the hottest fire of sight," and calls upon itself to "Exile desire / For what is not,"[73] but then ends up affirming, in the final section, a kind of masque in which

> the characters speak because they want
> To speak, the fat, roseate characters,
> Free, for a moment, from malice and sudden cry,
> Complete in a completed scene . . .[74]

The whole poem, as Vendler puts it, "may be seen as a meditation on the Keatsian moment in which the bees find that summer has o'erbrimm'd their clammy shells . . . and Stevens' response is exactly that of the humanized bees: to think that warm days will never cease, or to follow a devious logic of wish."[75] It is symptomatic—for reasons I'll come back to later—that those "characters" in the poem's final masque are figured earlier in the poem in terms of sovereignty—the "queen," the "bristling soldier," the "twelve princes," the "sun" (the same sun we find in "Sunday Morning," section VII), and the "king"—but for now I think we can agree with Vendler that the final section, and the poem as a whole, is answered and rebutted, in a way, by the later piece "The Ultimate Poem is Abstract," which is also "about a day which also seems plenary, full of revelation, placid, blue, roseate, ripe, complete."[76] Stevens begins the poem pointedly: "This day writhes with what? The lecturer / On This Beautiful World of Ours composes himself / And hems the planet rose and haws it ripe."[77] In a way, already, enough said. But Stevens makes the complaint a bit more technical, as it were: "It is not so blue as we thought. To be blue, / There must be no questions."[78] Moreover, the poem concludes, "It would be enough / If we were ever, just once, at the middle, fixed In This Beautiful World of Ours and not as now, // Helplessly at the edge."[79] For the rather technically binding reasons we have been exploring, however, we know that what is being described here—being "fixed" and in the "middle" of a unified sphere, an orb, a globe, where coherent stories of "This Beautiful World of Ours" are possible—is but a first-order observation that Stevens will subject to his own erosive and yet liberating second-order observation, itself but a moment in the framing and reframing "onwardness" that sustains the world in all its complexity through the failure of a final apprehension.

There are two further points to be made here. First, I would suggest that "the edge" here is the same edge, discussed earlier, in "Of Mere Being," where "the palm at the end of the mind" stands "at the edge of space." As I have argued elsewhere, *all* spaces have "edges," and unavoidably so, precisely because the observation of any space, any map, sets it off against *another* space, an outside, a "spacier" space, you might say, which only maintains its character by virtue of being the outside *of* an inside, precisely in the manner of a strange loop or Möbius strip.[80] And what is the relationship between "the edge" and Stevens's "question"? Both name the precise point at which what makes the world available—the form of meaning—is also what makes it unavailable, and *in* that unavailability resides what we call "environment," which then gets reframed ("resphered," as it were) as "world" through the form of meaning and its reentry of the system/environment difference on the side of the system itself.

But these lines from "The Ultimate Poem is Abstract" are important primarily because they link that iterability that creates the "edge of space" with the bird that "sings in the palm, without human meaning, / Without human feeling, a foreign song" in "Of Mere Being,"[81] and in doing so they remind us that "Credences" holds out another possibility that is presented very much at a tangent to the rest of the poem. It proposes the possibility of a different "now"—a different "*the* now" in "the now," you might say—that opens onto the reality of a larger environment not exhausted by either "desire for what is not" or "the barrenness / Of the fertile thing that can attain no more."[82] More precisely, this apparently epistemological question about the "edge" of knowledge is embedded in the much larger question of the embodied difference of the system/environment relation for other forms of life, other songs—songs we hear but that are not, in the hearing, exhausted. This aspect of the question is brought to bear in section IX of "Credences," which holds complex lines of relation to the crossing of nonhuman life with the question of second-order observation as staged in "Thirteen Ways of Looking at a Blackbird." Here, in "Credences," we find it in the imploration of the "cock bright" to "With one eye watch the willow, motionless," which is itself framed by the contrast between the "bean pole" in the section at hand and the tower presented earlier, in section III—all of which may be glossed in terms of our earlier discussion of the phallus and sovereignty as that is developed in the second set of seminars on *The Beast and the Sovereign*. This section of "Credences" also anticipates its companion section in "Notes Toward a Supreme Fiction," section VI, which we have already discussed in terms of its handling of the contrast between the "single text, granite monotony," in which all songs are one song, where the sparrow is "a bird // Of stone, that never changes," and the *augenblick* that unsettles the observer's sovereign position in relation to other forms of life.[83] "Credences" IX makes good on this latter gambit in its last stanza, where the "polished beast" (another iteration of the prostheticity of the bird and its song in "Of Mere Being") may "detect / Another complex of other emotions," one "not part of the listener's own sense."[84] And in this, we might say that section IX of "Credences" opens onto the exploratory space that is shared by Stevens's more successful later long poems, "Auroras of Autumn" and "Notes," which we will take up in more detail in the next chapter.

CHAPTER 6

"Premetaphysical Pluralism"

Dwelling in the Ordinary

THE FRAMEWORK I HAVE BEEN ADAPTING from Peter Sloterdijk's *Spheres* project (unwieldy though it sometimes is) enables me to explain something about Stevens's corpus that is otherwise quite difficult to articulate: why "An Ordinary Evening in New Haven" is a greater poem than "The Auroras of Autumn," and greater even than the poem most celebrated by Stevens's critics as his greatest achievement, "Notes Toward a Supreme Fiction." The easiest way to describe this in shorthand, following Sloterdijk's taxonomy, is to say that the essential movement that we find from "Sunday Morning," to "Notes," and then to "Ordinary Evening" is from a poetry of "globes" to a poetry of what Sloterdijk calls "foams." As for the former, Sloterdijk writes early in *Foams* that "the event called metaphysics" consisted at base of "the insight that local existence integrates itself into the absolute orb . . . the ensouled point swells up into the universal sphere," and "the two epitomes of totality, the world and God, were envisioned as an all-enclosing spheric volume" in which individuals found their concentric place—their "subordinate world shells," as Sloterdijk puts it—enabling philosophers from Plotinus to Leibniz to observe (in what is almost a Stevensian formulation itself), "*Tell me what you are immersed in, and I will tell you what you are.*"[1]

Against the backdrop of this conceptual cartography, we can see how the movement from "Sunday Morning" to the later long poems tracks the Emersonian trajectory we traced in the previous chapter from *Nature* to "Experience." At the end of *Nature*, the fourth of the "Orphic chants" provides one of the iconic visions in all of American literature of "the ensouled point" enlarging itself into "the universal sphere." But by the time of "Experience," the formula "Tell me what you are immersed in and I will tell you what you are" has become problematic if not untenable for Emerson, as the opening vertiginous question, "Where do we find ourselves?" turns out to be anything but rhetorical. And the issue, as Stanley Cavell reminds us, is precisely the subject's *lack* of "immersion" as "all things swim and glitter" and we confront "the evanescence and lubricity of all objects,"[2] propelling us toward the world of "foams" as Sloterdijk sketches it, where "'life' unfolds multifocally, multiperspectively and heterarchically," a "non-holistic" space that "can no longer be thought with the tools of ontological simplification, of collection in the smooth universal orb."[3] Though it thrusts us into a bewildering new space full of formal and conceptual challenges, the payoff of this historical and philosophical shift (as both Cavell and Sloterdijk recognize) is the possibility "to recover the premetaphysical pluralism of world-inventions postmetaphysically."[4] And this movement propels us not just outside the framework of "Sunday Morning" and its naturalized supernaturalism (to paraphrase Stevens) and its holism, but also outside the scaffolding of "Notes," which announces the end of the world organized by the "universal orb," but does so only by means of a countervailing commitment to continuing that project by other means: namely, in the felt necessity of a "Supreme Fiction." That is to say, "Notes" announces the end of the world of globes even as it hangs onto the need to assuage the globological urge that had previously been satisfied by religion, "the gods," and so on.

Indeed, when I go back and reread "Notes" now, the poem seems positively theatrical and even histrionic, with its numerous personae (General DuPuy, the planter, MacCullough, and so on) and the stage directing thereof. Similarly, it is easy to forget just how sustained is the allusive and intertextual dialogue in the poem with the Judeo-Christian tradition, beginning with the sun/Son homophone in the very first section; the repeated figure of the dove that comes and goes; Adam in canto IV of the first section; the cock crowing in section one, cantos VII and IX (thrice in the latter, and in April, no less); the several iterations of some version or echo of "I am that I am" that we find throughout; the seraph at the opening of the second section; the end of the second section's riff on Corinthians' "for now we see through a glass darkly," followed quickly by Saint Jerome at the opening of the next section, itself followed in canto II by the dogwood; and the list goes on. At the same time, "Notes" is certainly—in its poetics rather than its programmatic commitment to "Supreme Fiction"—about the dynamic and iterative processes (not products, including ones called "Supreme Fictions") of abstraction, change, and pleasure: the "living changingness" of the opening dedication that excavates "the central of our being," where "we sit at rest," but only "for a moment."[5] And that is in turn bookended by the remarkable final "fat girl" canto: "How is it I find you in difference, see you there / In a moving contour, a change not quite completed?"[6] We thus find a tension in "Notes" between the performative, processual, and iterative dimension that will find its maximal expression in "Ordinary Evening," and the thematizations and furniture of the era of globes and orbs that Stevens, at this juncture, continues to entertain and indeed invest in considerably.

"Ordinary Evening" will seek no recourse to such thematizations and furniture, directing our attention instead to the various "paths" and forms of "onwardness" (to reach back to Stanley Cavell's characterization of Emerson) that will constitute Stevens's most radical reconceptualization of what "dwelling," in a posthumanist sense, can mean. The question of suitable dwelling is raised, of course, in "Notes"— the "ennui of apartments"[7] and the "ephebe" at his "attic window" with a "rented piano"[8] early in the poem; the contrast between "my house" and the pretty landscapes of Franz Hals in canto VI, section I;[9] "The academies like structures in a mist" and the "castle-fortress-home" of MacCullough that immediately follow;[10] the remarkable canto on the planter and his environs;[11] even (in a different way) the figure of Ozymandias (with all of its Shelleyan echoes);[12] and the "angel in his cloud" late in the poem.[13] In this network of tropes, we find a growing (and increasingly textured) contrast to the picture of dwelling that we get from "Sunday Morning," beginning with its "complacencies," exoticisms, and ironic "green freedom," which, as the poem unfolds, needs to be haunted and spectralized (as the speaker suggests)—not just by the desire for paradise and transcendence inherited from religious tradition, but by the earth itself and its larger processes of which the spirit is but a part or vehicle. As I have already suggested, that contrast is resolved a little too easily in the closing lines of "Sunday Morning," but it is, happily (if that's the word), intensified in "Auroras" and "Ordinary Evening." Moreover, as noted in the previous chapter, part of the reason that many readers have felt "The Auroras of Autumn" to be a more successful poem than "Credences of Summer" is that the latter seems too certain, in a sense, of its own success and sufficiency, while the former calibrates more precisely the bare fact of the mind and what it contributes, locating the relationship between imagination and reality in a much more subtle and precise way, and thus achieving a kind of minimalism (in spite of its thematic theatrics) that "An Ordinary Evening in New Haven" will sustain on the level of its poetic procedure.

It's all the more important to illuminate the crucial differences in poetics in these, Stevens's greatest achievements, because, after all, the *argument* of the poems, from "Notes" through "Credences" and "Auroras" and finally to "Ordinary Evening," is—in philosophical or propositional terms, you might say—essentially the same argument regarding the relationship between mind and reality. But what I draw out here is the shifting nature of Stevens's poetics, *and why that shift is philosophically significant*, opening up the difference between poetry and philosophy and, more specifically, drawing our attention to how poetry can performatively handle problems of thinking the ecological and environmental that the propositional and logical procedures of philosophy can't achieve. Stevens's later long poems may be seen as an exploration—and an increasingly daring and sophisticated one, if I'm right—of this challenge to undertake a philosophically significant poetics after the end of the era of the "universal orb," and after (in Cavell's reading of Emerson) the end of philosophy itself as a foundational and totalizing enterprise.

We are ready, at this juncture, to move to a closer examination of "The Auroras of Autumn," because it reframes those questions of the relationship between mind and nature in terms of the problem of dwelling—quite explicitly in sections II–VI with its tropes of the cabin, the "one candle," the house "on flames," and the figures of the mother and father.[14] Sloterdijk's formulation early on in *Spheres* sets an especially apt framework for understanding the poem's trope of dwelling as an encounter with those "morpho-immunological constructs" where "humans continue their generational processes" in "the greenhouse of their autogenous atmosphere."[15] "Auroras" pivots on the transformative exposure of those immunological constructs to the force of the "outside" (as explored in the previous chapter), and the question for the poem then becomes what sort of posture the poet, and poetry, will adopt in the face of this challenge, one for which the resources to meet it—even the resources proposed by "Notes"—have been burned away. The poem begins this inquiry with its own relentless set of questions, where the figure of the aurora borealis is itself channeled through the topos of Plato and the cave, raising explicitly the questions of the relationship between medium and form and nature and mind, but all within the breaching (sometimes terrifying, sometimes exhilarating) of the "morpho-immunological" domain that had always ensured, in Sloterdijk's words, that "humans have never lived in a direct relationship with 'nature,' and their cultures have certainly never set foot in the realm of what we call the bare facts."[16] As "Auroras" begins, all of that has changed.

The egg and cave in the first section of the poem are, of course, "morpho-immunological" tropes, and they are elucidated in "Things of August," which follows "An Ordinary Evening in New Haven" in the *Collected Poems* and announces a premium on the radical outside (and the constructs that attempt to domesticate it) that will occupy the opening section of "Auroras." Invoking "the egg of the sea" and "the egg of the sky," "Things of August" tells us that "the egg of the earth lies deep within an egg," and implores us to "Crack the round dome. Break through," seizing a "liberty not as the air within a grave."[17] "Auroras," for its part, sets egg and cave going, too, in the first section, and the cracking of "the egg of the earth" that "lies deep within an egg" is what is at stake in the invocation of the aurora borealis itself, as the trope of dwelling (egg, cave) and the trope of fire are conjoined in a way that will occupy the rest of the poem.

As John Durham Peters notes in *The Marvelous Clouds*, fire has traditionally been regarded as central to the "arts and techniques" that allow human beings to dwell on the earth.[18] (As we will see, Peters's suggestion that we read technics and pyrotechnics, following the work of Bernard Stiegler, as a trope for the *techne* of *poiesis* is very much to the point of getting at the core concerns of "Auroras.") And when we add to this Peters's extrapolation of what Stephen J. Pyne calls "vestal fire," we can bring the distinctly Emersonian flavor of Stevens's ecopoetics in "Auroras" into sharper focus. As Peters notes, for Pyne, vestal fire is "Europe's key contribution to the history of fire practices." It "encompasses burning by human artifice" and "the hearth, one of the first container technologies, is its natural home."[19] Here, we find a kind of privileged medium for the concept of the *oikos* (of economy, of ecology) in relation to the question of dwelling: the hearth, the home, the dwelling, the father, the proper name, the law, and property, all bound together under one roof, as it were. But my point here is double. It's not just understanding, with Peters and with Pyne, "the all but universal victory

the radical outside

of vestal fire as a tragic metaphor for human blindness about nature's feedback loops and our rebellion against the renewing fertility of death and change."[20] It's also to underscore how the telescoping contrast between the two types of fire in "Auroras"—the borealis, on the one hand, and the hearth at the center of the "cabin" of "ancestral theme" in section II, on the other—takes on a distinctly Emersonian cast in figuring the vestal fire of the hearth and dwelling as cultural legacy in the form of a European mastery and domestication of fire, itself put under challenge by the exterior fire of the auroras, that *most* outside "outside," both exhilarating and terrifying in its serpentine unboundedness, much like Emerson's confrontation with "this new yet unapproachable America I have found in the West."[21]

We can thus hear the Emersonian undertones of Stevens's memorable pronouncement in section VI: "The scholar of one candle sees / An Arctic effulgence flaring on the frame / Of everything he is. And he feels afraid."[22] Given our discussion of fire as *techne*, we would do well to hear the word "frame" here precisely in the terms Heidegger uses in "The Question Concerning Technology" to describe technology as *gestell*, as "enframing."[23] And we would do well, too, to imagine the "one candle" here as a kind of hypercondensation of the vestal fire that lights Emerson's study by candlelight in the opening pages of *Nature*, when he says to the reader (sustaining his critique of "the sepulchres of the fathers," of "biographies, histories, and criticism," in the first two sentences of the essay) that "I am not solitary whilst I read and write, though nobody is with me." To which he responds, "But if a man would be alone, let him look at the stars"—or, in the case at hand, at the aurora borealis.[24] And now we can hear the full Emersonian resonance of Stevens's announcement in section III that "The house will crumble and the books will burn."[25]

This suggests that the primary ecopoetic work of the poem is not just to subject cultural legacy and vestal fire to the decreating and renovating force of the fire-from-outside figured as the auroras, but to ramify *how* that changes the thinking of dwelling, and how to bring that thinking into poetry. Here, it is useful to recall one of the most remarkable passages in all of Stevens's prose, from the important essay "Two or Three Ideas," where he writes of the transformation of "the classic repertory of poetic ideas,"

It is as if we had stepped into a ruin and were startled by a flight of birds that rose as we entered. The familiar experience is made unfamiliar and from that time on, whenever we think of that particular scene, we remember how we held our breath and how the hungry doves of another world rose out of nothingness and whistled away. We stand looking at a remembered habitation. All old dwelling-places are subject to these transmogrifications and the experience of all of us includes a succession of old dwelling-places: abodes of the imagination, ancestral or memories of places that never existed.[26]

"Where do we go from here?" is the question that then concerns Stevens, and his answer in the "Auroras" is to *liberate* fire or flame (distilled, as it were, from the borealis) as *techne* from the home, the hearth, and that which secures the immunological space of cultural legacy, and put it to work as a force for the temporizing activity of the poem, emphasizing not the products of the imagination (the cabin, the home, "the classic repertory of poetic ideas") but the *factum* of its process, where "the north is always enlarging the change" with its "gusts of great enkindlings."[27] Indeed, as Peters notes—in an observation that is illuminating for the crucial final line of "Auroras"—"like time, burning runs in only one thermodynamic direction," and fire, therefore, mocks any hope or fantasy of permanence that we might have for our species, or its artifacts.[28]

In this light, we are able to see how Stevens's "farewell to an idea" is met not with an embrace of the ongoing, cyclical natural process (such as we found in "Sunday Morning") of the auroras, but rather with an assertion that fire, if it is to be ours, has to be coupled to our finitude in the services of what Cavell, in his reading of Emerson's "Experience," calls "lasting," not in the sense of enduring like a house or stone hearth, but rather as moving on, taking steps (as in the "last" of a shoe): the transvaluation of "grounding as lasting," as he puts it, that has much in common with both Heidegger's notion of being "on the way" and Derrida's idea of "*sur-vivance*" (a bundle of terms I will take up in more detail later).[29] This is why section IV of "Auroras" ends in precisely the same way as sections II and III, with the emphasis on sand, wind, and "invincible sound."[30] And it is also why an art that simply affirms primal instinct or vitality is rejected in section V as an answer to the problem the poem sets itself, because the point, as we learn in the remarkable eighth section, is to "partake" of this "innocence of the earth," which is neither a "spell" nor a "saying."[31] What is read to the congregation in the poem's last section—which is very much about the poet helping people "to live their lives" (to remember Stevens's contention about the role of the poet in "The Noble Rider and the Sound of Words")[32]—is not just a "contrivance" but a contrivance contriving to contrive, as Stevens himself says (again, the focus is all on the activity, the performative). And what is contrived, what is "vital," is a "whole" whose purpose is not to reinstate a "hushful paradise" in "hall harridan" (there's dwelling as home again—finally rejected, again), but rather to open onto "a haggling of wind and weather, by these lights / Like a blaze of straw in winter's nick": a trope for the dynamic, onward, and fleeting fact of time if ever there was one (and in this context we have to hear the echoes—and I think we have to hear them all—of "nick" as "nick of time," and as slang for both a prison and the act of theft, as if stealing time from eternity).

But for all that, "Auroras" remains partially within a globological topography, the canonical vault of the night sky its setting, even as it begins to move in the more minimalist and discursively dismantling direction of "Ordinary Evening." It certainly shifts decisively away from the "major" and "central" theatrics of "Notes" and its globological project of "Supreme Fiction," with the abiding emphasis in "Auroras" (counterposed against the pageant of the poem's section V) on "slight caprice,"[33] "a thing of ether" met by a "flippant communication,"[34] on the "simplest word / Almost as part of innocence,"[35] and the work of the "never-failing genius" who, through the *techne* of the poem, converts the fire of the auroras to the fire of the imagination, but only by adding, in a sense, as little as possible—and certainly not by building another house or cabin (or "Supreme Fiction"). The question in Stevens is never one of escaping dwelling altogether. (What else, after all, is a poem but a dwelling, an enclosure—whether in Heidegger's classic formulation in late essays such as "Poetically Man Dwells," or in Luhmann's assertion that the poem begins with an absolutely contingent mark and by recursive self-reference builds up its own unique, unparaphrasable "internal necessity," so that it may be distinguished from all the other objects, and "quasi-objects," in the world.)[36] The challenge that Stevens sets himself is rather to poetically body forth a mode of dwelling predicated upon rejecting the idea of a final resting place, rejecting the idea that a dwelling would or could ever exhaustively describe or capture (or, in Heidegger's case, settle into) the larger environment in which it exists. And in that temporization of dwelling, the world is not so much transformed as revealed and illuminated.

This is precisely the challenge first broached in a major way in "Sunday Morning," which begins not just in a literal dwelling but with "The complacencies of the peignoir," which "mingle to dissipate" the pressure of a different kind of dwelling insisted on by the speaker: namely, the question of the relationship between earthly life, earthly existence, and the desire for "paradise" and divinity once the sacrificial symbolic logic of the Judeo-Christian answer to the question is no longer available after the "death of the gods." In Stevens's corpus, "The complacencies of the peignoir" turn out to be an insufficient response to the spherological challenge voiced by the poem, what Sloterdijk characterizes as the "rise of the external, the foreign, the fortuitous and those forces that threaten to burst the sphere," which is met by a reincorporation and redomestication of the environment's unruly multiplicity and specificity. "In this sense," he writes, "order is above all the effect of a transference from interior to exterior . . . Hegel's great synthesis is the last European monument to this will to draw all negativity and externality into the inside of a logically sealed dome."[37] In Stevens's poetry, sometimes this process is explored in terms of historical inheritance and cultural legacy—not just the death of the gods of "Sunday Morning" and elsewhere, but also just the "images" of "The Man on the Dump," "the rotted names" of "The Man with the Blue Guitar," and the houses and cabins of "Auroras"— but more often it is figured in the letter of the poetry as Stevens's refusal (not yet fully embraced at the end of "Sunday Morning") of the dialectical synthesis Hegel made possible.[38]

To make it clearer that this relationship between "foreign outside" and "expanded inside" *is* ecological, we should remember, as Michael Marder has noted, that in ecology, the hallmarks of metaphysics ("presence, assemblage, gathering into one") "are combined with the dwelling, the *oikos* belonging to the family and standing for property, the proper, *domus*, one's own domain,"[39] the "law that, in distinguishing it from the non-dwelling or from another dwelling, brings it into being. The 'yes' of the inside is the result of the 'no' directed to the outside."[40] In "The Auroras of Autumn," we see Stevens trying to deftly navigate "the admittedly porous boundaries between the house and the outside world (the fire of the hearth and cosmic fire)."[41] But in "An Ordinary Evening in New Haven," the focus shifts, it seems to me, to a different problem emphasized by Derrida's reading of the *oikos*: that "a fixed address where one dwells," as Marder puts it, "signifies no more and no less than a tomb," because its logic is the logic of the permanence and privation of property and propriety, which dictates "a death-like stability through an incessant rotation in a circle, coming back home over and over again"—a logic and trope that Derrida excavates on a grand scale in the second set of seminars on *The Beast and the Sovereign*.[42]

Here, I think, we find a useful framework for seeing how "An Ordinary Evening in New Haven," which Eleanor Cook calls Stevens's "evening-walking poem,"[43] is ecological in its *refusal* of "coming back home over and over again"—by descending to the street and "coming back and coming back" not to permanence but to transience and temporary dwelling, "to the hotel instead of the hymns."[44] But the ecological here extends beyond just the thematic level of the poem to what I called in earlier chapters its "topological" rather than "topographical" ecopoetics, with its ceaseless foregrounding of its own performativity, the relentless turning inside out of the world for which the term "reality" (as Harold Bloom has already noted) is actually a bit of an occlusion. (That term certainly will not help us make any headway on "the question that is a giant of himself: / Of what is this house composed if not of the sun." And then the poem immediately answers that "These houses, these difficult objects, dilapidate / Appearances" are "Dark things without a double, after all, / Unless a second giant kills the first— / A recent imagining of reality.")[45] As Cook notes, Stevens's "recent imagining of reality" will, in this poem, take the form of "a walk with various sounds and sights (such as seeing the evening star and hearing the rain), time in a hotel room, memories of the day, retiring to bed, thoughts of other cities compared with New Haven," and so on.[46] As is the norm in Stevens, the poem moves back and forth between exploring the priority of the imagination and the priority of reality—and the assertion of the differential relationship between the two whose name is "desire," as in canto III, where Stevens writes that "The point of vision and desire are the same. / It is to the hero of midnight that we pray / On a hill of stones to make beau mont thereof."[47]

Here, Emersonian "poverty" ("I am and I have, but I do not get") is transvalued into the engine of change and onwardness, the exit out of a dwelling that threatens otherwise to become a site of circular repetition and propriety: "But this cannot / Possess. It is desire, set deep in the eye, / Behind all actual seeing, in the actual scene."[48] But my larger point is that this dynamic of finitude and onwardness takes place in an ecology that is figured not just in terms of the ordinary, the plain, and the everyday, but more profoundly in terms of the difference between the topographical and the topological, discussed earlier, as in the important canto VI, where the Alpha and Omega of the book of Revelations are folded back upon themselves to form the fold or strange loop we saw in Serres's example of a baker's folding and kneading a ball of dough. "Reality is the beginning, not the end, / Naked Alpha," Stevens writes in the canto's opening lines. "It is the infant A standing on infant legs, / Not twisted, stooping, polymathic Z, / He that kneels always on the edge of space."[49]

Here, A and Z graphically figure not just the difference between "a baby's legs when it is learning to walk" and the "twisting, stooping" man of age,[50] as Cook notes, but also the topological folding and twisting of the "becoming space of time" (to use Derrda's phrase) that subtends the thematization we find here in terms of human generations—and it is in this dimension of time that old age finds, as Stevens finds in this poem, its zest and vitality. We explored in chapter 3 the underpinnings of this dynamic in theoretical biology, where the "unentailed" evolution of life creates the forms and frames that can only retroactively describe (as Stuart Kauffman argues) the conditions of its own emergence. But there is also, remarkably enough, a version of Stevens's argument in canto VI in Cavell's analysis of Emerson's "Experience," where he reads Emerson's complex relationship to the death of his son, Waldo, as a figure for the reversing or folding of the relationship between "founding" (as in philosophy as a "foundational" practice) and "finding" (as in leaving behind the grief that he feels for the death of his son, which Cavell reads as a trope for grief over the loss of the world under the truth of skepticism).[51] Waldo the child, like Stevens's "infant A," thus becomes the "founder" of Emerson's new philosophical practice of "onwardness" and "abandonment"; and as if this weren't enough, Cavell also reminds us that in the epigraph to the essay, Waldo's avatar, the "Little man, least of all," who is called "the founder thou," walks among "the lords of life," "among the legs of his guardians tall."[52]

But equally significant here is that Emerson writes about his grief over the death of his son (which is, if we believe Cavell, a grief about the loss of what Stevens will, in "Ordinary Evening," call "reality" and "the real") that "I cannot get it nearer to me."[53] This statement, Cavell suggests, opens onto the rather considerable Heideggerian resonances of the term "near" that we will explore in greater detail later,[54] but in the context I am developing here, I connect that topological folding and twisting of "nearness" with Stevens's assertion that "twisted" and "polymathic Z" "kneels always on the edge of space, / In the pallid perceptions of its distances."[55] This "edge of space" is the same edge of space, I suggest, that we have already analyzed in "Of Mere Being," where "The palm stands on the edge of space";[56] and what transforms topographically given, Cartesian space into the topological is precisely the contingency and finitude that we have explored in several different registers in earlier chapters: in the unentailed "creative" evolution of the biosphere; in the nonlinear, real-time complexities of the relations between the genetic and the epigenetic; and in the contingency of the "embodied enaction" of autopoiesis that creates human and nonhuman "worlds" (Uexküll's *umwelten*)—all of which the circularity of dwelling as *oikos*, that "coming home over and over again," attempts to guard against in immunitary protection. That immunitary space will be abandoned in "Ordinary Evening," not in a grand effort to transcend contingency and finitude, but rather to embrace them as the very engine of a poetic onwardness. Or, as Stevens puts it two cantos later, "We fling ourselves, constantly longing, on this form. / We descend to the street and inhale a health of air."[57]

The deathlike circle of the *oikos* understood as home, law, property and the proper—and the attempt to find an exit or a "path" out of it (to combine the terms of Heidegger, Cavell, and Derrida)—has considerable resonance for the biographical facts of Stevens's own "fixed address" and domestic life, of course. It provides a bridge to the otherwise strangely disconnected side of the Stevens dossier (disconnected from his lyricism, I mean) that we find in essays such as "Insurance and Social Change." But the connection makes a little more sense when we recall Sloterdijk's contention that modernity is "characterized by the technical production of its immunities and the increasing removal of its safety structures from the traditional theological and cosmological narratives," of the sort we find in "Sunday Morning" and even, in a different sense, in "Notes Toward a Supreme Fiction." What we find in industrial civilizations and the welfare state, Sloterdijk writes, is an "aim, in a shelless time, for an imitation of the now impossible, imaginary spheric security."[58] And in this light, "the early insurance system was one of the harbingers of systemic modernity, assuming one defines modernization as a progressive replacement of vague symbolic immune structures classifiable as final religious interpretations of human living risks with exact social and technical security services."[59]

The terms here are strikingly similar to Stevens's essay "Insurance and Social Change," where the problem of the *oikos* is engaged in not just economic but also social terms. Stevens opens the essay by asserting that "if each of us could put his hand on money whenever money was necessary: to repair any damage, to meet any emergency, we should all be willing to stop as far as money goes."[60] "The objective for all of us," he continues a few sentences later, "is to live in a world in which nothing unpleasant can happen. Our prime instinct"—and here the connections with Derrida on the *oikos* of dwelling, the economic, and the deathlike circle of life and repetition are clear—"is to go on indefinitely like the wax flowers on the mantelpiece. Insurance is the most easily understood geometry for calculating how to bring the thing about."[61] Such a world, however, is evacuated of its singularities and particulars, of the domain of the "ordinary" as Stevens will develop it in "An Ordinary Evening in New Haven." And we know, of course, that Stevens is no poet of "wax flowers," as poems such as "Study of Two Pears" remind us. Stevens continues:

> Compare the man who, as an individual, insures his dwelling against fire with that personality . . . who, at a stroke, insures all dwellings against fire; and who, without stopping to think about it, insures not only the lives of all those that live in the dwellings, but insures all people against all happenings of everyday life, even the worm in the apple or the piano out of tune . . . There is no difference between the worm in the apple and the tack in the can of sardines, and not the slightest difference between the piano out of tune and a person disabled.[62]

This is not just a world in which the ordinary is robbed of its texture and quality in the name of an immunized security; it is also a world evacuated of the singularity of what Derrida calls the "event." Indeed, as Sloterdijk notes, where "insurance-oriented thought has established itself . . . one witnesses the change of mentality that characterizes postmodern boredom societies: uninsured situations become rare and disturbances can be relished as an exception: the 'event' is positivized, and the demand for experiences of difference floods the market."[63] In "Insurance and Social Change," as in Derrida's discussion of *oikos*, the primary contrast is between an environment fraught with contingency and change, everywhere reminding us of our finitude and vulnerability, and an immunitary logic that describes the form of a circle. Indeed, as Derrida asserts (projecting forward, as it were, to Sloterdijk's architecture), "sovereignty is a circularity, indeed a sphericity."[64] As for Stevens's part, he writes,

> We should be able, by the payment of a trivial premium, to protect ourselves, our families and our property against everything. The procedure would necessarily be simple: Probably the dropping of a penny each morning in a box at the corner nearest one's place of residence on the way to one's place of employment. Each of us would have a personal or peculiar penny. What is the difference between a personal penny and a social security number? The circle just stated: income, insurance, the thing that happens and income again, would widen and soon become income, insurance, the thing that fails to happen and income again. In

other words, not only would all our losses be made good, but all our wishes would come true.[65]

What Stevens maps in the essay, in that strange and sometimes angular prose style of his, is a kind of dialectical relationship between the immunitary "wax flower" world, in which nothing bad can ever happen, and the world of the ordinary and everyday, where events (in Derrida's sense) from the outside, from the environment, can and do happen. As Stevens notes, discussing H. G. Wells, "it helps us to see the actual world to visualize a fantastic world," and when Wells "passes from the international to the interstellar, we hug the purely local."[66] The world needs poetry, in other words, not to provide the transcendence that previously resided "in God's hands alone," as Sloterdijk puts it, but rather, as Stevens writes in "Ordinary Evening," to enable us to come back again and again to "the real" and find it once more alive with change: "A view of New Haven, say, through the certain eye," "simple seeing, without reflection."[67] This domain of what "Ordinary Evening" calls "pure reality, untouched / By trope or deviation," "not merely the visible, / The solid, but the movable, the moment,"[68] may be viewed as an ecological dimension that is heterogeneous to the *oikos* not in the sense of a sealed-off (and, as it were, older and purer) zone of its own ("Nature"), but rather as a mode of individuation and elaboration, "the movable, the moment." As Marder characterizes the opposition between *oikos* and ecology, the latter "is not a collection of excluded leftovers, sacralized as the disavowed origins of the system that has spat them out, but a positive elaboration of the dwelling, respectful of the singularity and inner articulation" of its elements. And in this sense, "ecology is not a domain because the mode of dwelling it underwrites is not dominion, predicated on appropriation."[69] This "dwelling undecidably" is thus not a rejection of one sovereign domain (*oikos*) in favor of the fullness and positivity of another ("Nature"); rather (and this has considerable resonance for thinking together Stevens's insurance and Stevens's lyricism), it is "a shuttling between economy and ecology, interiority and exteriority, the circle and the line tending to infinity."[70] This is yet another way of clarifying the difference between what I have been calling a second-order (or topological) rather than first-order (or topographical) concept of ecology; here, holism, and "the gathering into presence" of an older concept of ecology ("Nature"), is unavoidably punctured and dispersed by the paradoxes attendant upon the radical finitude and embodied contingency that subtends observation—without redemption, without transcendence, and (as Marder notes) without the sacralizing logic of sacrifice.

Precisely this—and only this—keeps the "non-idealizable leftovers" of the *oikos* from taking on the status of an "as such": keeps us from turning "ecology" in the sense I have been developing here back into "Nature." And this allows us to deepen our understanding of the implications of this fact for art in a way consonant with Luhmann's nonrepresentationalist contention that "art can no longer be understood as an imitation of something that presumably exists along with and outside of art . . . To the extent that imitation is still possible, it now imitates the world's invisibility, a nature that can no longer be apprehended as a whole."[71] Or, as Derrida writes in his deconstruction of Kant on the role of the aesthetic in relation to nature, nature "folds itself, returns to itself, reflects itself through art. This specular flexion provides . . . the secret resource of *mimesis*—understood not, in the first place, as an imitation of nature by art, but as a flexion of the *physis*, nature's relation to itself."[72] As Marder notes, this "flexion" is "ecological" in the sense that we saw Stevens connoting above in "the movable, the moment"; it involves an individuating detour through heteronomy, a "return of nature to itself through us, humans, as well as through other living beings who inhabit the planet-wide house of this extremely extended family" (and here, of course, we should recall our discussion of nonhuman "worlds" in chapter 3).[73]

I have gone on at length about this matter of *oikos* and dwelling in Derrida not only because it enables us to see the stakes involved in holding onto the contingency of the self-reference and autopoiesis of human and nonhuman worlds that return "nature" to itself, but with a difference, turning it into "ecology" and "environment," but also because it enables us to make sense of the sustained commitment, in "Ordinary Evening" and also in "The Auroras of Autumn," to seeing art as the expression of an ecology that is precisely *not* "Nature" in the traditional sense, a desire in Stevens—and it never goes away—distilled in the announcement in "The Planet on the Table" that the poems "should bear / Some lineament or character" of "the planet of which they were a part."[74] We might say in this light that the "hotels" of "Ordinary Evening" are to the (insured) home and hearth as Sloterdijk's "foams" are to his "globes": the hotel room as a home, an *oikos*, that is always already divided against itself, displaced and temporary, already under abandonment.

The fact that this *is* an ecological undertaking is indexed by the "Ordinary" of the poem's title, which directs us away from anything "supreme" ("fiction" included). Writing of the recovery of a "premetaphysical pluralism"[75] by postmetaphysical means that animates the *Foams* project, Sloterdijk captures something of what Bloom calls the "clairvoyance"[76] of Stevens's later poetics when he muses in the "Prologue": "Almost nothing, yet not nothing. A something, if only a delicate web of cavities and subtle walls . . . [U]nder as yet unclarified circumstances, that which is dense, continuous, and massive is subject to an invasion by the hollow," that which "makes space on its own strength for strange places where previously there were none. What, then, would a first definition of foam have to be? Air in unexpected places?"[77] How apt a gloss this is for the many extraordinary moments we find in "Ordinary Evening," such as the suggestion that "The mobile and the immobile flickering / In the area between is and was are leaves,"[78] or the remarkable last stanza of section XVI, with its "exhalations in the eaves, so little / To indicate the total leaflessness,"[79] or the somewhat more programmatic "inchings of final form, / The swarming activities of the formulae / Of statement" of the poem's final section.[80]

Underneath it all, the poem forces us to begin by noting that if its procedure is one of dwelling-as-onwardness, then it is driven (to use the poem's own privileged term) by "desire." This is the desire beautifully articulated in section III, and it is the driver toward the "way" and the path in section VI that sets out from "reality," which is "the beginning not the end," Alpha and Omega linked in their ongoing process, but also the "spirit" in section X that is not "imprisoned" but "resides / in a permanence composed of impermanence"[81]—a reprise of the last line of "Auroras": dwelling here as *not* dwelling, a "residing" that is transitory, liberated from its own "nick," as it were.[82]

Stevens suggests, powerfully and poignantly, that that desire, that spirit, is born of finitude, the "crude collops," "bosom, beard, and being" put forward at the end of section I, rooting the extraordinary itinerary of the poem in a different kind of "ordinary" and "everyday": age, the bioenergetic life of the body, with "life" here (as Bloom notes in his pushback against Vendler)[83] being the accented term, "alive with age," as Stevens writes.[84] "Collop" denotes a slice of meat (and more specifically, sometimes, bacon), but also a traditional dish made of bacon and eggs typically served on what is called "Collop Monday," the day before Shrove Tuesday (thus doing a number, as they say, on the project of "Sunday Morning"), and also, and finally, to "a thick fold of flesh on the body as evidence of a well-fed condition."[85] The poem will then take this emphasis on age and finitude, and explicitly reframe it in terms of the question of generation and of dwelling via the by now familiar trope of the house: "These houses, these difficult objects, dilapidate."[86] And Stevens begins by unfolding the trope in section II of "Ordinary Evening" (as he had done in sections II and III of "Auroras") by musing, "Suppose these houses are composed of ourselves," itself a sort of answer to the question posed in the poem's second stanza, "Of what is this house composed if not of the sun."[87]

Immediately, then, the poem answers the question of whether the house is of nature or the self by its emphasis on age and finitude, through which nature returns to itself through us, as we noted of the "eco-" of "ecology" earlier, that slightest difference and detour through heteronomy that also makes all the difference in the world. And it thus moves to a solution, a suitable dwelling, *within* finitude, "beard and being," a particular (and sometimes particularly poignant) dimension of the "ordinary." The relationship between dwelling and finitude here could not be more different from what we find at the opening of "Sunday Morning." There, dwelling sets itself against the trauma of finitude—made all the more traumatic by the passing of traditional religion (in this case, Judeo-Christian)—and that trauma is solved, as it were, by the poem's recourse to "a naturalistic religion as a substitute for supernaturalism,"[88] wherein the finitude of the self is not so finite after all, becoming, as the poem unfolds, an epiphenomenon of the larger processes of nature ("Passions of rain, or moods in falling snow").[89]

It is worth emphasizing that this is how "An Ordinary Evening in New Haven"—audaciously and with the full force of poetic accomplishment and confidence—sets us on the path and way (as section VI puts it) of its remarkable itinerary. We can further amplify this by way of Derrida's extraordinary engagement of Heidegger's suggestion that *Dasein* involves a "nostalgia" for the world "in its totality," a desire that makes us always already on "the path under way, toward and in the whole that is the world," in which our human finitude consists of this "movement without repose" toward the "*Da-*" or "over *there*" of *Dasein*.[90] But it is a finitude "that is, if you will, both complicated and very simple." He continues, in what ends up being a footnote to the session:

> if there were no finitude, we would be simply "pushed" or simply "held back." If the movement were infinite, if we were infinite beings, well, the push would be endless, disturbed by nothing, or else being at rest would be disturbed by nothing. But given that we are finite, the drive is finite, and thus stopped: we are pushed up to a point, and thus held

back. The fact of being both pushed and held back is finitude. Infinite God either has an infinite push or is infinitely at rest; he cannot be both in movement and at rest. The finite being is this: neither . . . nor.[91]

We find this "neither . . . nor" all over the place in "Ordinary Evening"; indeed, it might be seen as the hallmark of Stevens's late mode, a poetry of what J. Hillis Miller, in an essay that I touched upon in chapter 1, calls "flickering mobility."[92] "No sooner has the mind created a new fictive world than this 'recent imagining of reality' becomes obsolete in its turn and must be rejected . . . There is one way to escape this impasse," Miller continues, "and the discovery of this way gives its special character to all Stevens' late poetry." It is an "oscillation" between "reality" and "imagination" that is "rapid enough" that it "becomes a blur in which opposites touch simultaneously, as alternating current produces a steady beam of light."[93]

This "oscillating" movement generates the recursions, temporizations, heapings, and partitionings of "Ordinary Evening," the "and yet, and yet, and yet"[94] that opens the poem by "introducing air in unexpected places" (to borrow Sloterdijk's felicitous phrase), leading us through the "Impalpable habitations" with which we are already familiar from "Auroras," the better to "descend to the street and inhale a health of air," where "Our breath is like a desperate element / That we must calm,"[95] and where "the profoundest forms / Go with the walker subtly walking there," "Free from majesty and yet in need / Of majesty," "A minimum of making in the mind" brought forth in "This endlessly elaborating poem" in "the intricate evasions of as, / In things seen and unseen, created from nothingness,"[96] and leading us finally to the pronouncement, which is also of course an *anti*-pronouncement, that ends the poem: "These are the edgings and inchings of final form."[97] And then, the poem's beguiling, minimalist, yet magnificent ending: "It is not in the premise that reality / Is a solid. It may be a shade that traverses / A dust, a force that traverses a shade."[98]

It is worth remembering, in light of Miller's "flickering mobility," that "Ordinary Evening" begins and ends with an accent on this transitive, performative element, which it sees no need to rescue or codify by means of the dicta we find in "Notes" regarding the "Supreme Fiction." In literary historical terms, the poem opens, as Bloom notes, with the inherited Emerson topos of vision reaching back to the "transparent eye-ball" of *Nature*: "The eye's plain version is a thing apart, / The vulgate of experience."[99] And as he also notes (in what is still the best engagement of the poem), that the first paragraph of Emerson's "Circles" would make a suitable epigraph for the poem: "The eye is the first circle; the horizon which it forms is the second; and throughout nature this primary figure is repeated without end . . . Our life is an apprenticeship to the truth that around every circle another can be drawn."[100] "Emerson's nature," Bloom continues, "is, as we will see, Stevens' 'reality,' and the fitting together on an ordinary evening in an ordinary city of the different degrees of reality will expose a volatile interplay of ocular circles."[101] This ocular circling of "Ordinary Evening" is not a globe-building project—even one that points to its own fictitious nature, to the fact that the globe *is* a globe, as in "Notes"—and it is in part this minimalism of "Ordinary Evening," embodied for many critics in Stevens's memorable phrase "so little / To indicate the total leaflessness," that marks the austere greatness of the poem.[102] I agree with Bloom's assessment (differing with Vendler's) that the poem is "threatened not by its own starvation but by its own copiousness, its abundance of invention that varies the one theme, which is the problematic Stevensian image that he unhelpfully always called 'reality.'"[103] And I agree with him, too, that Stevens's term "reality" "takes away more meaning that it tends to give."[104] More useful for Stevens's project is what Bloom detects in the poem's title: that "ordinary" "seems to mean 'true' or at least 'not false,' but true in the root sense of 'ordinary, *ar* or 'fitted together'"—an assertion of the poem as a performative *factum*, an *act* or process, a nonrepeating melodic line of modular assemblage and iteration.

This "fitting together" achieves what Cavell calls "the extraordinary of the ordinary" (a point I'll come back to later);[105] and equally resonant for my exploration of the relationship between the ecological, the ordinary, and the everyday is Bloom's observation that in the poem, "New Haven is simply any city that is not home, a city that unsettles the self just enough so that it is startled into meditation, but close enough to home so that the meditation keeps contact always with the commonplace"[106]—a shrewd and sensitive understanding, I think, of precisely how the poem calibrates itself, and one that will allow us to see how the minimalist procedure of "Ordinary Evening" (minimalist for Stevens, I mean) reaches forward to the handling of the ordinary and the everyday that we find in contemporary artists such as Thomas Demand and Jeff Wall as it gets glossed by Michael Fried. "Ordinary Evening" takes up what we might, following Fried and Cavell (and more distantly Wittgenstein), call the achievement or "prize" of the ordinary,[107] the "sublime in the everyday" (as Cavell puts it)—an achievement that Cavell associates with the photographic image, and from which we are blinded (or at least distracted) by the metapoetic scaffolding of "Notes" and the sheer natural spectacle of "Auroras."[108]

To tease this out a bit more, I would pair Bloom's observation about unsettling the self "just enough" so that the ordinary is recovered through poetic meditation, with a passage from Perry Miller's work on Jonathan Edwards, quoted by Michael Fried in *Another Light*—a passage I will eventually want to interpret quite otherwise than Fried by routing it not just through Cavell's work on Emerson and Wittgenstein, but also through Derrida and Luhmann. Miller writes,

> Edwards's journals frequently explored and tested a meditation he seldom allowed to reach print: if all the world were annihilated, he wrote . . . and a new world were freshly created, though it were to exist in every particular in the same manner as this world, it would not be the same. Therefore, because there is continuity, which is time, "it is certain with me that the world exists anew every moment; that the existence of things every moment ceases and is at every moment renewed." The abiding assurance is that "we every moment see the same proof of God as we should have seen if we had seen Him create the world at first."[109]

This incandescent quotation serves for Fried as a sort of parable about the primacy of intention in art—in particular, the intentionality that sometimes, and even especially, makes itself manifest in artworks that seem to deliver us over to a world that uncannily seems to be the same shared world we live in, but with a slight difference or displacement on which everything hinges. Fried finds the epitome of such art in the later work of Thomas Demand, who is famous for making paper-and-cardboard re-creations of various (sometimes notorious) scenes and then photographing or, in some cases, filming them in stop-action animation, as in Demand's remarkable late work *Pacific Sun*.[110] The question that interests Fried, of course, is why: why would an artist do such a thing?

Fried argues—in what amounts to a continuation of the attack on what he calls minimalist "theatricality" in his seminal essay "Art and Objecthood" (which is sustained and updated in the book *Why Photography Matters as Art as Never Before*)[111]—that we find here in Demand's images "allegories of intention," as though "the very bizarreness of the fact that the places and objects in the photographs, despite their initial appearance of quotidian 'reality,' have all been constructed by the artist throws into relief the determining force—also the inscrutability, one might say the opacity—of the intentions behind them."[112] Fried then goes on to say of Demand (in an argument a bit too technical for my purposes here) that "this, by the way, is why it matters that the photographs are understood to be rigorously indexical, that is, devoid of digital manipulation," even as he is forced to acknowledge that in the work of both Demand and Jeff Wall, there is manipulation aplenty to achieve the image quality the artist wants[113]—enough, of course, to completely disrupt Fried's claim about indexicality. And what would thus be revealed by that disruption is not so much an apotheosis or allegory of intentionality as a kind of *fantasy* or spectralizing of intention and indexicality.

This is not a bad way to characterize "Ordinary Evening"—as an interrogation ("philosophical," if you like) of the fantasy of intentionality in the service of what is bigger game, larger quarry. The poem is not about the apotheosis of intention in relation to the world that makes itself manifest in the artwork, but rather about how intentionality is refracted, you might say, by the ordinary, opening up the difference (often in the poem a quite minimal difference, as in the final two lines) between the world that one intends or wills and the world that one actually encounters. Stevens's entire point in "Ordinary Evening," after all, is that *nothing* can ever be *exactly* what the artist intends it to be (hence Hillis Miller's earlier point about Stevens's "oscillation"), and that—in contrast—the desire for "pure reality, untouched / By trope or deviation" generates a poetic itinerary that is *all* "trope" and "deviation." The world is thus possessed of a strange kind of doubleness revealed by the work of art, as Fried notes, but it is a different kind of doubleness: what Stevens, in an enigmatic line indeed, calls an "enigmatical beauty" that "becomes amassed in a total double-thing."[114] That's precisely why, as Stevens says, we have to "keep coming back and coming back / To the real,"[115] to "the inchings of final form"[116] at one end of the poem and the "never-ending meditation" [117] at the other, with the "intricate evasions of as" in between.[118]

What we find instead in those minimalist moments of "Ordinary Evening," such as the wonderful ending of the poem—"a shade that traverses / A dust, a force that traverses a shade"—is what we might call, with Cavell, a "glancing" or "indirection" that indicates the angle of egress or path "left open in the writer's confession, 'I cannot get it nearer,'" which is "precisely the direction of reception" of the ordinary: not an "apotheosis" of intention but rather a kind of "notice" or "noticing," if you will, that is also a kind of achievement.[119] This perspective calls for a shift of critical frames *away* from the question of epistemology (as so many of Stevens's critics have both noticed and desired) and in a way that gives poetry a kind of leverage on philosophy as a mode of knowing. As we saw in an earlier chapter, Critchley is only the latest in this line of readers of Stevens, and he captures this shift of critical perspective (which is also a shift in our understanding of philosophy's task) when he notes that for Stevens, "the world does not first and foremost show itself as an 'object' contemplatively and disinterestedly represented by a 'subject.' Rather, the world shows itself as a place in which we are completely immersed and from which we do not radically distinguish ourselves."[120] This means that underneath our representations of the world, we find not more precise, more refined representations, but rather, as Charles Taylor puts it, "a certain grasp of the world that we have as agents in it. This shows the whole epistemological construal of knowledge to be mistaken."[121] And it also helps explain why it matters that Stevens's poetics is not a representationalist enterprise.

Sebastian Gardner—in what is still one of the best essays on Stevens that I have come across—gives us an even more detailed account of how this sense of the ordinary maps onto Stevens's poetic procedure, specifically Stevens's dialectical "oscillation" (to use Miller's term) between the world of decreation and re-creation, the world of winter and the world of summer (to circle back to the thematics of Stevens's "mundo" in my very first chapter), the "contracted" world and the "expanded" world. "The world contracts," Gardner writes, "when, and only when, a distinction between appearance and reality is introduced which makes independence from the mind the criterion for reality . . . by, for instance, aligning it with physical causal efficacy, or with the property of being such as to figure essentially in idealized scientific theory." But this means, of course (thinking back now to Bateson's "map" vs. "territory" distinction), that "the real contents and features of the world may be identified with those that are grounded in, and implied by, those of our social and epistemic practices, habits of representation, accepted forms of discourse and so on." The desire for "reality" and the "contracted world" ultimately doubles back, then, to an acknowledgment that reality has to be "recognized as plural, as not having any one correct description. At the limit, where anti-realism becomes relativistic," Gardner concludes, "it will be said that the concepts of truth and reality have no genuine application outside some particular version of the world. And at this point it may seem that one has arrived at a philosophical picture that maps neatly onto Stevens' valorization of imagination and fiction."[122]

And indeed, I would say, one has—*but only insofar as one remains within the epistemological frame* we saw displaced a moment ago by Taylor and Critchley.[123] The issue is not "relativism," and what is of interest to me instead is Gardner's modulation of the question of "reality" and the "ordinary" into the domain of the social. In other words, not only is the ordinary *not* an epistemological issue; it is also, at base, not a "personal" one, even though it fully entails, even embroils, the personal. Cavell himself shifts this question of the "ordinary" and the "everyday" in what we might call a more social, cultural (even, in a sense, political) direction, but I'd prefer to call it "pragmatist" or "pragmatic." As Cavell puts it in a suggestive passage that is resonant with both Fried's reading of Demand and Wall and Bloom's sense of "Ordinary Evening," "Wittgenstein's insight is that the ordinary has, and alone has, the power to move the ordinary, to leave the human habitat habitable, the same transfigured. The practice of the ordinary," he continues, thus eventuates in "the familiar invaded by another familiar."[124] One way—an ecological way—to get at this "familiar invaded by another familiar" is to understand that world as a *shared* world, a domain of a "mine" embedded in a larger domain of a "not-ours" that we saw Bloom earlier associate with the Emersonian reality of the "not me" (in "Nature") composed of "one's own body, other selves, the external world, and the anteriority of art."[125]

That domain thus unavoidably entails questions of inheritance and legacy of the sort we will see Stevens explicitly engage, in the trope of home and dwelling, and for Cavell, it thus also includes the American inheritance of, and transformation of, the European legacy in art and philosophy, so central to his reading of Emerson, but also to what he calls "scenes of instruction" of the sort that open Wittgenstein's *Philosophical Investigations*. Remarking on the "attention to childhood and its inheritance" in the *Investigations*, Cavell writes, "I take its pervasive theme of the inheritance of language, the question, the anxiety, whether one will convey sufficient instruction in order that the other can go on (alone), as an allegory of the inheritability of philosophy."[126] Wittgenstein, like Cavell's Emerson, dramatizes how this refusal of philosophy as a foundational or transcendental enterprise constitutes a kind of "poverty," and in Emerson that poverty often gets thematized as "an idea specifically of America's deprivations, its bleakness and distance from Europe's achievements," which in turn means that "part of the task of discovering philosophy in America is discovering the terms in which it is given to us to inherit the philosophy of Europe."[127] This is exactly the zone in which Stevens operates, it seems to me: he whose prose writings are so replete with references to European and classical culture and so starved of those drawn from American culture (with few exceptions), all of which inflects and culturally transcodes, if you will, what Bloom calls "the obsessiveness of Stevens' lifelong anxieties concerning the rival authorities of philosophy and poetry."[128]

Indeed, the names "America" and "Europe" might be thought of as a kind of thematization of what Richard Eldridge identifies as the doubleness of the ordinary, one that we find throughout Stevens's work, as in the remarkable short poem "Tea" at the very end of "Harmonium," with its "umbrellas in Java" rising to frame "the leaves on the path" that "ran like rats."[129] The more mature Stevens, in such fully realized poems as "No Possum, No Sop, No Taters," no longer needs such exotic thematizations (though he certainly retains a taste for them). In that later poem, "The leaves hop, scraping on the ground," eliciting not the "seashades and sky-shades" of "Tea" but a kind of severity or poverty, "The last purity of the knowledge of good."[130] This uncanny doubleness—in which things are things and also more than things, and "more" insofar as they are all the more simply, sparsely themselves—is explored on a broader canvas in "Ordinary Evening," about which Stevens famously wrote in his letters, "my interest is to try to get as close to the ordinary, the commonplace and the ugly as it is possible for a poet to get. It is not a question of grim reality but of plain reality."[131] As Eldridge notes of the domain of the ordinary, the philosophical commitment here is to a "refusal" of "(a false) ascent," against which Cavell poses philosophy as "*descent*, the necessary faithfulness of philosophy to the common and the ordinary, as the only available repertoires of language, thought, and action."[132] But it is also the case that the actual, the ordinary, and the everyday can be experienced—as it is for Emerson in some of his more famous moments ("Self-Reliance," for example), and as it is for Stevens in many, many places (in his poetry and in his letters)—as "a scene of illusion and trance and artificiality (of need.)"[133] And hence, philosophy as "ascent" is also necessary, so that what is pursued "is an eventual or transfigured ordinary," what Cavell sometimes characterizes as the "achievement" of the ordinary.

The movement or itinerary that we thus find here is what Cavell calls "aversive" (as in Emerson's assertion that "self-reliance is the aversion of conformity");[134] it is a turning away at one moment for the purposes of a turning toward and returning later, in all its ongoingness. And that is precisely why the aversive movement I am describing here is not the circular, "self-same" movement of the wheel as a figure for the sovereignty of the *oikos* that we touched on earlier in Derrida's later writing. In what amounts to a Cavellian rendering of Derrida's conjugation of the immunitary and the auto-immunitary, Eldridge notes that at times we find ourselves pursuing visions or courses of action that are not "generally shared, hence seeking abandonment of or departure from the common." But at other times, we find ourselves "recoiling from the solipsistic madness of apocalyptic vision and returning to the common, accepting it as cure," so that we are left in an oscillating movement (to use Hillis Miller's phrase once more) between an aversion to "what is common with others in oneself, as decayed, vulgarized, inhibiting, and empty," and a return to "what is common with others in oneself, as what alone enables thought, recovery, conversation, and restoration."[135]

As Eldridge puts it—in what I think is an apt characterization for the intensity of Stevens's poetic desire, particularly in "Ordinary Evening"—we are caught up in this "joint disappointment and satisfaction" because "there is within us 'the human drive to transcend itself, make itself inhuman'" (in Cavell's words); and that is why, "for beings who are freighted with such wishes and responsibilities, arising in and through engagement with the ordinary," the ordinary itself is, in a phrasing Cavell adapts from Heidegger, "at bottom . . . not ordinary; it is extra-ordinary, uncanny."[136] Or, as Stevens puts it in "Ordinary Evening," "A celestial mode is paramount, // If only in the branches sweeping in the rain: / The two romanzas, the distant and the near, / Are a single voice."[137]

It is crucial to remember here—and this will lead in a moment to my coda—that the ordinary is thus not, as Timothy Gould puts it, "a sort of definite locale or a situation," but rather "a direction that we have to learn how to take."[138] It is, as Stevens puts it, "a never-ending meditation" carried out through "the intricate evasions of as," with "as" here being understood primarily in the sense of a doing, a *factum*, a process: a "while-ing," you might say (think back to Bateson's brilliant insight about the "then" in logic vs. living systems, in chapter 1).[139] But we need to add to this a couple of further embellishments regarding the ordinary that will be important for understanding the *gravitas*, if you will, of "Ordinary Evening." First (and again, we should bear in mind Fried's interest in Wall and Demand), Cavell finds "the obsessions of photography" anticipated in Emerson's insistence in "The American Scholar" that his students know the "ultimate reasons" of "the meal in the firkin; the milk in the pan; the ballad in the street; the news of the boat; the glance of the eye; the form and gait of the body." And "without the mode of perception inspired in Emerson (and Thoreau) by the everyday, the near, the low, the familiar," he continues, "one is bound to be blind to the poetry of film, to the sublimity of it," which would also "insure deafness to some of the best poetry of philosophy—not its mythological flights, nor its beauty or purity of argumentation, but its power of exemplification."[140] This is, I think, a wonderful way to frame not just the relationship between poetry and philosophy that we find in Stevens, but also the difference between "Auroras" ("mythological flights") and the more rigorous "exemplifying" power of "Ordinary Evening" that we find in minimal yet prismatic moments such as this, where Stevens wonders, "If it should be true that reality exists / In the mind: the tin plate, the loaf of bread on it, / The long-bladed knife, the little to drink and her / Misericordia," where the example is in fact more powerful than the "philosophical" conditional that introduces it.[141]

Another way to frame the challenge here is to say that the ordinary (to stay with the Cavellian frame a moment more) is a kind of answer to the problem of philosophical skepticism, with which Stevens is every bit as obsessed as Cavell (hence Bloom's complaint about the persistent term "reality" in Stevens's corpus). As Cavell puts it, "the ordinariness in question speaks of an intimacy with existence, and of an intimacy lost, that matches skepticism's despair of the world."[142] And in that light, he continues, "epistemologists who think to refute skepticism by undertaking a defense of ordinary beliefs, perhaps suggesting that there is a sense in which they are certain, or sufficiently probable for human purposes, have already given into skepticism, they are living it."[143] One way not to "live it" is to insist on opening the space, as Stevens does, for understanding how poetry can address this problem in a way that philosophy cannot—which is, I am arguing, the project (or one of the projects) of "Ordinary Evening." Why poetry? Because, poetry can "present," not represent, what Cavell calls the "uncanniness" or "the extraordinary of the ordinary," generating "a perception of the weirdness, or surrealism, of what we call, accept, adapt to, as the usual, the real."[144] Poetry is thus better equipped to explore the fact that "the ordinary is subject at once to autopsy and to augury, facing at once its end and its anticipation."[145] And this leads us directly back, of course, to our earlier discussion of the question of "dwelling."

In this light—to move now toward a conclusion—I suggest that it is actually Emerson's "Experience" that is the ur-text for "Ordinary Evening," with its concern with skepticism and, more important, with the *posture* one takes toward it; these are matched by the obsession with "reality" in "Ordinary Evening" and the postures (walking, dwelling as moving, descending and ascending, kneeling "on the edge of space") that it generates: in sections VII through IX, for example, where "We fling ourselves, constantly longing, on this form, / We descend to the street."[146] These are the answers, as it were, given by "Ordinary Evening" to the opening question of "Experience" ("where do we find ourselves?") and its image of the vertiginous "stair" stretching in both directions, "out of sight," which in time will open onto the "path" unfolded in Derrida's reading of Heidegger: "in the end and the way / To the end" plumbed in the Alpha and Omega of "Ordinary Evening," section VI.[147]

Cavell captures the poetic *modus operandi* of "Ordinary Evening" quite well, I think, when he observes that when Emerson says in "Experience," "I cannot get it nearer to me," he is sounding an "inflection" of "his problematic of the common, the low, the familiar, the everyday." He continues, in a remarkably rich passage,

> In specifying his inability to get something nearer, *he is leaving a direction open. I* cannot get "it" nearer . . . ; if it is to become nearer, *it* must come nearer, draw closer. But what can this mean? . . . With respect to nature [Stevens's "reality"], having spoken of objects slipping through our clutching fingers as the unhandsome part of our condition, Emerson says this: "Nature does not like to be observed . . . Direct strokes she never gave us power to make; all our blows glance, all our hits are accidents. Our relations to each other are oblique and casual." Unpacking a little: glancing is a way observing, an oblique way, one in which you do not see a thing coming, cannot predict it (as empiricists would prefer); a casual way, meaning a way of casualty, of fateful accident, means that no glancing hit is in itself essential. Such a picture of getting to know makes it indirect, negates the direction in which philosophy takes knowledge to come, namely what Emerson calls manipular efforts . . . Indirection thus negates the active direction of knowing and names the direction in which an approach is awaited from the object.[148]

When "an approach is awaited from the object," when what is wanted is for *it* to "come nearer," what does one do? In "An Ordinary Evening in New Haven," the answer is: one *observes*—looking, but perhaps even more important, *listening*, in the "actual landscape with its actual horns," "as if to hear, / Hear hard, gets at an essential integrity."[149] The poet "sits in his room, beside / The window, close to the ramshackle spout in which / The rain falls with a ramshackle sound."[150] Here, the poet finds "a single world," "In which he is and as and is are one," "its counterpart a kind of counterpoint" heard in "the wet wallows of the water-spout."[151] Why listening? Because, as Cavell puts it elsewhere, the world reveals itself to us *unbidden* in sound; "what is heard comes *from* someplace, whereas what you can see you can look *at*."[152] But most of all, one *walks*, "in a permanence composed of impermanence,"[153] the "spirit's alchemicana" that "goes roundabout."[154] And, therefore, we set out: "In the metaphysical streets, the profoundest forms / Go with the walker subtly walking there."[155] And in that walking, one dwells by moving on.

Indirections, on the Way

ONE WAY TO ALLOW THE "INDIRECTION" and "glancing" with which I concluded the last chapter to create the conditions in which "it" can "come nearer," "draw closer," is to transform dwelling into walking, a place into a path, in and through which we allow ourselves to receive the world, in the Emersonian mode of reception (which is also a kind of gratitude, if we believe Stanley Cavell and Jacques Derrida's reading of the common root of "thinking" and "thanking" in Heidegger, the open hand its signature, versus the "prehensile" grasping of the world via philosophical concepts that Emerson tells us is "unhandsome"). This nexus of dwelling-as-walking provides a means to connect Stevens with both his most important precursor (Emerson) and his most important post-cursor (A. R. Ammons)—and to connect them, moreover, in terms of the theory of ecological poetics I have been developing here. It also allows us to connect all three with the understanding of "world" developed in these pages, not least of all through Cavell and Derrida's mutual interest in Heidegger's work, and specifically the Heidegger who is focused on the "path" and the "way" (*denkweg*) of thought. But just as I suggested in the opening chapter with Stevens's "mundo," I have in mind here something a little different from a thematic reading, by which we might associate Stevens and Ammons—by comparing, for example, Stevens's "The Man on the Dump" with Ammons's great, late long poem *Garbage*, or by seeing Stevens's poem as a sort of parable for contemporary environmental decline.[1] Similarly, as we saw by way of illustration in the previous chapter, Stevens's "farewell to an idea" in "The Auroras of Autumn" doesn't open onto an embrace of ongoing, cyclical natural process (as in "Sunday Morning"), but rather harkens back to our fleetingness and our finitude in the service of what Cavell, in his reading of Emerson's "Experience," calls "lasting": not enduring like a house or stone hearth, but rather moving on, taking steps (as in the "last" of a shoe)—a rethinking of "grounding as lasting" that is directly linked (for him) to Heidegger's notion of being "on the way" and (for me) to Derrida's idea of "survivance" or "living-on."

No one has more strongly connected Ammons to the Emersonian genealogy than Harold Bloom. As he announced full-throatedly in his first essay on Ammons, from 1971, "in the lengthening perspective of American poetry, the year 1955 will be remembered as the end of Wallace Stevens's career and the beginning of Ammons's, himself not Stevens's heir, but like Stevens a descendent of the great originals of American Romantic tradition, Emerson and Whitman."[2] Bloom's decoupling of Ammons from Stevens is based in no small part, as Roger Gilbert notes, on Bloom's reservations about what he calls Ammons's "ecological and almost geological" focus on the physical particulars of nature (what Bloom called an "Ammonsian literalness"), which gets in the way of what Bloom thinks of as the poet's true job: as Gilbert puts it, "the visionary projection of a realm beyond or above nature."[3] As we have seen, things are a little more complicated than this for the poet of "An Ordinary Evening in New Haven," even though, in that poem, Stevens sometimes shares the Bloomian reservations just voiced (what in the previous chapter was called an "aversion"), when he writes in canto IV, for example, that "The plainness of plain things is savagery."[4] In my view, part of what joins Ammons to Stevens is a thoroughgoing deconstruction of the opposition between the "visionary" and the "plain"—a deconstruction that is carried out nowhere more exquisitely than in "Ordinary Evening," where walking provides its itinerary.

I have developed the theoretical infrastructure for that assertion in some detail in the foregoing pages, and I won't apply it now to Ammons's remarkable (and large) body of work to further make my case, in part because I did so, in condensed form, in the first essay I ever published, in 1989, called "Symbol Plural: The Later Long Poems of A. R. Ammons."[5] There, I attempted to put some distance between my reading of Ammons and Bloom's reading of Emerson (and his reading of

Ammons's relationship to Emerson), and I'd still emphasize the crucial differences between Bloom's framework and my own, even as I have found Bloom a gifted and insightful reader (and not just of Emerson, Stevens, and Ammons). In that early essay, I argued that in Ammons's later long poems (roughly from "Essay on Poetics" on) the conceptual form of what used to be called "nature" and what has been called here "environment" is drawn (as it is in this book) from systems theory (and in that essay, Gregory Bateson, who figures importantly in these pages, too, was my main exhibit). It is probably worth noting at this juncture—given the modulation of these questions out of an epistemological and into a biological and ecological frame in chapter 3—that Ammons's first book, from 1955, is called *Omateum with Doxology*: "omateum" referring to the Latin scientific nomenclature for the compound eye of an insect, which is composed of numerous microspheres angled in slightly different directions to form the whole, thus capturing neatly, for my purposes, the connection between Peter Sloterdijk's "foams" and the posthumanist sense of the contingency of observation (human and nonhuman) in systems theory.[6] Here, we might well be reminded of those strange lines from "Ordinary Evening" (strange even for Stevens) about the "barrenness" that is "a coming on and a coming forth," "not an empty clearness, a bottomless sight. / It is a visibility of thought, / In which hundreds of eyes, in one mind, see at once."[7]

As I noted in that earlier essay, and as I've argued here on a much larger scale, all this changes our concept of poetic form, but it also helps us see now why Bloom's opposition of the "visionary" and the "literal" (what "Ordinary Evening" calls the "plain") is misguided—because it helps us to see how the interest of Ammons and Stevens in the literal, plain, and ordinary, the things of this world, is not *representational*. To use the vocabulary of Cavell, there *is no such thing* as the "literal" and the "plain" *per se*, which is why we can talk of a "transfigured" or "uncanny" form of the "ordinary," something that Emerson, Stevens, and Ammons are keenly attuned to. Walking operates in the services of that attunement.

One way to mark the difference between Heidegger and Emerson (to stay with Cavell's reading a moment more, and refine it) is to notice what we might call the difference between the two regarding the gravitational pull of that walking, that path. As Derrida notes in the second set of seminars on *The Beast and the Sovereign*, for Heidegger that pull is about the tension between nostalgia for the world "as a whole" (in the sense, as I develop it here, reaching back to Uexküll, of an autopoietically generated whole) and the contingency of our finitude—this being "pushed" and "held back," as Derrida put it earlier—that creates the "oscillating," often circumambulating movement we find in Stevens, Emerson, and Ammons.[8] This is why, as David Farrell Krell puts it, Heidegger's trope of the *weg*, the way or path of thinking, "however linear it may appear to be often calls for an *Umweg*, a detour or way-around."[9] But this nostalgia is also the source of a sense of loss and mourning—the mourning that Derrida locates in Paul Celan's memorable line, "The world is gone, I must carry you," and the mourning that Cavell locates in Emerson's "Experience" over the loss of the world under the truth of skepticism, troped in that essay as grief over the dead son, Waldo, which in turn becomes the "founding" (by the child as father of the man, the "founder thou" in Emerson's epigraph) of philosophy reimagined as "finding."

As we have seen, Cavell wants to see Emerson's reinvention of philosophy as moving on from that grief, abandoning it, doing something else,[10] and that is the sense developed in Branka Arsić's remarkable book on Emerson, *On Leaving*, where she, too, notes the contrast with Heidegger's nostalgia—what I would call Heidegger's continuing attachment to "nature" versus the gravitational pull of "environment" in the sense I have developed here. As she puts it, "in contrast to Heidegger's claim that 'man is that inability to remain and is yet unable to leave his place,' Emerson will come to develop an astoundingly complex philosophy of leaving, culminating in the existential and ethical insistence that man has to be able to find the power to do what he is unable to do: leave his place."[11] This turns out to be more than a merely philosophical exercise. As Robert Bly once noted in an odd but insightful essay on Stevens, "Wallace Stevens and Dr. Jekyll," Stevens in his early insurance years would try to end his days in a town with a museum, where he could go look at pictures for a couple of hours. "This is a practical way of reawakening the senses," Bly writes, "as walks are."[12] He also notes what we noted at the end of the previous chapter: that "Stevens is careful of hearing"; he "pays more attention than most men to uniting the senses of color and smell," and he "works to join the eyes to the sense of touch." Stevens "works to become aware of weather, and its mergings with emotion," Bly writes, and he "begins to see how, if the senses are sharpened by labor, you begin to merge with the creatures and objects around you."[13] This is precisely what Arsić finds in Emerson's leaving, a movement "to reattach both the body and the mind to the world. In contrast to the skeptic, then, who lives in wounded detachment from objects, distanced from the world, Emerson's fugitive poet-walker finds the world by reattaching himself to it." Thus, "the Emersonian walk is a walk of self-renewal."[14]

This is the Emersonian Stevens that I find in "Ordinary Evening." And it is one that Ammons ecologically literalizes, if you will, in his essay "A Poem Is Walk," intervening in and sustaining the interest in the difference between poetry and philosophy that so captivated Stevens. As he puts it there (sounding very much like the Bateson of "Epistemology and Ecology" in my first chapter), "the statement, All is One, provides us no experience of manyness, of the concrete world from which the statement derived . . . Why should we be surprised that the work of art, which overreaches and reconciles logical paradox, is inaccessible to the methods of logical exposition? A world comes into being about which any statement, however revelatory, is a lessening."[15] As he notes about the analogy between poems and walks, his interest is in what we have seen Cavell call "glancing" and "indirection": "in clarification or intensification by distraction, seeing one thing better by looking at something else."[16] And he finds that analogy justified because, first, "I take the walk to be the externalization of an interior seeking," and second, "each makes use of the whole body"; the walk, like the poem, is "not simply a mental activity: it has body, rhythm, feeling, sound, and mind, conscious and subconscious." Third—and I think this is very much the tonic at work in "Ordinary Evening"—"every walk is unreproducible, as is every poem. Even if you walk exactly the same route each time—as with a sonnet— the events along the route cannot be imagined to be the same from day to day, as the poet's health, sight, his anticipations, moods, fears, thoughts cannot be the same."[17]

Or as Ammons puts it in one of his greatest early poems, "Corsons Inlet,"

> enjoying the freedom that
> Scope eludes my grasp, that there is no finality of vision,
> that I have perceived nothing completely,
> that tomorrow a new walk is a new walk.[18]

One wonders what the poet of "An Ordinary Evening in New Haven" could have desired any more.

Notes

PREFACE

1. Humberto Maturana and Bernhard Poersken, *From Being to Doing: The Origins of the Biology of Cognition*, trans. Wolfram Karl Koeck and Alison Rosemary Koeck (Heidelberg: Carl-Auer, 2004).

2. Wallace Stevens, "Adagia," in *Opus Posthumous: Poems, Plays, Prose*, ed. Milton J. Bates, revised and enlarged ed. (New York: Random House, 1990), 185. This book is hereafter cited as *OP*.

3. Maturana and Poersken, *From Being to Doing*, 34.

4. Jacques Derrida, *The Beast and the Sovereign, Vol. 2*, ed. Michel Lisse, Marie-Louise Mallet, and Ginette Michaud, trans. Geoffrey Bennington (Chicago: University of Chicago Press, 2011), 99; Donna J. Haraway, "Situated Knowledges: The Science Question in Feminism and the Privilege of Partial Perspective," in *Simians, Cyborgs, and Women: The Reinvention of Nature* (New York: Routledge, 1991), 183–202. On this point—situatedness in relation to the question of observation—Haraway and Derrida have something to teach Maturana, who opines that "observing is for me a human operation that requires language" in terms that end up being similar to those of Heidegger, which Derrida engages in some detail, as we will see later (Maturana and Poersken, *From Being to Doing*, 35).

5. Stacy Alaimo, *Exposed: Environmental Politics and Pleasures in Posthuman Times* (Minneapolis: University of Minnesota Press, 2016), 144.

6. Alaimo, *Exposed*, 169–70.

7. Quoted in Alaimo, *Exposed*, 150.

8. Derrida, *The Beast and the Sovereign, Vol. 2*, 8.

9. Derrida, *The Beast and the Sovereign, Vol. 2*, 267.

10. Harold Bloom, *The Poems of Our Climate* (Ithaca, NY: Cornell University Press, 1976), 23.

11. I thank Marjorie Levinson for helping me to articulate this very important point in precisely this way.

12. Richard Rorty, *Objectivity, Relativism, and Truth: Philosophical Papers, Vol. 1* (Cambridge: Cambridge University Press, 1991), 109.

13. Lawrence Buell, "Ecocriticism: Some Emerging Trends," *Qui Parle: Critical Humanities and Social Sciences* 19, no. 2 (Spring–Summer 2011): 89.

14. Buell, "Ecocriticism," 90–91.

15. Buell, "Ecocriticism," 91.

16. Buell, "Ecocriticism," 91, 95.

17. Amitav Ghosh, *The Great Derangement* (Chicago: University of Chicago Press, 2016), 7.

18. *The Collected Poems of Wallace Stevens* (New York: Random House, 1982), 381. Hereafter cited as *CP*.

19. Ghosh, *The Great Derangement*, 76–77. Exhibit A for him, in his critique of John Updike, is that the novel as a genre is above all about the moral trajectory of an individual character.

20. Ghosh, *The Great Derangement*, 68–69.

21. Ghosh, *The Great Derangement*, 25.

22. My view—and mobilization—of Stevens and insurance has little in common with the primary book on the topic, Thomas Grey's *The Wallace Stevens Case: Law and the Practice of Poetry* (Cambridge, MA: Harvard University Press, 1991), whose aims are quite different from my own.

23. Frank Lentricchia has made perhaps the most sustained and compelling attempt to address this question in *Ariel and the Police: Michel Foucault, William James, Wallace Stevens* (Madison: University of Wisconsin Press, 1989).

24. Ghosh, *The Great Derangement*, 15.

25. *CP*, 489.

26. *CP*, 294.

27. *CP*, 381.

28. *OP*, 234.

29. Frank Lentricchia, *Ariel and the Police*, 147–58.

30. Timothy Campbell, *Improper Life: Technology and Biopolitics from Heidegger to Agamben* (Minneapolis: University of Minnesota Press, 2011), 90.

31. Campbell, *Improper Life*, 93.

32. *OP*, 234.

33. Peter Sloterdijk, "Rules for the Human Zoo: A Response to the *Letter on Humanism*," *Environment and Planning D: Society and Space* 27 (2009): 114.

34. Sloterdijk, "Rules for the Human Zoo," 114–15.

35. Peter Sloterdijk, with Hans-Jürgen Heinrichs, *Neither Sun nor Death*, trans. Steve Corcoran (Los Angeles: Semiotext[e], 2007), 105.

36. Sloterdijk and Heinrichs, *Neither Sun nor Death*, 104.

37. Sloterdijk and Heinrichs, *Neither Sun nor Death*, 106.

38. Sloterdijk and Heinrichs, *Neither Sun nor Death*, 114.

39. In a differently oriented discussion, this would eventually lead us to Derrida's meditation on the "desert" of the *khora* in his essay "Faith and Knowledge: The Two Sources of Religion at the Limits of Reason Alone," in *Religion*, ed. Jacques Derrida and Gianni Vattimo (Stanford, CA: Stanford University Press, 1996), 1–78.

40. Jacques Derrida, *Of Spirit: Heidegger and the Question*, trans. Geoffrey Bennington and Rachel Bowlby (Chicago: University of Chicago Press, 1989).

41. Stanley Cavell, "Aversive Thinking: Emersonian Representations in Heidegger and Nietzsche," in *Emerson's Transcendental Etudes*, ed. David Justin Hodge (Stanford, CA: Stanford University Press, 2003), 141–70.

42. Katy Waldman, "Does Having a Day Job Mean Making Better Art?," *New York Times*, March 22, 2018, https://www.nytimes.com/2018/03/22/t-magazine/art/artist-day-job.html (accessed July 15, 2018).

43. Wallace Stevens, "The Noble Rider and the Sound of Words," in *The Necessary Angel: Essays on Reality and the Imagination* (New York: Random House, 1951), 29.

CHAPTER 1

1. Sebastian Gardner, "Wallace Stevens and Metaphysics: The Plain Sense of Things," *European Journal of Philosophy* 2, no. 3 (1994): 326.

2. Gardner, "Wallace Stevens and Metaphysics," 327.

3. Gardner, "Wallace Stevens and Metaphysics," 328.

4. George Lensing, "Stevens' Seasonal Cycles," in *The Cambridge Companion to Wallace Stevens*, ed. John N. Serio (Cambridge: Cambridge University Press, 2007), 118.

5. J. Hillis Miller, "Wallace Stevens' Poetry of Being," in *The Act of the Mind: Essays on the Poetry of Wallace Stevens*, ed. Roy Harvey Pearce and J. Hillis Miller (Baltimore: Johns Hopkins University Press, 1965), 149–50.

6. Miller, "Wallace Stevens' Poetry of Being," 150.

7. Miller, "Wallace Stevens' Poetry of Being," 150–51.

8. Miller, "Wallace Stevens' Poetry of Being," 151.

9. Richard A. Macksey, "The Climates of Wallace Stevens," in *The Act of the Mind*, ed. Pearce and Miller, 187.

10. Macksey, "The Climates of Wallace Stevens," 187–88.

11. Specifically, in Cary Wolfe, *What Is Posthumanism?* (Minneapolis: University of Minnesota Press, 2010), 268–70.

12. This is, unfortunately, the case with Charles Altieri's recent book on Stevens, which is why I do not engage it in these pages (Charles Altieri, *Wallace Stevens and the Demands of Modernity: Toward a Phenomenology of Value* [Ithaca,

NY: Cornell University Press, 2013]). Following Nietzsche, and against both pragmatism and deconstruction, Altieri writes that his "version of phenomenology would try to locate affective states in our self-reflexive attention to the basic grammatical forces that adapt language to the world and the world to language" (36). He continues, "Stevens seeks at every moment a sense that a poet's eloquence can participate in a spirit of discovery. The work of imagination becomes a mode of participating in the reality it encounters, so Stevens can plausibly believe that this new style affords a possible union between the states of making and finding that most modernist poetics labors to reconcile" (42). I do not see how this marks an advance beyond the position of Gelpi that I criticize in *What Is Posthumanism?* nor do I see how the position outlined in the first quotation can survive the critique of phenomenology that we find in either Derrida or Luhmann, which I develop in detail below—a critique invited by Altieri's "basic grammatical forces." My discussion of Stevens's essay "The Irrational Element in Poetry" in chapter 2 will explore this question in some detail.

13. Macksey, "The Climates of Wallace Stevens," 192.

14. Wallace Stevens, *The Necessary Angel: Essays on Reality and the Imagination* (New York: Random House, 1951), 65–66.

15. *CP*, 194.

16. See, for a primer, Andy Clark, *Supersizing the Mind: Embodiment, Action, and Cognitive Extension* (Oxford: Oxford University Press, 2011).

17. "Nature," in *Emerson's Prose and Poetry*, ed. Joel Porte and Saundra Morris (New York: W. W. Norton, 2001), 29.

18. Jacques Derrida, "Typewriter Ribbon," in *Without Alibi*, trans. Peggy Kamuf (Stanford, CA: Stanford University Press, 2002), 136.

19. *CP*, 440, 442.

20. *CP*, 532–33.

21. Joan Richardson, *A Natural History of Pragmatism: The Fact of Feeling from Jonathan Edwards to Gertrude Stein* (Cambridge: Cambridge University Press, 2007), 11.

22. "Mereological" relationships are those that involve whole-to-part and part-to-whole relationships, which turn out to be importantly asymmetrical and dynamically generative of emergent and self-organizing forms of order, rather than holistic. See Alicia Juarrero, "What Does the Closure of Context-sensitive Constraints Mean for Determinism, Autonomy, Self-determination, and Agency?," *Progress in Biophysics and Molecular Biology* 119 (2015): 510.

23. I am thus sympathetic with Matthew Griffiths's suggestion, in his chapter on Stevens in *The New Poetics of Climate Change*, that Stevens's work is "a reminder that the experience of nature cannot be separated from the human imagination" (Matthew Griffiths, *The New Poetics of Climate Change: Modernist Aesthetics for a Warming World* [London: Bloomsbury, 2017], 59). But the problem is that this general claim does not lead to a sufficient understanding of Stevens's unique poetics. And so we end up, on the one hand, with formulations such as

the following (familiar from the Stevens literature): "By trying to see the sun in its own terms, we have to adopt a solar intensity of vision, and we then *become* the environment in the way that the 'mind' of the Snow Man is 'of winter.' At the same time, we can only achieve that identity through the human device of metaphor" (65). And, on the other hand, we end up with the claim that the entanglement of mind and nature is "a process that intersects with, but is not limited to, the practices of scientific and literary climate modelling" (74)—which is perhaps true, but so general as to be of little use in helping us locate the ecological dimension of Stevens's poetics in a compellingly specific way.

24. Richard Poirier, *Poetry and Pragmatism* (London: Faber & Faber, 1992), 11.

25. Poirier, *Poetry and Pragmatism*, 17.

26. Poirier, *Poetry and Pragmatism*, 17–18.

27. Poirier, *Poetry and Pragmatism*, 18.

28. Richardson, *Natural History*, 1.

29. Richardson, *Natural History*, 11.

30. "The Man on the Dump," *CP*, 201.

31. Quoted in Poirier, *Poetry and Pragmatism*, 26.

32. Stanley Cavell, "Finding as Founding: Taking Steps in Emerson's 'Experience,'" in *Emerson's Transcendental Etudes* (Stanford, CA: Stanford University Press, 2003), 117, 130, 133.

33. *OP*, 140.

34. Poirier, *Poetry and Pragmatism*, 27.

35. Poirier, *Poetry and Pragmatism*, 31.

36. Poirier, *Poetry and Pragmatism*, 133.

37. See, for example, my *What Is Posthumanism?*, 31–48; *Animal Rites: American Culture, the Discourse of Species, and Posthumanist Theory* (Chicago: University of Chicago Press, 2003), 78–94; and *Before the Law: Humans and Other Animals in a Biopolitical Frame* (Chicago: University of Chicago Press, 2013), 63–86.

38. Poirier, *Poetry and Pragmatism*, 133.

39. Poirier, *Poetry and Pragmatism*, 40.

40. Cavell, "Finding as Founding," 139.

41. Quoted in Poirier, *Poetry and Pragmatism*, 151–52.

42. Helen Hennessy Vendler, "The Qualified Assertions of Wallace Stevens," in *The Act of the Mind: Essays on the Poetry of Wallace Stevens*, ed. Pearce and Miller, 163–64.

43. Vendler, "The Qualified Assertions of Wallace Stevens," 174–75.

44. Beverly Maeder, "Stevens and Linguistic Structure," in *The Cambridge Companion to Wallace Stevens*, 151.

45. Roger Gilbert, "Verbs of Mere Being: A Defense of Stevens' Style," *Wallace Stevens Journal* 28, no. 2 (Fall 2004): 193, 194.

46. Gilbert, "Verbs of Mere Being," 193.

47. Maeder, "Stevens and Linguistic Structure," 154.

48. Maeder, "Stevens and Linguistic Structure," 153.

49. Mac Hammond, "On the Grammar of Wallace Stevens," in *The Act of the Mind: Essays on the Poetry of Wallace Stevens*, ed. Pearce and Miller, 179.

50. Simon Critchley, *Things Merely Are: Philosophy in the Poetry of Wallace Stevens* (London: Routledge, 2005), 58.

51. Poirier, *Poetry and Pragmatism*, 11.

52. Joan Richardson, *Pragmatism and American Experience: An Introduction* (Cambridge: Cambridge University Press, 2014), 12.

53. Richardson, *Pragmatism and American Experience*, 61.

54. Richardson, *Pragmatism and American Experience*, 62.

55. Richardson, *Pragmatism and American Experience*, 60.

56. Elizabeth Grosz, *Time Travels: Feminism, Nature, Power* (Durham, NC: Duke University Press, 2005), 21.

57. Richardson, *Pragmatism and American Experience*, 13.

58. Angus Fletcher, *A New Theory for American Poetry: Democracy, the Environment, and the Future of Imagination* (Cambridge, MA: Harvard University Press, 2004), 2.

59. Fletcher, *A New Theory for American Poetry*, 9.

60. Fletcher, *A New Theory for American Poetry*, 9.

61. Fletcher, *A New Theory for American Poetry*, 12.

62. Though it should be well noted here—for reasons I will develop in due course—that, as J. Hillis Miller notes, Stevens's poetry "is not dialectical, if that means a series of stages which build on one another, each transcending the last and moving on to a higher stage, in some version of the Hegelian sequence of thesis, antithesis, synthesis. At the beginning Stevens is as far as he ever goes" (Miller, "Wallace Stevens' Poetry of Being," 146). This, I will argue, is precisely what makes him (or part of what makes him) an Emersonian poet.

63. And it's the same problem, on different terrain, with the phenomenological framework to which he refers when he assimilates Emerson's "Circles" to Husserl's concept of the "horizon," for reasons already discussed. Miller, "Wallace Stevens' Poetry of Being," 17.

64. Fletcher, *A New Theory for American Poetry*, 165, 206.

65. Humberto R. Maturana and Francisco J. Varela, *The Tree of Knowledge The Biological Roots of Human Understanding*, rev. ed., trans. Robert Paolucci (Boulder, CO: Shambhala, 1992), 130–31. They dismantle this view in painstaking detail on, for example, 169, 196.

66. Joseph N. Riddell, *The Clairvoyant Eye: The Poetry and Poetics of Wallace Stevens* (Baton Rouge: LSU Press, 1965).

67. This lacuna in Fletcher's argument is all the more striking because he invokes the old chestnut of Gödel's Incompleteness Theorem as a paradigm of the "inconsistent coherence" of the environment-poem: "the coherent environment-poem is necessarily inconsistent at some point, and for this reason it coheres" (Fletcher, *A New Theory for American Poetry*, 11). These problems make themselves manifest in Fletcher's attempt, for example, to describe "understanding

the common as a function of poetic form and language" in relation to "the role of environment as what is *around*, as what is *surrounding* the poet's seeing eye" (25). The problem, of course, is that we cannot take seriously a Gödelian idea of the paradoxical self-reference that provides the environment-poem its inconsistent incompleteness *and* at the same time leaves the idea of "the common" untouched by it, for what is "common" is the *difference* between different observers (and not just *human* observers, as Stevens emphasizes in so many of his bird poems—"Thirteen Ways of Looking at Blackbird" would be canonical here, but so would be "No Possum, No Sop, No Taters"): that is to say, the difference between observing system and environment in each iteration of self-referential observation. And that difference is not, crucially, the "same," generic difference because of the radically different modes of embodied being-in-the-world. Instead, what we get with Fletcher's account is a very familiar strategy of trying to "split the difference" between what these new theoretical vocabularies demand and an older theoretical lexicon that simply smuggles back in the very problems Fletcher is trying to move beyond. So, on the one hand, Fletcher will admirably suggest that "such poems are not *about* the environment. In some sense they share the same character, the same intrusion, the same coextension in our lives as has the environment." And this means that we find in the environment-poem "a breakdown of the old distinction—a classical distinction through critical history, no matter how complex its profile at different historical periods—between the world within the poem and the world 'out there,' outside the poem" (227). But, on the other hand, "the old distinctions" are precisely what plague Fletcher's attempt to theorize the "environment-poem," when he writes that "the poem, like the system, adapts *by itself* to meet communicative needs at many levels of contact with the environment"; "the work finally organizes itself . . . Mind and nature thus converge on the plane of complex non-linear aggregates" (206).

68. Roy Harvey Pearce, "Wallace Stevens: The Last Lesson of the Master," in *The Act of the Mind: Essays on the Poetry of Wallace Stevens*, ed. Pearce and Miller, 129.

69. Pearce, "Wallace Stevens: The Last Lesson of the Master," 127.

70. *OP*, 276, quoted in Pearce, "Wallace Stevens: The Last Lesson of the Master," 127.

71. Quoted in Pearce, "Wallace Stevens: The Last Lesson of the Master," 130; *OP*, 140.

72. *CP*, 532–33.

73. Pearce, "Wallace Stevens: The Last Lesson of the Master," 131.

74. Gregory Bateson, *A Sacred Unity: Further Steps to an Ecology of Mind*, ed. Rodney E. Donaldson (New York: Harper Collins, 1991), 181.

75. Bateson, *A Sacred Unity*, 204.

76. Bateson, *A Sacred Unity*, 188.

77. Bateson, *A Sacred Unity*, 182.

78. Bateson, *A Sacred Unity*, 205.

79. Bateson, *A Sacred Unity*, 264, emphasis added.
80. Bateson, *A Sacred Unity*, 188.
81. Bateson, *A Sacred Unity*, 189–90.
82. See *What Is Posthumanism?*, xxi–xxv.
83. Bateson, *A Sacred Unity*, 222.
84. *OP*, 135–36.

CHAPTER 2

1. Robert Lehmann, "Abstract Pleasures: Romanticism and Finitism in the Poetry of Wallace Stevens," *Modern Philology* 111, no. 2 (November 2013): 315–16.
2. In this chapter, I will reprise some of the theoretical groundwork for this reading of the Emerson/Stevens genealogy that I undertook in chapter 10 of *What Is Posthumanism?* (Minneapolis: University of Minnesota Press, 2010), 265–82.
3. Stanley Cavell, "Finding as Founding: Taking Steps in Emerson's 'Experience,'" in *Emerson's Transcendental Etudes* (Stanford, CA: Stanford University Press, 2003), 111.
4. Joseph Riddell, *The Clairvoyant Eye: The Poetry and Poetics of Wallace Stevens* (Baton Rouge: Louisiana State University Press, 1965), 225, 224.
5. Cavell, "Finding as Founding," 79.
6. Stanley Cavell, "Emerson, Coleridge, Kant (Terms as Conditions)," in *Emerson's Transcendental Etudes*, 63.
7. Cavell, "Emerson, Coleridge, Kant (Terms as Conditions)," 62.
8. Cavell, "Finding as Founding," 117.
9. Harold Bloom, *Wallace Stevens: The Poems of Our Climate* (Ithaca, NY: Cornell University Press, 1976), 306.
10. Bloom, *Wallace Stevens: The Poems of Our Climate*, 306–7.
11. Quoted in Bloom, *Wallace Stevens: The Poems of Our Climate*, 307.
12. "An Ordinary Evening in New Haven," in *CP*, 465.
13. Stanley Cavell, "Aversive Thinking: Emersonian Representations in Heidegger and Nietzsche," in *Emerson's Transcendental Etudes*, 147.
14. See my discussion of this cluster of texts in *Animal Rites: American Culture, The Discourse of Species, and Posthumanist Theory* (Chicago: University of Chicago Press, 2003), 63–64.
15. Ralph Waldo Emerson, *Emerson's Prose and Poetry*, ed. Joel Porte and Saundra Morris (New York: W. W. Norton, 2001), 212.
16. "Sermon CLXII [The Lord's Supper], Romans 14:17, September 9, 1832," in *Emerson's Prose and Poetry*, ed. Porte and Morris, 17–26.
17. Quoted in Paul Jay, *Contingency Blues: The Search for Foundations in American Criticism* (Madison: University of Wisconsin Press, 1997), 26, 29.
18. Jay, *Contingency Blues*, 28.
19. *OP*, 259.
20. Cavell, "Finding as Founding," 111–12.

21. Richard Rorty, *Objectivity, Relativism, and Truth: Philosophical Papers, Vol. 1* (Cambridge: Cambridge University Press, 1991), 4.

22. Rorty, *Objectivity, Relativism, and Truth*, 96.

23. Rorty, *Objectivity, Relativism, and Truth*, 5.

24. Richard Rorty, *Philosophy and the Mirror of Nature* (Princeton, NJ: Princeton University Press, 1979), 368.

25. Rorty, *Objectivity, Relativism, and Truth*, 100.

26. Cavell, "Finding as Founding," 113.

27. Stanley Cavell, "Being Odd, Getting Even (Descartes, Emerson, Poe)," in *Emerson's Transcendental Etudes*, 84, 87. Cavell reminds us that most readers will "remember or assume the cogito always to be expressed in words that translate as 'I think, *therefore* I am.' But in Descartes's Second Meditation, where I suppose it is most often actually encountered, the insight is expressed: '*I am, I exist*, is necessarily true every time that I pronounce or conceive it in my mind.' Emerson's emphasis on the *saying* of 'I' is precisely faithful to this expression of Descartes's insight" (85).

28. Cavell, "Being Odd, Getting Even (Descartes, Emerson, Poe)," 87.

29. Cavell, "Being Odd, Getting Even (Descartes, Emerson, Poe)," 89.

30. Stanley Cavell, "Introduction: Staying the Course," in *Conditions Handsome and Unhandsome: The Constitution of Emersonian Perfectionism* (Chicago: University of Chicago Press, 1990), 12.

31. Cavell, "Aversive Thinking," 160. I think this formulation has remarkable traction for thinking about Stevens's complicated and vexing relationship to the political and social domain, and how those, in turn, are related to his own biographical peculiarities, the lawyer and insurance executive who at the same time, in his poetry, voiced relentlessly the need to leave behind the self, and the perceptions and tropes of that self, of an earlier moment, both culturally and existentially—a bundle of complications that I'll try to unpack later with the help of Peter Sloterdijk and his *Spheres* project.

32. Cavell, "Finding as Founding," 115.

33. *Emerson's Prose and Poetry*, ed. Porte and Morris, 29.

34. Maurice Gonnaud, *An Uneasy Solitude: Individual and Society in the Work of Ralph Waldo Emerson*, trans. Lawrence Rosenwald (Princeton, NJ: Princeton University Press, 1987), 299.

35. Gonnaud, *An Uneasy Solitude*, 301, 302.

36. Lee Rust Brown, *The Emerson Museum: Practical Romanticism and the Pursuit of the Whole* (Cambridge, MA: Harvard University Press, 1997), 73.

37. Brown, *The Emerson Museum*, 71, 72.

38. Brown, *The Emerson Museum*, 47.

39. Brown, *The Emerson Museum*, 45–46.

40. *Emerson's Prose and Poetry*, ed. Porte and Morris, 123.

41. Niklas Luhmann, "Cognition as Construction," trans. Hans-Georg Moeller, "Appendix B" in Moeller, *Luhmann Explained: From Souls to Systems*

(Chicago: Open Court Press, 2006), 250. As Luhmann summarizes the point, if "God is beyond all distinctions, even beyond the distinction between distinctness and indistinctness" (250), then the problem becomes, how can that which is transcendent insofar as it transcends distinctions be observed to be compatible with Christian dogma ("identifiable as a person and as the trinity," and so on) (251)? "One had, in God, to save the possibilities of observation and thus on the one hand to be careful not to ascribe to God the impossibility of self-observation, and, on the other hand, to avoid to come close to the devil who was the boldest observer of God . . . The escape route came fatally close to the assumption that God needed creation and the damnation of the devil in order to be able to observe himself, and it led to writings that Nicolaus believed unprepared minds with their weak eyes had better not read" (251).

42. Niklas Luhmann, *Art as a Social System*, trans. Eva M. Knodt (Stanford, CA: Stanford University Press, 2000), 90.

43. Harro Muller, "Luhmann's Systems Theory as a Theory of Modernity," *New German Critique* 61 (Winter 1994): 40.

44. Luhmann, *Art as a Social System*, 89.

45. Wallace Stevens, "The Noble Rider and the Sound of Words," in *The Necessary Angel: Essays on Reality and the Imagination* (New York: Random House, 1951), 29.

46. Niklas Luhmann, *Social Systems*, trans. John Bednarz, Jr. with Dirk Baecker, foreword by Eva M. Knodt (Stanford, CA: Stanford University Press, 1995), 25.

47. Niklas Luhmann, "The Paradoxy of Observing Systems," *Cultural Critique* 31 (Fall 1995): 41–42.

48. Luhmann, *Social Systems*, 60.

49. Luhmann, *Social Systems*, 63.

50. *Emerson's Prose and Poetry*, ed. Porte and Morris, 84.

51. Luhmann, *Art as a Social System*, 158.

52. Luhmann, *Social Systems*, 26.

53. Luhmann, *Social Systems*, 17.

54. Niklas Luhmann, "A Redescription of 'Romantic Art,'" *MLN* 111, no. 3 (1996): 508, 511.

55. *Emerson's Prose and Poetry*, ed. Porte and Morris, 142.

56. Niklas Luhmann, "The Cognitive Program of Constructivism and a Reality That Remains Unknown," in *Selforganization: Portrait of a Scientific Revolution*, ed. Wolfgang Krohn et al. (Dordrecht: Kluwer Academic Publishers, 1990), 76.

57. Luhmann, *Art as a Social System*, 92.

58. *Emerson's Prose and Poetry*, ed. Porte and Morris, 174, emphasis added.

59. Luhmann, *Art as a Social System*, 91.

60. Luhmann, *Art as a Social System*, 96.

61. Luhmann, "A Redescription of 'Romantic Art,'" 517.

62. Jacques Derrida, *The Beast and the Sovereign, Vol. 2*, ed. Michel Lisse, Marie-Louise Mallet, and Ginette Michaud, trans. Geoffrey Bennington (Chicago: University of Chicago Press, 2011), 269.

63. Derrida, *The Beast and the Sovereign, Vol. 2*, 270.

64. Derrida, *The Beast and the Sovereign, Vol. 2*, 268.

65. Niklas Luhmann, "Notes on the Project 'Poetry and Social Theory,'" trans. Kathleen Cross, *Theory, Culture, and Society* 18, no. 1 (2001): 15–27.

66. Wimsatt argues that the fundamental dynamic of rhyme in English poetry is one that yokes acoustic similarity and semantic contrast, and that, canonically, the more extreme the contrast, the better, as in the classic rhyme "king/thing." His essay is part of *The Verbal Icon: Studies in the Meaning of Poetry* (Lexington: University of Kentucky Press, 1954).

67. Niklas Luhmann, "How Can the Mind Participate in Communication?," in *Materialities of Communication*, ed. Hans Ulrich Gumbrecht and K. Ludwig Pfeiffer, trans. William Whobrey (Stanford, CA: Stanford University Press, 1994), 372, 374.

68. Luhmann, "How Can the Mind Participate in Communication?," 379.

69. Luhmann, *Art as a Social System*, 374.

70. Dietrich Schwanitz, "Systems Theory and the Difference between Communication and Consciousness: An Introduction to a Problem and Its Context," *MLN* 111, no. 3 (1996): 494. See also Luhmann, *Art as a Social System*, 8–9.

71. Luhmann, *Art as a Social System*, 14.

72. Luhmann, *Art as a Social System*, 142.

73. Luhmann, *Art as a Social System*, 22.

74. Luhmann, *Art as a Social System*, 26.

75. Luhmann, *Art as a Social System*, 141.

76. Luhmann, *Art as a Social System*, 25.

77. Luhmann, *Art as a Social System*, 18.

78. Luhmann, *Art as a Social System*, 19, 22.

79. Luhmann, *Art as a Social System*, 26.

80. Luhmann, *Art as a Social System*, 125, emphasis added.

81. Luhmann, *Art as a Social System*, 120.

82. Luhmann, *Art as a Social System*, 91.

83. Luhmann, *Art as a Social System*, 91.

84. Luhmann, *Art as a Social System*, 29.

85. Niklas Luhmann, *Observations on Modernity*, trans. William Whobrey (Stanford, CA: Stanford University Press, 1998), 48, emphasis added.

86. Luhmann, *Art as a Social System*, 92.

87. Luhmann, *Art as a Social System*, 149.

88. Luhmann, *Art as a Social System*, emphasis added.

89. Mac Hammond, "On the Grammar of Wallace Stevens," in *The Act of the Mind: Essays on the Poetry of Wallace Stevens*, ed. Roy Harvey Pearce and J. Hillis Miller (Baltimore: Johns Hopkins University Press, 1965), 179.

90. *CP*, 326.

91. *CP*, 129–30, emphasis added.

92. *CP*, 129.

93. On why this is not a Hegelian schema, but quite the contrary, see my *Critical Environments: Postmodern Theory and the Pragmatics of the "Outside"* (Minneapolis: University of Minnesota Press, 2003), 68.

94. Niklas Luhmann, "Sthenography," trans. Bernd Widdig, *Stanford Literature Review* 7 (1990): 135.

95. Stevens, "The Noble Rider and the Sound of Words," in *The Necessary Angel*, 29. Such is the drift too, I think, of one recent critic's observation that Stevens's function in this regard is not so much philosophical as "pragmatic": "Stevens can speak to the lawyer or legal theorist as a kind of therapist for the habitual and institutional rigidities of binary thought." Thomas C. Grey, *The Wallace Stevens Case: Law and the Practice of Poetry* (Cambridge, MA: Harvard University Press, 1991), 6–7, quoted in Bart Eeckhout, "Stevens and Philosophy," in *The Cambridge Companion to Wallace Stevens*, 114. Grey's observation is especially appropriate in this context, given the common habit of misreading Luhmann as a rigidly binary thinker, rather than one who precisely deontologizes binaries by making them momentary, functional distinctions that systems use to try to reduce overwhelming environmental complexity by virtualizing and temporalizing it.

96. Luhmann, "Notes on the Project 'Poetry and Social Theory,'" 26.

97. *CP*, 193–94.

98. Luhmann, "Sthenography," 135.

99. *OP*, 220.

100. *OP*, 221, emphasis added.

101. Luhmann, *Social Systems*, 61.

102. Luhmann, *Social Systems*, 61.

103. *OP*, 222.

104. *OP*, 224.

105. *OP*, 224.

106. *OP*, 226–27.

107. And here we can't help but recall Emerson's reminder in "The Poet" that "[t]he spirit of the world, the calm presence of the Creator, comes not forth to the sorceries of opium or of wine. The sublime vision comes to the pure and simple soul in a clean and chaste body. This is not an inspiration, which we owe to narcotics, but some counterfeit excitement and fury" (*Emerson's Prose and Poetry*, ed. Porte and Morris, 192).

108. *OP*, 225.

109. *OP*, 226.

110. Luhmann, *Art as a Social System*, 120.

111. *OP*, 227–28.

112. Luhmann, *Art as a Social System*, 147–48.

113. *OP*, 229–30.

114. *OP*, 230–31.

115. Luhmann, "Cognitive Program," 77.

116. Gregory Bateson, *Steps to an Ecology of Mind* (New York: Ballantine Books, 1972), 410.

117. *OP*, 231–32.

118. Richard Poirier, *Poetry and Pragmatism* (London: Faber & Faber, 1992), 149.

119. *CP*, 526.

120. Poirier, *Poetry and Pragmatism*, 162–63.

121. Poirier, *Poetry and Pragmatism*, 294.

CHAPTER 3

1. Martin Hägglund, "The Trace of Time: A Critique of Vitalism," *Derrida Today* 9, no. 1 (2016): 36.

2. Vicki Kirby, "Grammatology: A Vital Science," *Derrida Today* 9, no. 1 (2016): 48.

3. Kirby, "Grammatology: A Vital Science," 47.

4. Humberto Maturana and Francisco Varela, *The Tree of Knowledge: The Biological Roots of Human Understanding*, rev. ed., foreword by J. Z. Young (Boston: Shambhala Press, 1992), 169.

5. Maturana and Varela, *The Tree of Knowledge*, 133.

6. Maturana and Varela, *The Tree of Knowledge*, 135–36.

7. Humberto R. Maturana, "Science and Daily Life: The Ontology of Scientific Explanations," in *Research and Reflexivity*, ed. Frederick Steier (London: Sage, 1991), 34.

8. Michael Marder, "Ecology as Event," in *Eco-Deconstruction: Derrida and Environmental Philosophy*, ed. Matthias Fritsch, Phillip Lynes, and David Wood (New York: Fordham University Press, 2018), 143.

9. Makoto Katsumori, "Derridean Deconstruction and the Question of Nature," *Derrida Today* 3, no. 1 (May 2010): 59.

10. Jacques Derrida, *The Beast and the Sovereign, Vol. 2*, ed. Michel Lisse, Marie-Louise Mallet, and Ginette Michaud, trans. Geoffrey Bennington (Chicago: University of Chicago Press, 2011), 9.

11. Ana M. Soto, Giuseppe Longo et al., "Toward a Theory of Organisms: Three Founding Principles in Search of a Useful Integration," *Progress in Biophysics and Molecular Biology* 122 (2016): 79. See also Louis H. Kauffman, "Self-reference, Biologic, and the Structure of Reproduction," *Progress in Biophysics and Molecular Biology* 119 (2015): "In living systems there is an essential circularity that is the living structure. Living systems reproduce themselves from themselves and the materials and energy of the environment. There is a strong contrast in how we avoid circularity in mathematics and how nature revels in

biological circularity. One meeting point of biology and mathematics is knot theory and topology. This is no accident, since topology is indeed a controlled study of cycles and circularities in primarily geometical systems" (386).

12. Russell Winslow, *Organism and Environment: Inheritance and Subjectivity in the Life Sciences* (London: Lexington Books, 2017), 70.

13. Winslow, *Organism and Environment*, xiv.

14. Denis Noble, *Dance to the Tune of Life: Biological Relativity* (Cambridge: Cambridge University Press, 2017), 222.

15. Quoted in Winslow, *Organism and Environment*, 117.

16. Winslow, *Organism and Environment*, 123.

17. Quoted in Derek Woods, "What Is Ecotechnology?" (PhD diss., Rice University, 2017). As Alexander Wilson puts it, "selection and adaptation do not take place on a single playing field: each basin of selection is nested within other selecting systems. There is thus a whole hierarchy of nested selection principles at work in each given adaptation . . . On the side of the environment and ecology, the genomic organism is subject to conditioning from its avatars (or actual incarnations of the genome within an individual), these avatars are conditioned by their local ecosystems, and these local ecosystems by their wider regional ecosystems. On the side of evolution and genealogy, the organism's genome is contained and conditioned within the individual's own developmental individuality. The individual is conditioned by the *demes* its immediate ancestry has emerged from, the demes are limited and constrained by the species and its boundaries, and the species is itself constrained by more general phyletic constraints such as *body plans*. This nested aspect of the selection units and the causal relations between the reservoirs of information they select from, make the correlation of a specific trait to a specific adaptive goal that much more difficult. They also leave open the possibility of *substrate independent* selections: i.e. symmetry breaks in null regions, which result in 'emergent' expressions that are irreducible to the specific pressures of the lower selective basin." Alexander Wilson, *Aesthesis and Perceptronium* (Minneapolis: University of Minnesota Press, 2019).

18. Alicia Juarrero, "What Does the Closure of Context-sensitive Constraints Mean for Determinism, Autonomy, Self-determination, and Agency?," *Progress in Biophysics and Molecular Biology* 119 (2015): 510.

19. Juarrero, "What Does the Closure of Context-sensitive Constraints Mean," 511.

20. Juarrero, "What Does the Closure of Context-sensitive Constraints Mean," 519.

21. Juarrero, "What Does the Closure of Context-sensitive Constraints Mean," 512–13.

22. Juarrero, "What Does the Closure of Context-sensitive Constraints Mean," 518.

23. Juarrero, "What Does the Closure of Context-sensitive Constraints Mean," 518.

24. Juarrero, "What Does the Closure of Context-sensitive Constraints Mean," 520.

25. See, for example, Jacques Derrida, *The Animal That Therefore I Am*, ed. Marie-Louise Mallet, trans. David Wills (New York: Fordham University Press, 2008), 47, 56, 67.

26. Quoted in Cary Wolfe, *Animal Rites: American Culture, the Discourse of Species, and Posthumanist Theory* (Chicago: University of Chicago Press, 2003), 94. For a fuller discussion of these issues, see 78–94.

27. Vicki Kirby, "Autoimmunity: The Political State of Nature," *Parallax* 23, no. 1 (2017): 55, 56.

28. Carsten Strathausen, *Bioaesthetics: Making Sense of Life in Science and the Arts* (Minneapolis: University of Minnesota Press, 2017), 1, 3.

29. Strathausen, *Bioaesthetics*, 9.

30. Noble, *Dance to the Tune of Life*, 262.

31. Christopher Johnson, *System and Writing in the Philosophy of Jacques Derrida* (Cambridge: Cambridge University Press, 1993), 4.

32. Johnson, *System and Writing in the Philosophy of Jacques Derrida*, 165.

33. François Jacob, *The Logic of Life: A History of Heredity*, trans. Betty E. Spillmann (New York: Pantheon, 1973), 1–2.

34. Jacques Derrida, *Of Grammatology*, trans. Gayatri Chakravorty Spivak (Baltimore: Johns Hopkins University Press, 1976), 7, 9.

35. Jacques Derrida and Elisabeth Roudinesco, "Violence against Animals," in *For What Tomorrow . . . : A Dialogue*, trans. Jeff Fort (Stanford, CA: Stanford University Press, 2004), 63, emphasis added.

36. "'Eating Well,' or the Calculation of the Subject: An Interview with Jacques Derrida," in *Who Comes after the Subject?*, ed. Eduardo Cadava, Peter Connor, and Jean-Luc Nancy (New York: Routledge, 1991), 116–17.

37. Matthias Fritsch, "An Eco-Deconstructive Account of the Emergence of Normativity in 'Nature,'" in *Eco-Deconstruction: Derrida and Environmental Philosophy*, ed. Fritsch, Lynes, and Wood, 286.

38. Derrida, "*Différance*," 7. See Martin Hägglund, *Radical Atheism: Derrida and the Time of Life* (Stanford, CA: Stanford University Press, 2008).

39. I am indebted to Derek Woods for drawing my attention to the Vernadsky reference in Bataille's text.

40. Noble, *Dance to the Tune of Life*, 147–48.

41. Noble, *Dance to the Tune of Life*, 147.

42. Noble, *Dance to the Tune of Life*, 180.

43. Johnson, *System and Writing in the Philosophy of Jacques Derrida*, 7–8.

44. As Ana Soto and others note, part of the story here is that "during most of the twentieth century experimental and theoretical biologists lived separate lives." The "Central Dogma" of molecular biology "was a theory, except that it was not usually formulated as such. It was presented as fact, a *fait accompli*. Meanwhile the pages of journals of theoretical and mathematical biology

continued to be filled with fascinating and difficult papers to which experimentalists, by and large, paid little or no attention." Anna Soto, Giuseppe Longo, and Denis Noble, "Preface to 'From the Century of the Genome to the Century of the Organism: New Theoretical Approaches,'" *Progress in Biophysics and Molecular Biology* 122 (2016): 1, 2.

45. Derrida and Roudinesco, *For What Tomorrow*, 63. For more on "double finitude," see the introductory chapter to my *What Is Posthumanism?* (Minneapolis: University of Minnesota Press, 2010).

46. See Niklas Luhmann, *Social Systems*, trans. John Bednarz, Jr., with Dirk Baecker, introd. Eva M. Knodt (Stanford, CA: Stanford University Press, 1995), 12–58.

47. Namely, in *What Is Posthumanism?*, xx–xxv.

48. Quoted in Johnson, *System and Writing in the Philosophy of Jacques Derrida*, 146.

49. Denis Noble, "Conrad Waddington and the Origin of Epigenetics," *Journal of Experimental Biology* 218 (2015): 816.

50. Noble, "Conrad Waddington and the Origin of Epigenetics," 816. As Susan Squier notes, "The epigenetic landscape originated as a charcoal drawing by the British landscape artist John Piper, commissioned in 1940," during the London blitz, and although Waddington considered other visual models, by 1957 he had settled on the iconic image of the "chreode." Susan M. Squier, "Epigenetic Landscape," in *Posthuman Glossary*, ed. Rosi Braidotti and Maria Hlavajova (London: Bloomsbury, 2018), 132.

51. Noble, "Conrad Waddington and the Origin of Epigenetics," 816. As Noble points out, a standard neo-Darwinian explanation would be that random mutations in the population accounted for the change, but that is extremely unlikely, given the time scale of the experiment (only a few generations). And in any event, random mutations would manifest in individuals, not in the whole group at once. A much simpler explanation, Noble says (816), is that Waddington's experiment "exploited plasticity that is already present in the population," suggesting "that all the alleles (gene variants) necessary for the inheritance of the characteristic were already present in the population, but not initially in any particular individuals in the correct combination. The experiment simply brings them together."

52. Gregory Bateson, *Steps to an Ecology of Mind* (New York: Ballantine, 1972), 451.

53. Noble, *Dance to the Tune of Life*, 259.

54. Bateson, *Steps to an Ecology of Mind*, 460. Bateson takes this in a direction that sometimes courts a kind of vitalism—and a vitalism that is indissociable from his holism:

I now localize something which I am calling "Mind" immanent in the large biological system—the ecosystem. Or, if I draw the system boundaries at a different level, then mind is immanent in the total evolutionary structure. If this identity between mental and evolutionary units is broadly right, then we face a number of shifts in our thinking . . . The individual mind is immanent but not only in in the body. It is immanent also in the pathways and messages outside the body; and there is a larger Mind of which the individual mind is only a sub-system. This larger Mind is comparable to God and is perhaps what some people mean by God, but it is still immanent in the total interconnected social system and planetary ecology. (*Steps to an Ecology of Mind*, 461)

Bateson's project is thus roughly split between this sort of neo-vitalist holism and the *other* side of his work—closer to Kauffman, Derrida, and second-order systems theory in general—which emphasizes time and again that "the map is not the territory." Waddington himself rejected vitalism for the same reasons that the term does not apply to Kauffman. As Waddington put it, "vitalism amounted to the assertion that living things do not behave as though they were nothing but mechanisms constructed of mere material components; but this presupposes that one knows what mere material components are and what kind of mechanisms they can be built into." As Roger Levin points out in his book on complexity theory, "Waddington was an emergentist, but not a vitalist. He believed that the assembly of a living organism is subject to physical laws, but that their product is not derivable from the laws themselves." Roger Lewin, *Complexity* (New York: Collier, 1992), 179. Interestingly enough, Bateson hypothesizes that the takeaway from Waddington's work, which "can be read in various ways" (*Steps to an Ecology of Mind*, 256), is framed in terms of what Bateson calls "stochastic" process. As he puts it:

to achieve a result by trial and error which could have been achieved in any more direct way necessarily consumes time and effort in some sense of these words. Insofar as we think of adaptability as achieved by stochastic process, we let in the notion of an economics of adaptability. In the field of mental process, we are very familiar with this sort of economics, and in fact a major and necessary saving is achieved by the familiar process of habit formation. We may, in the first instance, solve a given problem by trial and error; but when similar problems recur later, we tend to deal with them more and more economically by taking them out of the range of stochastic operation and handing over the solutions to a deeper and less flexible mechanism, which we call "habit." It is, therefore, perfectly conceivable that some analogous phenomenon may obtain in regard to the production of bithorax characteristics. It may be more economical to produce these by the rigid mechanism of genetic determination rather than by the more wasteful, more flexible (and perhaps less predictable) method of somatic change. (*Steps to an Ecology of Mind*, 257)

Bateson's point here leads directly to the discussion we have already had regarding Derrida's work on "scripts," archives, "writing," and their *machinalité* and automaticity in relation to the question of "life" and, more specifically still, the difference between "response" and mere "reaction" as a means of protecting the ontological domain of the "human." And in this connection, it is worth noting that Derrida *insists* on the cross-contamination of the genetic and epigenetic—a cross-contamination highly specific to the environmental factors of what he calls, in "Signature Event Context," the "pragmatic instance" that Bateson, still laboring under the Weismannian hegemony (*Steps to an Ecology of Mind*, 346), purifies in his reassertion of the then-Weismannian orthodoxy that "no message can pass from the more superficial somatic system to the germ plasm" (*Steps to an Ecology of Mind*, 258).

55. Stuart Kauffman, *Humanity in a Creative Universe* (Oxford: Oxford University Press, 2017), 74.

56. Kauffman, *Humanity in a Creative Universe*, 15, 16.

57. Kauffman, *Humanity in a Creative Universe*, 17.

58. Kauffman, *Humanity in a Creative Universe*, 40.

59. Kauffman, *Humanity in a Creative Universe*, 42.

60. Kauffman, *Humanity in a Creative Universe*, 43.

61. Kauffman, *Humanity in a Creative Universe*, 64.

62. Kauffman, *Humanity in a Creative Universe*, 67.

63. Kauffman, *Humanity in a Creative Universe*, 65.

64. Kauffman, *Humanity in a Creative Universe*, 66.

65. Kauffman, *Humanity in a Creative Universe*, 67.

66. Kauffman, *Humanity in a Creative Universe*, 69.

67. Kauffman, *Humanity in a Creative Universe*, 70.

68. Kauffman, *Humanity in a Creative Universe*, 71.

69. Kauffman, *Humanity in a Creative Universe*, 72.

70. Kauffman, *Humanity in a Creative Universe*, 73.

71. Kauffman, *Humanity in a Creative Universe*, 73.

72. Johnson, *System and Writing in the Philosophy of Jacques Derrida*, 169.

73. Johnson, *System and Writing in the Philosophy of Jacques Derrida*, 163.

74. Kauffman, *Humanity in a Creative Universe*, 75.

75. Martin Hägglund, "The Trace of Time," 39.

76. Hägglund, "The Trace of Time," 43.

77. Hägglund, "The Trace of Time," 43.

78. Bateson, *Steps to an Ecology of Mind*, 418–19.

79. Kauffman, *Humanity in a Creative Universe*, 79.

80. Kauffman, *Humanity in a Creative Universe*, 205.

81. Kauffman, *Humanity in a Creative Universe*, 206–7.

82. William Rasch, *Niklas Luhmann's Modernity: The Paradoxes of Differentiation* (Stanford, CA: Stanford University Press, 2000), 39, 49.

83. See Hägglund, "The Trace of Time," 37.

84. Peter Sloterdijk, *Spheres, Vol. 3: Foams: Plural Spherology*, trans. Wieland Hoban (South Pasadena, CA: Semiotext[e]), 59–60.

85. Sloterdijk, *Spheres, Vol. 3: Foams: Plural Spherology*, 60.

86. Sloterdijk, *Spheres, Vol. 3: Foams: Plural Spherology*, 60. Sloterdijk's recourse, here and elsewhere in the *Spheres* project (sometimes explicit, sometimes tacit, but always at hand) to the Spinozan figure of the monad is far from fortuitous. Denis Noble, in fact, argues that Spinoza is a precursor to systems biology and its opposition to the mechanistic reductionism that derives from Descartes. See *Dance to the Tune of Life*, 164–68.

87. Derrida, *The Animal That Therefore I Am*, 29.

88. Sloterdijk, , *Spheres, Vol. 3: Foams: Plural Spherology*, 60.

CHAPTER 4

1. Jacques Derrida, *The Beast and the Sovereign, Vol. 1*, ed. Michel Lisse, Marie-Louise Mallet, and Ginette Michaud, trans. Geoffrey Bennington (Chicago: University of Chicago Press, 2009), 236.

2. Jacques Derrida, *The Animal That Therefore I Am*, ed. Marie-Louise Mallet, trans. David Wills (New York: Fordham University Press, 2008), 24, 28, 30, 125.

3. Derrida, *The Animal That Therefore I Am*, 39.

4. Derrida, *The Animal That Therefore I Am*, 39.

5. Derrida, *The Animal That Therefore I Am*, 39.

6. *The Poetry of Robert Frost: The Collected Poems, Complete and Unabridged*, ed. Edward Connery Latham (New York: Henry Holt & Co., 1979), 338.

7. John Hollander, *Vision and Resonance: Two Senses of Poetic Form* (Oxford: Oxford University Press, 1975), 42.

8. See, in this connection, Derrida's *The Animal That Therefore I Am* and the well-known discussion of "carnophallogocentrism" in "'Eating Well,' or the Calculation of the Subject: An Interview with Jacques Derrida," in *Who Comes after the Subject?*, ed. Eduardo Cadava, Peter Connor, and Jean-Luc Nancy (New York: Routledge, 1991), 96–119.

9. Slavoj Žižek, *Looking Awry: An Introduction to Jacques Lacan through Popular Culture* (Cambridge, MA: MIT Press, 1992), 36–37.

10. Robert Kern, "Frost and Modernism," *American Literature* 60, no. 1 (March 1988): 15.

11. Hollander, *Vision and Resonance*, 43.

12. See Cary Wolfe, *Animal Rites: American Culture, the Discourse of Species, and Posthumanist Theory* (Chicago: University of Chicago Press, 2003), 78–94.

13. For Stevens's review of Williams, see the essay "Williams," in *OP*, 213–15.

14. Robert Morgan, "Mockingbird," in *Trunk & Thicket* (Fort Collins, CO: L'Epervier Press, 1978), 35.

15. Quoted in Jennifer Ackerman, *The Genius of Birds* (New York: Penguin, 2016), 140.

16. Ackerman, *The Genius of Birds*, 140.

17. Ackerman, *The Genius of Birds*, 141.

18. David Wills, *Inanimation: Theories of Inorganic Life* (Minneapolis: University of Minnesota Press, 2016), 266–67, 258.

19. Ackerman, *The Genius of Birds*, 141.

20. Ackerman, *The Genius of Birds*, 144.

21. Ackerman, *The Genius of Birds*, 144–45.

22. See, for example, Harold Bloom, *Wallace Stevens: The Poems of Our Climate* (Ithaca, NY: Cornell University Press, 1976), 371.

23. In this connection, see the notes on the poem in Eleanor Cook, *A Reader's Guide to Wallace Stevens* (Princeton, NJ: Princeton University Press, 2007), 314.

24. Martin Hägglund, "The Arche-Materiality of Time: Deconstruction, Evolution, and Speculative Realism," in *Theory after "Theory,"* ed. Jane Elliott and Derek Attridge (London: Routledge, 2011), 270.

25. Hägglund, "The Arche-Materiality of Time," 274.

26. Quoted in Hägglund, "The Arche-Materiality of Time," 274–75.

27. Hägglund, "The Arche-Materiality of Time," 275.

28. Ackerman, *The Genius of Birds*, 145, 147. And here I think it's worth noting that even Morgan's poem, beginning as it does, comes around to the same assertions, unpacking and ramifying iteration and recombination in the situated organism/environment relationship, handled here more in terms of phylogenesis than the ontogenesis that opened the poem so stunningly, and ramping up the premium on how the technicity of the trace traverses the organic/inorganic relation. Morgan writes in "Mockingbird":

> Don't try
> to filibuster nature. The art of culture
> is always substitution. The knife must
> turn to keep its honey. Note nature's
> formality and the million intersections
> in a piece of cloth. Slice the terrain in
> strips evading fungus and depletion, and
> play them like bands of the spectrum.
> Recombination captures more sunlight
> and mineral. People on mountaintops
> age slower, says Einstein. The clock's heart
> knocks in its cabinet. Think of vegetal
> glass and optical flesh. Though time's a
> potentate and clay a tyrant, the law
> of conservation means the world's
> an anagram of each stage of evolution. (38)

29. Ackerman, *The Genius of Birds*, 153.

30. Ackerman, *The Genius of Birds*, 153.

31. Humberto Maturana and Francisco Varela, *The Tree of Knowledge: The Biological Roots of Human Understanding*, rev. ed., trans. Robert Paolucci, foreword by J. Z. Young (Boston: Shambhala Press, 1998), 29.

32. Cary Wolfe, *Before the Law: Humans and Other Animals in a Biopolitical Frame* (Chicago: University of Chicago Press, 2013), 57.

33. Derrida's characterization occurs in *Limited Inc*, ed. Gerald Graff, trans. Jeffrey Mehlman and Samuel Weber (Evanston, IL: Northwestern University Press, 1988), 113.

34. Derrida, *The Animal That Therefore I Am*, 37–39.

35. *CP*, 82, 13, 18, 318.

36. Simon Critchley, *Things Merely Are: Philosophy in the Poetry of Wallace Stevens* (London: Routledge, 2005), 4.

37. *CP*, 486.

38. Critchley, *Things Merely Are*, 19.

39. Critchley, *Things Merely Are*, 58.

40. *OP*, 189.

41. Jacques Derrida, "The University without Condition," in *Without Alibi*, ed., trans., and introd. Peggy Kamuf (Stanford, CA: Stanford University Press, 2002), 209.

42. Derrida, "The University without Condition," 214.

43. *CP*, 247.

44. *CP*, 203.

45. *CP*, 202.

46. *CP*, 203.

47. Jacques Derrida, "Afterword," in *Limited Inc*, 119.

48. *CP*, 204.

49. *CP*, 394.

50. Derrida's most important and best known discussion of *augenblick* is in his early work *Speech and Phenomena: And Other Essays on Husserl's Theory of Signs*, trans. and introd. David B. Allison, preface by Newton Garver (Evanston, IL: Northwestern University Press, 1973), 52–64, which is ably summarized in Leonard Lawlor's entry for Derrida in the online *Stanford Encyclopedia of Philosophy*, http://plato.stanford.edu/entries/derrida/, last accessed September 28, 2015. As Lawlor explains,

> for Derrida, Husserl's descriptions imply that the living present, by always folding the recent past back into itself, by always folding memory into perception, involves a *difference* in the very middle of it (*Voice and Phenomenon*, p. 56). In other words, in the very moment, when silently I speak to myself, it must be the case that there is a minuscule hiatus differentiating me into the speaker and into the hearer. There must be a hiatus that differentiates

me from myself, a hiatus or gap without which I would not be a hearer *as well as* a speaker. This hiatus also defines the trace, a minimal repeatability. And this hiatus, this fold of repetition, is found in the very moment of hearing-myself-speak. Derrida stresses that "moment" or "instant" translates the German "Augenblick," which literally means "blink of the eye." When Derrida stresses the literal meaning of "Augenblick," he is in effect "deconstructing" auditory auto-affection into visual auto-affection. When I look in the mirror, for example, it is necessary that I am "distanced" or "spaced" from the mirror. I must be distanced from myself so that I am able to be *both* seer *and* seen. The *space* between, however, remains obstinately invisible. Remaining invisible, the space gouges out the eye, blinds it. I see myself over there in the mirror and yet, that self over there is other than me; so, I am not able to see myself as such. What Derrida is trying to demonstrate here is that this "spacing" (*espacement*) or blindness is essentially necessary for all forms of auto-affection.

Emerson's "transparent eye-ball" occurs in the essay *Nature*, in *Emerson's Prose and Poetry*, ed. Joel Porte and Saundra Morris (New York: W. W. Norton, 2001), 29.

51. *CP*, 93.

52. See Niklas Luhmann, *Social Systems*, trans. John Bednarz, Jr., with Dirk Baecker, introd. Eva M. Knodt (Stanford, CA: Stanford University Press, 1995), 12–58.

53. Namely, in Wolfe, *What Is Posthumanism?*, xx–xxv.

54. Luhman, *Social Systems*, 26.

55. The characterization of "correlationism" is from Ian Bogost, *Alien Phenomenology, Or What It's Like to Be a Thing* (Minneapolis: University of Minnesota Press, 2013), 5, summarizing Quentin Meillassoux's definition of the term in his book *After Finitude*. But as Raoni Padui explains in an exacting and careful essay that traces this problem through the history of philosophy since Kant, "one can maintain a materialist standpoint, namely, that the entity and the real are ontologically prior to thought, while denying that direct and immediate access of thought to such an entity. In other words, one can be a materialist and an anti-realist at the same time." He continues, "Materialism is an ontological thesis that posits that being can be independent of thinking, while realism posits the thinkability of this being independent of thinking. If correlationist skepticism is an anti-realism, it does not necessarily need to be an anti-materialism. In the argument from facticity, Meillassoux moves from one to the other, claiming that the existence of something prior or independent of thought (materialism) can only be maintained if we can think or access being prior to thought (realism). This move is clearly illegitimate, insofar as it involves the claim that there can be matter prior to thought if and only if one can think the being of matter prior to thought. In other words, it is grounding ontology in epistemology."

Raoni Padui, "Realism, Anti-Realism, and Materialism," *Angelaki: Journal of the Theoretical Humanities* 16, no. 2 (2011): 91–92.

56. Richard Rorty, *Objectivity, Relativism, and Truth: Philosophical Papers, Vol. 1* (New York: Cambridge University Press, 1991), 159.

57. Rorty, *Objectivity, Relativism, and Truth*, 101.

58. Rorty, *Objectivity, Relativism, and Truth*, 97.

59. *CP*, 203.

60. One might further note, to put a finer point on my reading of the pigeons' "ambiguous undulations," that "ambiguity," as Gerald Graff reminds us, is a much more domesticated concept than "indeterminacy," which doesn't simply offer a choice between two finite meanings, but rather obeys a much more radical logic of a different kind of finitude: not the finitude of discrete and bounded meanings between which we can choose, but the finitude of our inability to limit and fix meaning, or meanings, in this way. See his essay "Determinacy/Indeterminacy" in *Critical Terms for Literary Study*, ed. Frank Lentricchia and Thomas McLaughlin (Chicago: University of Chicago Press, 1990), 163–76.

61. *OP*, 141.

62. Jacques Derrida, "The Principle of Reason: The University in the Eyes of Its Pupils," in *Eyes of the University: The Right to Philosophy 2*, trans. Jan Plug et al. (Stanford, CA: Stanford University Press, 2004), 132.

63. Derrida, "The Principle of Reason," 139.

64. *OP*, 141.

65. David Ferrell Krell, *Derrida and Our Animal Others: Derrida's Final Seminar, "The Beast and the Sovereign"* (Bloomington: Indiana University Press, 2013), 38.

66. See, for example, Jacques Derrida, *Rogues: Two Essays on Reason*, trans. Pascale-Anne Brault and Michael Naas (Stanford, CA: Stanford University Press, 2005), 84.

67. Derrida, *The Beast and the Sovereign, Vol. 1*, 223.

68. *CP*, 63.

69. Jakob von Uexküll, *A Foray into the Worlds of Animals and Humans, with A Theory of Meaning*, trans. Joseph D. O'Neil, introd. Dorion Sagan (Minneapolis: University of Minnesota Press, 2010). Alva Noë, *Out of Our Heads: Why You Are Not Your Brain, and Other Lessons from the Biology of Consciousness* (New York: Hill & Wang, 2009), xiii.

70. For more on how these questions cross-pollinate with Derrida's work, see Cary Wolfe, *Animal Rites: American Culture, the Discourse of Species, and Posthumanist Theory* (Chicago: University of Chicago Press, 1998), 78–94; and, more recently, Wolfe, *Before the Law: Humans and Other Animals in a Biopolitical Frame* (Chicago: University of Chicago Press, 2013), 60–86.

71. Noë, *Out of Our Heads*, 43.

72. Derrida, *The Beast and the Sovereign, Vol. 2*, 8.

73. Derrida, *The Beast and the Sovereign, Vol. 2*, 8–9.

74. See, for example, Timothy Morton, *The Ecological Thought* (Cambridge, MA: Harvard University Press, 2012); and Morton, *Hyperobjects: Philosophy and Ecology after the End of the World* (Minneapolis: University of Minnesota Press, 2013).

75. See Wolfe, *Before the Law*, 63–86.

76. For an expanded discussion of what falls between the dashes here—and in relation to Stevens's poetry—see Wolfe, *What Is Posthumanism?*, chap. 10.

77. Derrida, *The Beast and the Sovereign, Vol. 2*, 105.

78. *CP*, 203.

79. Steven D. Brown, "A Topology of the Sensible," *New Formations* 72 (January 2011): 165.

80. Michel Serres with Bruno Latour, *Conversations on Science, Culture, and Time*, trans. Roxanne Lapidus (Ann Arbor: University of Michigan Press, 1995), 60.

81. Paul Harris, "The Itinerant Theorist: Nature and Knowledge/Ecology and Topology in Michel Serres," *SubStance* 26, no. 2 (1997): 44.

82. But for a very brief summary, see Wolfe, *What Is Posthumanism?*, 91–93, 132–33, 292–95.

83. Derrida, *The Beast and the Sovereign, Vol. 2*, 62.

84. Gregory Bateson, *Steps to an Ecology of Mind* (New York: Ballantine, 1972), 449.

85. *OP*, 141.

86. Derrida, *The Beast and the Sovereign, Vol. 2*, 62–63, 72–73.

87. Serres and Latour, *Conversations*, 65.

88. Serres and Latour, *Conversations*, 64.

89. Harris, "The Itinerant Theorist," 45.

90. *CP*, 534.

91. Serres and Latour, *Conversations*, 65.

92. Serres and Latour, *Conversations*, 66.

93. Quoted in Derrida, *The Beast and the Sovereign, Vol. 2*, 86.

94. Quoted in Derrida, *The Beast and the Sovereign, Vol. 2*, 86.

95. Derrida, *The Beast and the Sovereign, Vol. 2*, 86.

96. Derrida, *The Beast and the Sovereign, Vol. 2*, 87.

97. Michael Naas, *The End of the World and Other Teachable Moments: Jacques Derrida's Final Seminar* (New York: Fordham University Press, 2015), 94. See David Farrell Krell's amusing discussion of this moment in *Derrida and Our Animal Others*, 49.

98. Krell, *Derrida and Our Animal Others*, 50.

99. Brown, "A Topology of the Sensible," 164.

100. Harris, "The Itinerant Theorist," 37.

101. Quoted in Brown, "The Itinerant Theorist," 164; emphasis added.

102. Derrida, *The Beast and the Sovereign, Vol. 2*, 88.

103. For a more detailed handling of this issue in relation to pragmatism, see Wolfe, *What Is Posthumanism?*, 244–45.

104. Naas, *The End of the World*, 98.

105. Maturana and Varela, *The Tree of Knowledge*, 242.

106. Hans-Georg Moeller, *The Radical Luhmann* (New York: Columbia University Press, 2012), 70–72.

107. Derrida, *The Beast and the Sovereign, Vol. 2*, 105.

108. For more on this question in Derrida in relation to ethics and nonhuman animals, see Wolfe, *Before the Law*, chaps. 7 and 8.

109. Derrida, *The Beast and the Sovereign, Vol. 2*, 268.

110. Derrida, *The Beast and the Sovereign, Vol. 2*, 269–70.

111. Derrida, *The Beast and the Sovereign, Vol. 2*, 8.

112. See Kelly Oliver's foregrounding of this aspect of the seminars, which is somewhat different in emphasis from my own, in "The Poetic Axis of Ethics," *Derrida Today* 7, no. 2 (2014): 121–36, especially 125, 129.

113. *OP*, 189.

114. Stevens, *The Necessary Angel*, 29.

CHAPTER 5

1. Stuart Elden gives an able summary of the *Spheres* project and its major contours. One of the more novel features of the project, he notes, is its tracing of the relationship between the birth of the child and the birth of "world" that Sloterdijk lays out in volume one, *Bubbles*. As Elden puts it, for Sloterdijk,

> we are born, but too soon. We are the aborted creatures that are thrown into a world that is partly established and is partly to be accomplished. Neoteny, for Sloterdijk, is another name for this being aborted, always too early, always too violently. It is this coming into the world, being born into the world, after being thrown and ripped from the warm amniotic fluid which we breath and feed on that Sloterdijk finds philosophically fecund. For Sloterdijk, therefore, phenomenological analysis has to be preceded by a philosophical gynaecology, of what he calls in the first volume of *Sphären*, a negative gynaecology that is an analysis of the process of being ejected from, thrown out of the uterus. We are thus strange and estranged (*verfremdetet*) creatures, who must arrive in a world, but who in so doing are already abandoning it. We are creatures of distance . . . We are mangled creatures, who survive because of the generosity and gratitude of the Other, who welcomes us, who nourishes us, who gives us an abode and refuge. We are born of someone, and someone receives us . . . Coming to the world is a form of coupling: being-with is a being-with-another which forms a couple. But being born before time means we are always arriving in the world. This arrival

is met with the project of fashioning a dwelling. To come into the world is to build a home. In contrast to Heidegger, for Sloterdijk the *Mit-sein* is always being-alongside-others in a dwelling that has been built and in which we are enclosed. Being-with is always being inside of a dwelling. *Dasein's* neoteny and always dwelling alongside another means that the subject is always in a process of autogenesis that is simultaneously a making of worlds. *Dasein's* ex-stasis, its being always ahead of itself, is simultaneously a worlding, a bringing-forth of worlds, whether they be poetic, literary, or material and real, such as glasshouses, palaces, or caves.

Stuart Elden, "Being-with as Making Worlds: The 'Second Coming' of Peter Sloterdijk," *Environment and Planning D: Society and Space* 27 (2009): 5–6. One need not buy into Sloterdijk's "negative gynaecology" to perceive the project's utility for mapping the tropological architecture and trajectory of Stevens's poetry—and, importantly, mapping it in terms that allow us to see "world-historical" developments that express themselves, however obliquely, in Stevens's work. (This is important because, as many critics have noted, when Stevens himself tried to forcibly shoehorn his lyricism into a mode of "social relevance," or attempted to situate his poetry in relation to "world events," the result was almost always disappointing, with *Owl's Clover* being Exhibit A, of course (as in, for example, Joseph Riddel's discussion in *The Clairvoyant Eye: The Poetry and Poetics of Wallace Stevens* [Baton Rouge: LSU Press, 1965], 109, 122–23).

2. Timothy Campbell, *Improper Life: Technology and Biopolitics from Heidegger to Agamben* (Minneapolis: University of Minnesota Press, 2011), 86.

3. Peter Sloterdijk, *Spheres, Vol. 2: Globes—Macrospherology* (South Pasadena, CA: Semiotext[e], 2014), 126, 128. For readers who are especially interested in the theoretical arguments in this book, let me situate my relationship to Sloterdijk's work more precisely. As one might already guess, Sloterdijk's diverse commitments in the *Spheres* project embroil him in a battle on multiple fronts to differentiate his position from those of Lacan (to whom much attention is devoted in *Bubbles*), Derrida (to whom Sloterdijk has devoted a slender and largely insignificant book), and Luhmann, with whom he has an especially productive and provocative relationship. More specifically, a commitment to a "polycontextural logic" (to use Luhmann's characterization of Gotthard Günther's work, which is also central to Sloterdijk) grounds the posthumanism of both Luhmann and Sloterdijk, and Sloterdijk returns to it at the end of the book of interviews entitled *Neither Sun Nor Death*, where he observes:

That one is in situation and belongs to it is the *a priori* assumption of chaos theory. In actual fact, we can live nowhere else than in chaos—in a chaos compensated through orders. If we bring the Heideggerian formula of "being-in-the-world" into play, then the resulting statement is: *Dasein*, or being-there, means to be in complexity or to be in chaos . . . What is missing is a logic with enough power and versatility to accommodate complexity, indeterminacy, and immersion . . . The murderous ideologies of the 20th century are . . . nothing other than desperate endgames of bivalency, and militant denials of complex thinking, which were announced in many various forms. Their indispensibility need not be doubted today, but how they could be operatively accomplished is something for which hitherto there exist only a few suggestive propositions—for example, on the basis of cybernetics, systems theory, and bio-informatics (Peter Sloterdijk with Hans-Jürgen Heinrichs, *Neither Sun Nor Death*, trans. Steve Corcoran [Los Angeles: Semiotext(e), 2007], 351).

At the same time, however, Sloterdijk is at pains in many places to differentiate his position, most of all, from Luhmann. Earlier in the interviews, for example, he writes that "we remain captives of substance fetishism to the extent that we first address things in an isolated form and then their relations with one another." This "individualist substantialism," as he puts it, appears "in a practically perfect incognito, in the form of systems theory," where systems "are assessed as quasi-monads that are distinguished from their specific environments; but strict heed is paid to the following succession: first and above all the internal relations of the system with itself, then external relations" (*Neither Sun Nor Death*, 150–51). As we have already seen in some detail in the earlier chapters, this is true as far as it goes—but only as far as it goes. First of all, it is hard to imagine a less apt characterization of Luhmann than "substance fetishism," given that, for him, the fundamental elements of social systems are not substances but *communications*, and given as well, as we have seen, his insistence on the *difference* between psychic and social systems and *how* that difference must affect any theory of meaning, which in turn necessitates a quite elaborate theory of meaning in terms of the actual and the possible, the triadic relations of utterance, information, and understanding, and so on (which need not concern us in their technical details here). Second, it is the thinking of *complexity* that is paramount for Luhmann (that is, after all, where Sloterdijk sees their common cause as theorists of the social); for Luhmann, it is the radically asymmetrical distribution of complexity across the system/environment divide that necessitates "monadic" system closure, selection, and so on, which means that the entire "internal"/"external" topography used by Sloterdijk is subjected, as discussed earlier, to a topological folding or torsion in systems theory.

But be that as it may, Sloterdijk's chief means for distancing himself from Luhmann's "quasi-monads" is, of course, the purchase provided by the fundamental dyadic relation laid out in the "negative gyneaecology" of volume 1 of the *Spheres* project, *Bubbles*, but here a few brief observations are in order. First, it seems quite a stretch to contend that *Luhmann*—who is quite clear that elements in a system have a conferred and not given character—is a "fetishist of substance," especially when put alongside Sloterdijk's commitment to the gynecological/foundational project of *Bubbles*, which simply means that for Sloterdijk, complexity, and the confrontation with complexity, is always already domesticated by a fundamentally onto-subjective scenario, as is the case in psychoanalysis (in short, complexity loses its radical alterity because it is always already domesticated by the phenomenological and psychoanalytic foundation of the gynecological/dyadic relation of subject formation). (And this is to leave aside the not insignificant point that such a scenario fundamentally subordinates sexuality to reproduction and, indeed, to heteronormativity, even if it is obviously weighted in the direction of the mother/child relationship: *canonically* weighted, one might say.) Moreover—and this would be one of the very first deconstructive points to make, of course—there is no isomorphic scalability from the formal commitment to complexity shared by both thinkers to (or from) the dyadic gynecology at the foundation of the *Spheres* project. Why not? Precisely for the reasons we discussed in chapter 3, which leads to a third and separate point: in terms of theoretical biology, we have to understand that the question is not the dyadic relationship of the self and its (m-)other—the primal relationship of which multiplicity and difference are but epiphenomena—but rather, to borrow from Donna Haraway's phrasing, the self *and all its others* (as we saw in chapter 3). And this fact—what we might call the "othering of the other," the retention of the alterity of the other (in Derrida's terms)—actually opens onto not just the more radical and deconstructive consequences of the paradoxes of self-reference that Stevens himself is so interested in, but also onto the *machinalité* of the biological and the body that obtains at a more fundamental level, a nonisomorphic and nonscalable multiplicity that obtains well beneath Sloterdijk's fundamental dyadic relation (and entangling it in, as Derrida well demonstrates, the domain of the animal, the nonhuman, the mammalian existence that resides beneath the domain of the [m-]other, and so on). Which is to say that what is needed here (for these are Sloterdijk's *own* terms, finally) is a much more layered, nuanced, and concatenated analysis of the immunity/autoimmunity relation as that obtains *beneath* the level of "the body," "the person," and so on. This is, after all, one of Roberto Esposito's main points in his rethinking of the problem of biopolitics. See my discussion of "flesh" vs. "the body" in Esposito's work, in Cary Wolfe, *Before the Law: Humans and Other Animals in a Biopolitical Frame* (Chicago: University of Chicago Press, 2013), 50.

4. *CP*, 68.

5. *OP*, 260.

6. *CP*, 412.

7. Peter Sloterdijk, *Spheres, Vol. 1: Bubbles—Microspherology* (Los Angeles, Semiotext[e], 2011), 25.

8. Emerson writes at the end of "Nature," "Man is the dwarf of himself Once

he was permeated and dissolved by spirit. He filled nature with his overflowing currents . . . But, having made for himself this huge shell, his waters retired; he no longer fills the veins and veinlets; his is shrunk to a drop. He sees, that the structure still fits him, but fits him colossally." *Emerson's Poetry and Prose*, ed. Joel Porte and Saundra Morris (New York: W. W. Norton, 2001), 53. For the relevant passage in "Fate," see 278.

9. Sloterdijk, *Spheres, Vol. 1: Bubbles—Microspherology*, 28.

10. *CP*, 66.

11. Harold Bloom, *The Poems of Our Climate* (Ithaca, NY: Cornell University Press, 1980), 23.

12. Sloterdijk, *Spheres, Vol. 2: Globes—Macrospherology*, 774.

13. Sloterdijk, *Spheres, Vol. 2: Globes—Macrospherology*, 777.

14. *CP*, 94.

15. Sloterdijk, *Spheres, Vol. 2: Globes—Macrospherology*, 778–79.

16. Sloterdijk, *Spheres, Vol. 2: Globes—Macrospherology*, 779.

17. Campbell, *Improper Life*, 88.

18. Sloterdijk, *Spheres, Vol. 2: Globes—Macrospherology*, 779.

19. Christopher Schaberg, *The Textual Life of Airports: Reading the Culture of Flight* (London: Bloomsbury, 2013), 118.

20. Riddell, *The Clairvoyant Eye*, 86–87.

21. Bloom, *The Poems of Our Climate*, 105.

22. *CP*, 70.

23. Vilém Flusser, *Natural:Mind*, ed. Siegfried Zielinski, trans. Rodrigo Maltez Novaes (Minneapolis: Univocal, 2013), 27.

24. *CP*, 411, 420.

25. Bloom. *The Poems of Our Climate*, 270–71.

26. *CP*, 532–33.

27. Niklas Luhmann, *Art as a Social System*, trans. Eva M. Knodt (Stanford, CA: Stanford University Press, 2000), 92.

28. Niklas Luhmann, *Introduction to Systems Theory*, ed. Dirk Baecker, trans. Peter Gilgen (Cambridge: Polity, 2013), 168.

29. Luhmann, *Introduction to Systems Theory*, 170.

30. *CP*, 380.

31. *CP*, 381.

32. *CP*, 440–41.

33. *CP*, 443.

34. See Richard Poirier's discussion in *Poetry and Pragmatism* (London: Faber & Faber, 1992), 37, 160.

35. *CP*, 442.

36. *CP*, 443.

37. Helen Vendler, *On Extended Wings: Wallace Stevens' Longer Poems* (Cambridge, MA: Harvard University Press, 1969), 237.

38. Vendler, *On Extended Wings* 231–32.

39. Luhmann, *Introduction to Systems Theory*, 160.

40. Luhmann, *Introduction to Systems Theory*, 161.

41. Luhmann, *Introduction to Systems Theory*, 161.

42. Luhmann, *Introduction to Systems Theory*, 163.

43. *CP*, 403.

44. *CP*, 404.

45. *CP*, 373.

46. *CP*, 203.

47. *CP*, 199.

48. *CP*, 198.

49. Sloterdijk, *Spheres, Vol. 1: Bubbles—Microspherology*, 71.

50. See Jacques Derrida, *The Beast and the Sovereign, Vol. 2*, ed. Michel Lisse, Marie-Louise Mallet, and Ginette Michaud, trans. Geoffrey Bennington (Chicago: University of Chicago Press, 2011); and Derrida, *Rogues: Two Essays on Reason*, trans. Pascale-Anne Brault and Michael Naas (Stanford, CA: Stanford University Press, 2005).

51. Sloterdijk, *Spheres, Vol. 1: Bubbles—Microspherology*, 71.

52. Bloom, *The Poems of Our Climate*, 148.

53. *CP*, 202; Bloom, *The Poems of Our Climate*, 144.

54. Riddell, *The Clairvoyant Eye*, 155.

55. Riddell, *The Clairvoyant Eye*, 155.

56. Riddell, *The Clairvoyant Eye*, 156.

57. *CP*, 215.

58. *CP*, 215.

59. Luhmann, *Introduction to Systems Theory*, 171.

60. *CP*, 216.

61. *CP*, 391.

62. *CP*, 76.

63. *CP*, 193–94.

64. On this cluster of terms and commitments in Emerson, see the essay "Aversive Thinking: Emersonian Representations in Heidegger and Nietzsche," in Stanley Cavell, *Emerson's Transcendental Etudes*, ed. David Justin Hodge (Stanford, CA: Stanford University Press, 2003), 140–70.

65. Jacques Derrida, "Justices," trans. Peggy Kamuf, *Critical Inquiry* 31 (2005): 700.

66. Sloterdijk, *Spheres, Vol. 1: Bubbles—Microspherology*, 541.

67. Quoted in Derrida, "Justices," 700.

68. Derrida, "Justices," 701.

69. *Emerson's Prose and Poetry*, ed. Porte and Morris, 29.

70. Gregory Bateson, *Steps to an Ecology of Mind* (New York: Ballantine, 1972), 410.

71. Vendler, *On Extended Wings*, 232.

72. *CP*, 374.
73. *CP*, 373.
74. *CP*, 378.
75. Vendler, *On Extended Wings*, 242.
76. Vendler, *On Extended Wings*, 244.
77. *CP*, 429.
78. *CP*, 429.
79. *CP*, 430.
80. Cary Wolfe, "Elemental Relations at the Edge," in *Elemental Ecocriticism*, ed. Jeffrey J. Cohen and Lowell Duckert (Minneapolis: University of Minnesota Press, 2015), 234–48.
81. *OP*, 141.
82. *CP*, 373.
83. *CP*, 394.
84. *CP*, 377.

CHAPTER 6

1. Peter Sloterdijk, *Spheres, Vol. 3: Foams—Plural Spherology*, trans. Wieland Hoban (South Pasadena, CA: Semiotext[e], 2016), 16–17.
2. *Emerson's Prose and Poetry*, ed. Joel Porte and Saundra Morris (New York: W. W. Norton, 2001), 198, 200.
3. Sloterdijk, *Spheres, Vol. 3: Foams—Plural Spherology*, 23.
4. Sloterdijk, *Spheres, Vol. 3: Foams—Plural Spherology*, 25.
5. *CP*, 380.
6. *CP*, 406.
7. *CP*, 381.
8. *CP*, 384.
9. *CP*, 385.
10. *CP*, 386.
11. *CP*, 393.
12. *CP*, 395.
13. *CP*, 404.
14. *CP*, 412–16.
15. Peter Sloterdijk, *Spheres, Vol. 1: Bubbles—Microspherology* (Los Angeles: Semiotext[e], 2011), 46.
16. Sloterdijk, *Spheres, Vol. 1: Bubbles—Microspherology*, 46.
17. *CP*, 490.
18. John Durham Peters, *The Marvelous Clouds: Toward a Philosophy of Elemental Media* (Chicago: University of Chicago Press, 2015), 115.
19. Peters, *The Marvelous Clouds*, 125.
20. Peters, *The Marvelous Clouds*, 125.
21. *Emerson's Prose and Poetry*, ed. Porte and Morris, 208.

22. *CP*, 417.

23. Martin Heidegger, "The Question Concerning Technology," in *Basic Writings*, ed. David Farrell Krell (New York: Harper & Row, 1977), 301.

24. *Emerson's Prose and Poetry*, ed. Porte and Morris, 27–28.

25. *CP*, 413.

26. *OP*, 258.

27. *CP*, 412–13.

28. Peters, *The Marvelous Clouds*, 118.

29. Stanley Cavell, *Emerson's Transcendental Etudes*, ed. David Justin Hodge (Stanford, CA: Stanford University Press, 2003), 138–39. Regarding the question of finitude here, Michael Naas notes that "as Derrida will argue, the category of life cannot be thought without appealing to a concept of repetition and, thus, of the trace, the possibility of the trace or of archivization begins not after life but already with the emergence of life itself . . . This means that *survivance* does not simply follow upon life but is coextensive with it, that life and death must be thought together as survival." Michael Naas, *The End of the World and Other Teachable Moments* (New York: Fordham University Press, 2015), 13.

30. *CP*, 414.

31. *CP*, 418.

32. Wallace Stevens, *The Necessary Angel: Essays on Reality and the Imagination* (New York: Random House, 1951), 29.

33. *CP*, 417.

34. *CP*, 418.

35. *CP*, 420.

36. Martin Heidegger, *Poetry, Language, Thought*, trans. Albert Hofstadter (New York: Harper & Row, 1971).

37. Sloterdijk, *Spheres, Vol. 1: Bubbles—Microspherology*, 56.

38. Theoretically speaking, that refusal, as I have clarified elsewhere, is predicated (to use the terms of systems theory) on the contingency of the mark (in Spencer Brown's sense), which ensures not the "identity of identity and nonidentity" (as in Hegel), but the *nonidentity* of identity and nonidentity. Cary Wolfe, *What Is Posthumanism?* (Minneapolis: University of Minnesota Press, 2010), 223.

39. Michael Marder, "Ecology as Event," in *Eco-Deconstruction: Derrida and Environmental Philosophy*, ed. David Wood, Philip Lynes, and Matthias Fritsch (New York: Fordham University Press, 2018), 143.

40. Marder, "Ecology as Event," 143.

41. Marder, "Ecology as Event," 143.

42. Marder, "Ecology as Event," 146. See Jacques Derrida, *The Beast and the Sovereign, Vol. 2*, ed. Michel Lisse, Marie-Louise Mallet, and Ginette Michaud, trans. Geoffrey Bennington (Chicago: University of Chicago Press, 2011); and Derrida, *Rogues: Two Essays on Reason*, trans. Pascale-Anne Brault and Michael Naas (Stanford, CA: Stanford University Press, 2005).

43. Eleanor Cook, *A Reader's Guide to Wallace Stevens* (Princeton, NJ: Princeton University Press, 2007), 259.

44. *CP*, 471.

45. *CP*, 465.

46. Cook, *Reader's Guide*, 259.

47. *CP*, 466.

48. *CP*, 467.

49. *CP*, 469.

50. Cook, *Reader's Guide*, 262.

51. Cavell, *Emerson's Transcendental Etudes*, 132–33.

52. *Emerson's Prose and Poetry*, ed. Porte and Morris, 198.

53. *Emerson's Prose and Poetry*, ed. Porte and Morris, 200.

54. Cavell, *Emerson's Transcendental Etudes*, 133, 139.

55. *CP*, 469. Harold Bloom has noted this connection with "Of Mere Being" as well. See *The Poems of Our Climate* (Ithaca, NY: Cornell University Press, 1977), 316.

56. *OP*, 141.

57. *CP*, 470.

58. Sloterdijk, *Spheres, Vol. 1: Bubbles—Microspherology*, 25.

59. Peter Sloterdijk, *Spheres, Vol. 2: Globes—Macrospherology* (South Pasadena, CA: Semiotext[e], 2014), 845.

60. *OP*, 233.

61. *OP*, 234.

62. *OP*, 234.

63. Sloterdijk, *Spheres, Vol. 2: Globes—Macrospherology*, 867.

64. Derrida, *Rogues*, 13.

65. *OP*, 234.

66. *OP*, 234.

67. *CP*, 471.

68. *CP*, 471–72.

69. Marder, "Ecology as Event," 156.

70. Marder, "Ecology as Event," 156.

71. Niklas Luhmann, *Art as a Social System*, trans. Eva M. Knodt (Stanford, CA: Stanford University Press, 2000), 92.

72. Quoted in Marder, "Ecology as Event," 150.

73. Marder, "Ecology as Event," 150.

74. *CP*, 532–33.

75. Sloterdijk, *Spheres, Vol. 3: Foams—Plural Spherology*, 25.

76. Bloom, *The Poems of Our Climate*, 23.

77. Sloterdijk, *Spheres, Vol. 3: Foams—Plural Spherology*, 28.

78. *CP*, 474.

79. *CP*, 477.

80. *CP*, 488.

81. *CP*, 472.

82. *CP*, 421.

83. Bloom, *The Poems of Our Climate*, 306.

84. *CP*, 466.

85. *Oxford English Dictionary, Vol. 1, Compact Edition* (Oxford: Oxford University Press, 1971), 468. I am indebted to Jonathan Burt for drawing my attention to these connotations of these lines.

86. *CP*, 465.

87. *CP*, 465.

88. *Letters of Wallace Stevens*, ed. Holly Stevens (Berkeley: University of California Press, 1966), 464n7.

89. *CP*, 67.

90. Derrida, *The Beast and the Sovereign, Vol. 2*, 99, 101.

91. Derrida, *The Beast and the Sovereign, Vol. 2*, 100n13.

92. J. Hillis Miller, "Wallace Stevens' Poetry of Being," in Roy Harvey Pearce and J. Hillis Miller, *The Act of the Mind: Essays on the Poetry of Wallace Stevens* (Baltimore: Johns Hopkins University Press, 1965), 153.

93. Miller, "Wallace Stevens' Poetry of Being," 151.

94. *CP*, 465.

95. *CP*, 470.

96. *CP*, 486.

97. *CP*, 488.

98. *CP*, 489.

99. *CP*, 465; Bloom, *The Poems of Our Climate*, 308.

100. Quoted in Bloom, *The Poems of Our Climate*, 310.

101. Bloom, *The Poems of Our Climate*, 310.

102. *CP*, 477.

103. Bloom, *The Poems of Our Climate*, 306.

104. Bloom, *The Poems of Our Climate*, 306.

105. Cavell, *Emerson's Transcendental Etudes*, 39.

106. Bloom, *The Poems of Our Climate*, 306.

107. Cavell, *Emerson's Transcendental Etudes*, 34.

108. Cavell, *Emerson's Transcendental Etudes*, 25.

109. Quoted in Michael Fried, *Another Light: Jacques-Louis David to Thomas Demand* (New Haven: Yale University Press, 2014), 258.

110. *Pacific Sun* uses paper and cardboard models to re-create the contents of the bar inside a large cruise ship, the *Pacific Sun*—tables, chairs, a bookcase, a credenza, a refrigerator, but also a flowerpot, a mop-trolley and mop, a hanging lamp, cups, plastic ketchup bottles, lemon slices, pencils or straws, napkins, and so on—which in 2008 was buffeted by large waves and wind, during which the ensuing chaos of all these items and more shifting to and fro in the bar was captured on a closed-circuit security camera. That video went viral on YouTube, and Demand decided on a project that, on the face of it, seems almost insane:

to re-create the entire 2 minutes and 2 seconds in a 2,944-frame stop-action video involving hundreds of paper and cardboard items of various sizes in a set of shifting interactions that could hardly be more complex.

111. Michael Fried, *Art and Objecthood: Essays and Reviews* (Chicago: University of Chicago Press, 1998), 40.

112. Fried, *Another Light*, 254. And "it is worth stressing," he continues, "that the role of photography in this operation is crucial, indispensable: as actual things in the world, occupying real, three-dimensional space, Demand's constructions would be no more 'saturated' with his intentions (to use a well-chosen verb of Régis Durand's) than would be any other made thing, of art or non-art, with the intentions of its maker or makers; in other words, they would be ontologically on a par with the larger real-world context in which they were encountered. Whereas by photographing the objects and situations he constructs, Demand effectively replaces the real-world context with a merely depicted one, every detail and aspect of which, including lighting and point of view, is *exactly* what he intends it to be" (255).

For Fried, then—and this is to reprise the argument of "Art and Objecthood"—intentionality is what characterizes, indeed defines, the artwork as such, as opposed to "the Minimalist/Literalist and, more broadly, the Post-Modernist advocacy of an aesthetic of indeterminacy, an aesthetic that gave primacy to the viewing or reading subject's experience of the works in question rather than to the internal relations that make those works what they are (or, more simply, to the works themselves). Essentially, such an aesthetic conceives of the subject as constituting the work or text in and by his/her experiencing of it; put another way, the work is in effect replaced by the experience, which in the case of 'visual' art is of the larger situation in which the encounter takes place" (257). For Fried, the apotheosis of artwork qua "allegory of intention" is High Modernist painting of the sort we find in Morris Louis, Kenneth Noland, Frank Stella and so on (its Minimalist/Literalist enemy, the work of Donald Judd, Tony Smith, et al.). But more importantly for my purposes, he cites an interesting passage from Baudelaire's essay "Why Sculpture is Tiresome" that makes it clear why the sort of artwork Fried praises—or rather, more simply (as he might say), his concept of art as such—is in fact *anti*-ecopoetical in the sense I am developing here. Baudelaire writes:

Sculpture has several disadvantages, which are a necessary consequence of its means and materials. Though as brutal and positive as nature herself, it has at the same time a certain vagueness and ambiguity, because it exhibits too many surfaces at once. It is in vain that the sculptor forces himself to take up a unique point of view; the spectator who moves around the figure can choose a hundred different points of view, except for the right one, and it often happens that a change trick of the light, an effect of the lamp, may discover a beauty which is not at all the one that artist had in mind—and this is a humiliating thing for him. A picture, however, is only what it wants to be; there is no other way of looking at it than on its own terms. Painting has but one point of view; it is exclusive and despotic, and therefore the painter's expression is much more forceful (256).

As this quotation makes clear in the specificity of its diction—which Baudelaire, being Baudelaire, would tune quite finely—the relationship between the work of art and its environment should be first and foremost one of exclusion, where the "unique point of view," "the right one," asserts itself in all its uniqueness against the positivity of "nature herself," "on its own terms," and by doing so, it is "exclusive and despotic" in relation to the viewer in a way that sculpture—subject as it is to the play of environmental contingency and the contingency of its own three-dimensional materiality—could never be. Now I take it that such a characterization of the "proper" work of art could not be more different than the ecopoetics we find in "An Ordinary Evening in New Haven," with all of the resonances of "ordinary" and "everyday" in play that we have been exploring—a fact that "Ordinary Evening" signals not just by beginning and ending with an emphasis on paradoxical observation, performativity, and the spectral nature of both, but also in its entire opening flourish:, where the gap between "The eye's plain version" and "experience" generates "an and yet, and yet, and yet— // As part of the never-ending meditation," which Fried would contrast with what he calls the "*presentness*" of the art work itself, in which "*at every moment the work itself is wholly manifest*" (257–58).

113. As in *Pacific Sun* itself, where, Fried notes, "it was also necessary to make adjustments to his camera so that the entire space from near to far would be in sharp focus" (*Another Light*, 256).

114. *CP*, 472.

115. *CP*, 471.

116. *CP*, 488.

117. *CP*, 465.

118. *CP*, 486. The point I am making here has *something* to do, of course, with the differences between poetry, painting, and photography as a medium, but *only* something, as Fried's references to Rilke in his essay on Demand make clear. The differences here don't hinge on that difference of medium, in other words.

119. Cavell, *Emerson's Transcendental Etudes*, 134.

120. Simon Critchley, *Things Merely Are: Philosophy in the Poetry of Wallace Stevens* (London: Routledge, 2005), 29–30.

121. Quoted in Critchley, *Things Merely Are*, 30.

122. Sebastian Gardner, "Wallace Stevens and Metaphysics: The Plain Sense of Things," *European Journal of Philosophy* 2, no. 3 (1994): 333.

123. Gardner goes on to offer a refutation of this view on the same page, which is not very convincing, and perhaps this is not surprising, given that Gard-

ner takes the debate between "realism" and "idealism" far too seriously. What is needed here, instead, is Rorty's debunking of "relativism" itself in *Objectivity, Relativism, and Truth* as "trying to put a metanarrative in the postmodernist's mouth," which opens in turn onto Rorty's redescription of the Kantian transcendental subject as Fish's "interpretive communities," thus shifting the conversation from an epistemological to an ethical frame, which leads us, in turn, to Stevens's "poetry helps people to live their lives." See Richard Rorty, *Objectivity, Relativism, and Truth: Philosophical Papers, Vol. 1* (Cambridge: Cambridge University Press, 1991).

124. Stanley Cavell, *This New Yet Unapproachable America: Lectures after Emerson and Wittgenstein* (Albuquerque, NM: Living Batch Press, 1989), 47.

125. Bloom, *The Poems of Our Climate*, 307.

126. Cavell, *This New Yet Unapproachable America*, 67–68.

127. Cavell, *This New Yet Unapproachable America*, 68.

128. Bloom, *The Poems of Our Climate*, 327. As Henry Staten points out in his fine book on Wittgenstein and Derrida, it is true that all of this—in a Cavellian light, especially—raises the question of "ordinary language, but "the question is not, however, whether the language of a given text is 'ordinary' in any fixed or predetermined fashion." Rather, the issue is getting "unstuck from a too literal or uncritical or fixated attachment to the formulas of traditional philosophy," so that we can see how "the peculiar verbal usages of philosophers, properly read, give us a new apprehension of the familiar, a claim that sounds exactly like what literary critics say about the peculiar usages of poets." Henry Staten, *Wittgenstein and Derrida* (Lincoln: University of Nebraska Press, 1986), xiv. And this is Stevens's charge, I am arguing, in "Ordinary Evening." We can thus be reminded of just how impressive Stevens's achievement is in the later long poems by remembering just how differently "the same" set of philosophical questions is handled in "Ordinary Evening" vs. "Auroras," not just in terms of scene, setting, and theme—the overwhelming spectacle of the aurora borealis in one, the underwhelming "ugliness" and "commonness" of New Haven, Connecticut, in the other—but also in terms of how those differences pose very different challenges for how the poetry works though the same set of ecological or ecopoetic concerns.

129. *CP*, 112.

130. *CP*, 294.

131. *Letters of Wallace Stevens*, 636.

132. Richard Eldridge, "Introduction: Between Acknowledgment and Avoidance," in *Stanley Cavell*, ed. Richard Eldridge (Cambridge: Cambridge University Press, 2003), 2.

133. Eldridge, "Introduction: Between Acknowledgment and Avoidance," 2.

134. Cavell, *Emerson's Transcendental Etudes*, 2.

135. Cavell, *Emerson's Transcendental Etudes*, 2.

136. Cavell, *Emerson's Transcendental Etudes*, 4.

137. *CP*, 480–81.

138. Timothy Gould, "The Names of Action," in *Stanley Cavell*, ed. Eldridge, 74.

139. *CP*, 465, 486.

140. Cavell, *Emerson's Transcendental Etudes*, 25–26.

141. *CP*, 485.

142. Cavell, *This New Yet Unapproachable America*, 34.

143. Cavell, *This New Yet Unapproachable America*, 34.

144. Cavell, *This New Yet Unapproachable America*, 39.

145. Cavell, *This New Yet Unapproachable America*, 40.

146. *CP*, 470.

147. *CP*, 469.

148. Cavell, *Emerson's Transcendental Etudes*, 244–45, first emphasis added.

149. *CP*, 474–75.

150. *CP*, 475.

151. *CP*, 476.

152. Stanley Cavell, *The World Viewed: Reflections on the Ontology of Film*, enlarged ed. (Cambridge, MA: Harvard University Press, 1979), 18. For a fuller discussion of this question, see Wolfe, *What Is Posthumanism?*, chap. 8.

153. *CP*, 472.

154. *CP*, 471–72.

155. *CP*, 473.

CODA

1. For example, Gyorgyi Voros, "Wallace Stevens and A. R. Ammons as Men on the Dump," *Wallace Stevens Journal* 24, no. 2 (2000): 161–75; and J. Hillis Miller, "Anachronistic Reading," *Derrida Today* 3, no. 1 (2010): 75–91.

2. Harold Bloom, "When You Consider the Radiance," in Harold Bloom, *The Ringers in the Tower: Studies in Romantic Tradition* (Chicago: University of Chicago Press, 1971), 257.

3. Roger Gilbert, "'I Went to the Summit': The Literary Bromance of A. R. Ammons and Harold Bloom," *Genre* 45, no. 1 (2012): 173. Ammons expresses this Bloomian perspective in the poem that gives Gilbert's essay its title, "For Harold Bloom," which concludes the *Selected Poems* from 1977, where Ammons writes, "having been brought this far by nature I have been / brought out of nature / and nothing here shows me the image of myself." *A. R. Ammons, The Selected Poems 1951–1977* (New York: W. W. Norton, 1977), 105.

4. *CP*, 467.

5. Cary Wolfe, "Symbol Plural: The Later Long Poems of A. R. Ammons," *Contemporary Literature* 30, no. 1 (1989): 78–94.

6. A. R. Ammons, *Omateum with Doxology* (Philadelphia: Dorrance, 1955).

7. *CP*, 488.

8. Jacques Derrida, *The Beast and the Sovereign, Vol. 2*, ed. Michel Lisse, Marie-Louise Mallet, and Ginette Michaud, trans. Geoffrey Bennington (Chicago: University of Chicago Press, 2011), 101, 100n13.

9. David Farrell Krell, *Derrida and Our Animal Others: Derrida's Final Seminar, "The Beast and the Sovereign"* (Bloomington: Indiana University Press, 2013), 51. As he points out, following a suggestion by Michael Naas, "Derrida is always and everywhere perturbed by Heidegger's apparent confidence in proximity—for example, in the proximity of Dasein to the question of the meaning of being, or the proximity of the mortal to its own death, proximities denied to all other life forms—may we dare to hope that Heidegger's emphasis here on the remoteness of the path will assuage that perturbation?" (123).

10. As Cavell puts it, "the substantive disagreement with Heidegger shared by Emerson and Thoreau, is that the achievement of the human requires not habitation and settlement but abandonment, leaving. Then everything depends on your realization of abandonment." Stanley Cavell, *Emerson's Transcendental Etudes* (Stanford, CA: Stanford University Press, 2003), 19.

11. Branka Arsić, *On Leaving: A Reading in Emerson* (Cambridge, MA: Harvard University Press, 2010), 3.

12. Robert Bly, *A Little Book on the Human Shadow*, ed. William Booth (San Francisco: Harper & Row, 1988), 66.

13. Bly, *A Little Book on the Human Shadow*, 66–68.

14. Arsić, *On Leaving*, 70.

15. A. R. Ammons, *Set in Motion: Essays, Interviews, and Dialogues*, ed. Zofia Burr (Ann Arbor: University of Michigan Press, 1996), 13. As Ammons notes, interestingly enough, in an interview in that volume, "I have read very little Stevens, and basically he's not one of my favorite poets, though I think he's a good poet" (63–64).

16. Ammons, *Set in Motion*, 16.

17. Ammons, *Set in Motion*, 16–17.

18. Ammons, *The Selected Poems 1951–1977*, 46.

Index

Ackerman, Jennifer, 92–93, 96
Alaimo, Stacy, xi–xii, xix
Ammons, A. R., 7, 166–70
animal, concept of, xv, xix–xx, 13, 64,
    70, 83–87, 92–93, 104–8, 124, 126,
    196n3, 209n9
Aristotle, xiii, 49, 104–5
Arsić, Branka, 169–70
autoimmunity, concept of, xvii, 113,
    122, 196n3
autopoiesis, concept of, x–xi, xiii–xiv,
    20, 37–38, 41–43, 66–68, 73, 77–79,
    102, 113, 130, 134, 152, 168

Bateson, Gregory, xv, 22–25, 37, 49, 56,
    65, 74–75, 81, 89, 103, 110, 113, 135, 159,
    162, 168, 170, 186n54
Bloom, Harold, vii, xii, 6, 7, 26–27, 101,
    122–24, 131–32, 147, 153, 155–57, 160–
    61, 163, 167–68, 208n3
Bly, Robert, 169–70
Brown, Lee Rust, 33–34

Buell, Lawrence, xiv–xv
Burke, Kenneth, 13

Campbell, Timothy, xviii, 120, 123
Cavell, Stanley, xxi, 5, 12, 14, 26–29,
    30–33, 36, 39, 57, 119, 133, 139–41,
    144, 148–49, 156–58, 160–65, 166–70,
    179n27, 209n10
Celan, Paul, 52, 64, 108–9, 169
Coleridge, Samuel Taylor, 26, 33
complexity, concept of, xvi, 19–20,
    23, 34, 36–38, 45, 50, 55–56, 64, 70,
    73–77, 82, 102, 127, 130, 132–33, 136,
    182n95, 186n54, 196n3
correlationism, 101–3
Critchley, Simon, 16, 98–99, 101,
    159–60

Darwinism, xiv, 17–18, 68, 71–72, 74–
    75, 79, 95, 186n51
Dawkins, Richard, 65, 78
Defoe, Daniel, 105, 112–13

Demand, Thomas, 156–58, 160, 162, 204n110, 205n112, 206n118

Derrida, Jacques, x–xiii, xv, xx–xxi, 5, 7, 17–18, 28, 35, 40–41, 47, 52, 62–64, 67, 69–72, 80, 83, 84–88, 92, 94–95, 97–101, 104–16, 126, 130–31, 133–34, 144, 146, 149–52, 154, 157, 161, 164, 166–69, 171n4, 173n39, 186n54, 191n50, 196n3, 202n29, 207n128, 209n9

Descartes, René, 31, 148, 179n27, 189n86

dwelling, concept of, xviii, xxi, 14, 31, 119–21, 140–54, 160, 163, 166, 195n1. See also *oikos*, concept of

ecology, concept of, vii–viii, ix–xvi, xix–xx, 9–10, 14–16, 18, 20, 22–23, 50, 61–66, 68, 71–72, 75–76, 83, 106–9, 113–15, 128–30, 132, 134, 141–42, 146–47, 151–52, 154–56, 160, 170, 174n23, 184n17, 186n54, 207n128

Eldridge, Richard, 161–62

Emerson, Ralph Waldo, xxi, 5, 7, 9, 11–14, 16–20, 26–39, 46, 51, 57–58, 100–101, 119, 121–22, 127, 131–34, 139–44, 147–48, 155–57, 160–63, 164–70, 176n62, 176n63, 179n27, 182n107, 199n8, 209n10

environment, concept of, viii, ix–xiii, xiv, xvi, xix–xx, 6, 9, 19–20, 36–38, 50, 52–53, 55–56, 58, 62, 64–67, 70–71, 73–75, 81–83, 96–97, 102, 107, 113, 122, 129–30, 132, 135–37, 145–46, 150–52, 168–69, 175n23, 176n67, 182n95, 183n11, 184n17, 190n28, 196n3. *See also* world, concept of

epistemology, concept of, xii–xiii, 5, 12, 22, 24–25, 29, 34, 58, 61, 65–68, 97–98, 101–3, 114–16, 137, 158–60, 168, 192n55, 206n123

Fletcher, Angus, 18–20, 23, 176n67

form, concept of, ix, xii, 6–9, 19–20, 22, 33, 37, 39–47, 49, 51–56, 66, 70–71, 82, 85, 89, 111, 125–31, 133, 135–36, 142, 150, 168, 174n22, 196n3

Fried, Michael, 156–58, 160, 162, 205n112, 206n113, 206n118

Fritsch, Matthias, 70–71

Frost, Robert, 86–93, 97

Gardner, Sebastian, 3–4, 159–60, 206n123

Ghosh, Amitav, xvi–xvii

Gilbert, Roger, 5, 15, 46, 167

Gonnaud, Maurice, 32–33

Hägglund, Martin, 62, 71, 80–81, 83, 94–95

Hammond, Mac, 15, 46–47

Haraway, Donna, x, 171n4, 198

Harris, Paul, 110–11, 113

Hegel, G. W. F., 39, 53, 88, 127, 146, 176n62, 182n93, 202n38

Heidegger, Martin, xi, xiv–xv, xvii, xix–xxi, 28, 32, 35, 40, 64, 83, 86, 107–9, 134, 143–45, 148–49, 154, 162, 164, 166–69, 171n4, 195n1, 196n3, 209n9, 209n10

Hollander, John, 87–90

Hopkins, Gerard Manley, 8, 86, 133–34

human, concept of, xv, xvii, xix–xxi, 9–14, 64, 68, 70, 72, 83, 84–89, 92–93, 96–97, 103–9, 122–24, 126, 141–43, 149, 152–54, 162–63, 171n4, 176n67, 186n54, 209n10

Husserl, Edmund, 5, 39, 69, 125–26, 128, 176n63, 191n50

immunity, concept of, xi, xvii–xviii, xxi, 113, 119, 121–23, 125, 141–42, 144, 149–51, 162, 196n3

insurance, xii, xvii–xviii, 120–21, 149–51, 169, 179n31

Jacob, François, 69, 71

James, William, 9–14, 17, 57–58, 127

Jaurrero, Alicia, 66–67, 76, 82
Johnson, Christopher, 69, 72–73, 80

Kant, Immanuel, 27, 29–32, 39–40, 47,
    77–79, 115, 152, 192n55, 206n123
Kauffman, Stuart, 64, 67, 71–73, 75–82,
    86, 148, 186n54
Keats, John, 26, 135
Kermode, Frank, 26, 28
Kirby, Vicki, 62, 68
Krell, David Ferrell, 105, 113, 169,
    194n97, 209n9

Latour, Bruno, xvi, 102, 110–11, 114
Lehmann, Robert, 5, 26, 49
Lentricchia, Frank, xviii, 172n23
life, concept of, xiii–xiv, xix–xx, 11, 18,
    22–23, 61–62, 65–72, 78, 83, 86, 88,
    92, 95–97, 107, 109, 113, 134, 139, 148,
    186n54, 202n29, 209n9
Longo, Giuseppe, 65, 82, 185n44
Luhmann, Niklas, ix, xvi, 10, 13, 17, 23,
    32–50, 53–56, 62, 73, 102, 108, 125–29,
    130–33, 135, 145, 152, 157, 179n41,
    182n95, 196n3

Macksey, Richard, 4–5
Maeder, Beverly, 15–16, 47
Marder, Michael, 63, 146, 151–52
Maturana, Humberto, ix–x, 19–20, 62,
    68, 97, 102, 115, 171n4
Miller, J. Hillis, 4, 26, 128, 133–34, 155,
    158–59, 162, 176n62
Monod, Jacques, 69, 71
Moore, Marianne, 42, 49
Morgan, Robert, 91, 190n28
Morton, Timothy, vi, 108

Naas, Michael, 112, 114, 202n29,
    209n9
Nietzsche, Friedrich, 17, 173n12
Noble, Denis, 65, 69, 71–74, 82, 186n51
Noë, Alva, 107–8

observation, concept of, ix–x, 5, 18,
    27, 32–34, 37, 39–41, 44–48, 54, 58,
    62, 69, 82, 108, 110, 115, 120, 124, 127,
    129–30, 132, 134–37, 151, 168, 171n4,
    176n67, 179n41, 205n112. See also
    topology (vs. topography)
oikos, concept of, xx, 123, 130, 142,
    146, 149–52, 161. See also dwelling,
    concept of
ontology, concept of, xiii, xx–xxi, 15–
    16, 35–36, 38, 44, 53, 65–68, 72, 83, 92,
    97, 102, 120, 139, 186n54, 192n55
ordinary, the, 147, 150–51, 156–63

paradox, concept of, ix, xii, xviii, 7, 9,
    15, 19–22, 27–29, 31–35, 37–48, 66,
    94, 103, 115, 119, 134, 151, 170, 176n67,
    196n3, 206n112
Pearce, Roy Harvey, 20–22
Peirce, Charles Sanders, 17
Peters, John Durham, 142, 144
phenomenology, concept of, xv, 5,
    21–23, 35, 37, 41, 61, 85, 97, 173n12,
    176n63, 195n1, 196n3
Plato, xiii, 54, 124, 142
Poirier, Richard, 9–14, 16–17, 57, 131

representationalism, concept of, viii,
    xiii, xvi, 11, 13, 15–19, 23, 30–32, 36, 52,
    56, 62–63, 100, 103–4, 114, 159, 168
Richardson, Joan, 9, 16–18
Riddell, Joseph, 20, 26
Romanticism, viii, xiv, 12, 18, 20–21,
    26–27, 29, 32–35, 39, 49–50, 89–90,
    167
Rorty, Richard, xiii–xiv, 30–31, 63, 103,
    206n123

Serres, Michel, 110–11, 113–14, 147
Sloterdijk, Peter, xi, xvii–xxi, 38, 83,
    119–24, 127, 129–30, 134, 138–39,
    141–42, 146, 149–53, 155, 168, 189n86,
    195n1, 196n3

Soto, Ana, 65, 82, 185n44
Staten, Henry, 95, 207n128
Stevens, Wallace, works of: "Adagia,"
116; "Add This to Rhetoric," 129;
"Anecdote of the Jar," 130, 133;
"Auroras of Autumn, The," xvii–
xviii, 10, 121, 124–25, 127, 135, 137–38,
140–46, 152–55, 157, 163, 167, 207n128;
"Autumn Refrain," 13, 101; "Collect
of Philosophy, A," 20–21; "Con-
noisseur of Chaos," 130, 132–33;
"Credences of Summer," 13, 127,
129, 135–37, 141; "Depression Before
Spring," 106; "Disillusionment of
Ten O'Clock," 122; "Domination of
Black," 125; "Esthétique du Mal,"
46; "Figure of the Youth as Virile
Poet, The," 6, 8, 35; "Idea of Order
at Key West, The," 46–47, 108; "In-
surance and Social Change," xvii,
149–50; "Invective Against Swans,"
98; "Irrational Element in Poetry,
The," 9, 14, 49–57, 126; "Man on the
Dump, The," xvi, 12, 99–101, 103,
127, 129–32, 146, 166; "Man with the
Blue Guitar, The," 16, 24, 98, 146;
"Noble Rider and the Sound
of Words, The," xxii, 35, 40, 47–48,
116, 144; "No Possum, No Sop, No
Taters," xvii, 58, 161, 177; "Notes
Toward a Supreme Fiction," xvi,
49, 100–101, 120, 126–29, 133, 137–41,
145, 149, 155–57; "Not Ideas About
the Thing But the Thing Itself," 13,
20, 90, 93, 98, 101, 106, 111, 122, 129;
"Of Mere Being," 93, 98, 103–6,
111, 122, 136, 137, 148; "On the Road
Home," 100–101, 106, 109, 111;
"Ordinary Evening in New Haven,
An," xvii, 25, 119–20, 138, 140–64,
168–70, 205n112, 207n128; "Planet
on the Table, The," 8, 9, 21–22, 125,
128, 152; "Poems of Our Climate,

The," 6, 8–9, 48, 130, 133; "Poet That
Matters, A," 49–50; "Primitive Like
an Orb, A," 8, 126; "Reality Is an
Activity of the Most August Imag-
ination," 25; "Region November,
The," 12, 21; "Rock, The," vii, 20, 57–
58; "So-and-So Reclining on Her
Couch," 25; "Study of Two Pears,"
25, 150; "Sunday Morning," 10, 98,
103, 120, 122, 124, 135–36, 138–40,
144–46, 149, 153–54, 167; "Tea," 161;
"Things of August," 142; "Thirteen
Ways of Looking at a Blackbird,"
x, 58, 98, 101, 105, 122–24, 129, 137,
177; "Two or Three Ideas," 29, 120,
143–44; "Ultimate Poem is Abstract,
The," 136; "Well Dressed Man with
a Beard, The," 99
Surrealism, 53, 57, 163

temporality, concept of, 22–23, 36–37,
39, 48–49, 64, 81, 94–95, 100–101,
127–29
topology (vs. topography), 9, 20, 46,
65–66, 83, 110–11, 114, 127, 147–48,
151, 183n11, 196n3. See also observa-
tion, concept of

Uexküll, Jakob von, 40, 64, 83, 107, 134,
149, 168

Varela, Francisco, 19–20, 62, 68, 97, 115
Vendler, Helen, vii, 5, 15, 26, 47, 127,
131, 135–36, 153
virtual, concept of, x–xii, 21–22, 182n95

Waddington, Conrad, 72–75, 81,
186n50, 186n51, 186n54
Wall, Jeff, 156, 158, 160, 162
Whitman, Walt, 18, 98, 167
Wills, David, 92–93
Wimsatt, W. K., 7, 41, 181n66
Winslow, Russell, 65–66

Wittgenstein, Ludwig, 119, 156–57, 160

world, concept of, viii–xii, xiv–xv, xvii, xix–xxi, 3–6, 8–16, 19–20, 22–25, 27–28, 32, 35, 37–40, 43–45, 47–48, 50, 52, 61–64, 79, 83, 85, 97–100, 102–3, 107–9, 113–16, 122, 124, 126–27, 129–30, 132–34, 136, 138–39, 147–49, 151–52, 154, 157–60, 164–65, 166, 168–70, 176n67, 195n1, 196n3. *See also* environment, concept of

Yeats, William Butler, 93–94, 104–5

Žižek, Slavoj, 87–88